Decision Analytics: Microsoft® Excel®

Conrad Carlberg

800 E. 96th Street
Indianapolis, Indiana   46240

Decision Analytics: Microsoft® Excel®

ISBN-13: 978-0-7897-5168-3
ISBN-10: 0-7897-5168-2

Library of Congress Control Number: 2013942294

Printed in the United States of America

First Printing: November 2013

Trademarks

All terms mentioned in this book that are known to be trademarks or service marks have been appropriately capitalized. Que Publishing cannot attest to the accuracy of this information. Use of a term in this book should not be regarded as affecting the validity of any trademark or service mark.

Warning and Disclaimer

Every effort has been made to make this book as complete and as accurate as possible, but no warranty or fitness is implied. The information provided is on an "as is" basis. The author and the publisher shall have neither liability nor responsibility to any person or entity with respect to any loss or damages arising from the information contained in this book.

Bulk Sales

Que Publishing offers excellent discounts on this book when ordered in quantity for bulk purchases or special sales. For more information, please contact

U.S. Corporate and Government Sales
1-800-382-3419
corpsales@pearsontechgroup.com

For sales outside of the U.S., please contact

International Sales
international@pearsoned.com

Editor-in-Chief
Greg Wiegand

Executive Editor
Loretta Yates

Development Editor
Charlotte Kughen

Technical Editor
Michael Turner

Managing Editor
Kristy Hart

Project Editor
Elaine Wiley

Copy Editor
Geneil Breeze

Senior Indexer
Cheryl Lenser

Proofreader
Debbie Williams

Editorial Assistant
Cindy Teeters

Cover Designer
Anne Jones

Compositor
Nonie Ratcliff

Table of Contents

About the Author

Conrad Carlberg lives near San Diego with his wife, not too far from the beach, but high enough that the rise in the sea level is unlikely to convert their home to waterfront property. Two cats round out the indoor menagerie; the three rabbits are required to stay outside.

Dedication

Once again, to my beloved and beautiful Toni, who laughs with me.

Acknowledgments

My thanks once again to Loretta Yates for skillfully directing this book through the acquisition process, and for her steady hand and even temper. Michael Turner, of the University of Colorado's REM lab, provided a fine technical edit, one that kept me from embarrassing myself in print and that got me back on track when necessary. Anne Jones...what can I say? Her brilliant cover artwork for Statistical Analysis: Microsoft Excel 2010 and for Predictive Analytics: Microsoft Excel surely drove as many sales as the contents did, and she's done it again. Geneil Breeze's copy edit gently reminded me to leave the pedantry behind, in the first draft where it belongs. Elaine Wiley, for shepherding the project through all its incarnations. My heartfelt thanks to each of you.

We Want to Hear from You!

As the reader of this book, *you* are our most important critic and commentator. We value your opinion and want to know what we're doing right, what we could do better, what areas you'd like to see us publish in, and any other words of wisdom you're willing to pass our way.

We welcome your comments. You can email or write to let us know what you did or didn't like about this book—as well as what we can do to make our books better.

Please note that we cannot help you with technical problems related to the topic of this book.

When you write, please be sure to include this book's title and author as well as your name and email address. We will carefully review your comments and share them with the author and editors who worked on the book.

Email: feedback@quepublishing.com

Mail: Que Publishing
        ATTN: Reader Feedback
        800 East 96th Street
        Indianapolis, IN 46240 USA

Reader Services

Visit our website and register this book at quepublishing.com/register for convenient access to any updates, downloads, or errata that might be available for this book.

Introduction

I'd like to get something off my chest right away: Excel workbooks are waiting for you to download them from the publisher's website, quepublishing. com/title/9780789751683. The download links are sometimes a little tough to distinguish from regular text, but both the links and the workbooks are there.

Starting with Chapter 2, "Logistic Regression," each chapter in this book has its own Excel workbook, and each figure in each chapter appears as a separate worksheet. A few additional workbooks carry out cluster analysis, discriminant function analysis, and other analytics procedures that don't have their own worksheet functions.

Okay, with that item out of the way:

This is *not* a book about acquiring, storing, and partitioning so-called big data. This book is about how to make sense of the numbers, be they big data or small beer.

We've all been confronted by situations in which we have, say, 30 variables to deal with, each potentially important and each with a slightly different slant on the really interesting phenomenon, whether that's 12-month survival, or probability of profiting from an investment, or seeing a new hire make good. Regardless of whether you have 200 or 200,000 records at your disposal, the real question is how to handle those 30 variables. How to combine or discard them so as to make the right decisions about the effects of a medication, about whether to extend the financing, or about which candidate to hire.

What's in the Book

That's what *Decision Analytics: Microsoft Excel* is about: finding the best mix of the variables you have at hand, so that your decision is as informed as you can make it.

That's an exercise in using quantitative classification techniques, and there are several, as follows.

Discriminant function analysis has a long and generally honorable history. It's been used for a broad array of purposes, from identifying the party affiliations of nineteenth century politicians on the basis of their legislative records, to flagging possibly fraudulent Form 1040s based on patterns of deductions and adjustments. Chapter 5, "Discriminant Function Analysis: The Basics," and Chapter 6, "Discriminant Function Analysis: Further Issues," of this book walk you through this sort of analysis and explore the data reduction techniques involved. They show you, in the context of both worksheets and charts, how discriminant function analysis goes about its business.

Because discriminant analysis depends on a multivariate approach to handling the continuous variables, I have included Chapter 7, "Principal Components Analysis." This helps you get your arms around concepts such as eigenvalues and eigenvectors as they pertain to correlation matrixes—again, in the familiar context of Excel worksheets and charts.

There's also a workbook for you to download with VBA code that runs a complete discriminant function analysis and outputs the significance tests, the function coefficients, canonical correlations, and other bells and whistles, which are each explained in the text and further illustrated in the chapter's workbooks.

The best way to approach a discriminant analysis is by way of multivariate analysis of variance, or *MANOVA*. As you'll see, MANOVA helps you decide whether it even makes sense to carry out a discriminant function analysis—whether the correlations between the dependent variables, and their ability to distinguish between different groupings of people and actions, support further analysis at all. Therefore, Chapter 4, "Multivariate Analysis of Variance (MANOVA)," discusses MANOVA, and you can download a separate workbook that runs a one-factor MANOVA with multiple dependent variables.

If it's been a while since you gave any thought to either ANOVA or MANOVA, you might want to run through Chapter 3, "Univariate Analysis of Variance (ANOVA)." As background to MANOVA, it's helpful to see, in the context of a worksheet, what's going on with the way ANOVA manages variability.

Besides discriminant function analysis, another method of classifying people or market activities (or politicians, or houseplants) is by way of *logistic regression*. That's a useful method, and it avoids some of the pitfalls that discriminant analysis might put in your way. For example, logistic regression doesn't make all the assumptions about how the data is distributed that discriminant analysis does. So if you're concerned that your data violates those assumptions (and honestly, it doesn't necessarily invalidate your analysis even if the assumptions get trampled), you can often use logistic regression instead, as the analytic basis for your decisions.

On the other hand, those assumptions are what give discriminant analysis its statistical power—its ability to successfully and reliably distinguish between different groupings of subjects. Other things being equal, discriminant analysis is a more sensitive guide to classification than is logistic regression.

I give two chapters to logistic regression in my previous book *Predictive Analytics: Microsoft Excel*. I cover it here in Chapter 2, "Logistic Regression," more as a review than as a full discussion.

Chapter 8, "Cluster Analysis: The Basics," and Chapter 9, "Cluster Analysis: Further Issues," go into yet another approach to decision analytics. In logistic regression and discriminant analysis, you know going in what your groups are. You have a sample of data, be it large or small, with observations that include group membership (survives/doesn't, makes a profit/doesn't, wins/loses) and variables that you hope will position you to make good decisions (demographic data, financials, purchasing history).

But in cluster analysis you don't know what your groups are. You have a set of, for example, demographic variables and you'd like to know how they classify people. You turn one of the variations of cluster analysis loose on your data set, hoping that it will cluster those people such that differences on demographics will be relatively small within clusters, and relatively large between clusters.

Leland Wilkinson gave an apt description of this sort of decision analysis way back in 1986, when he wrote, "In rough terms, it is like doing a one-way analysis of variance where the groups are unknown and the largest F-value is sought by reassigning members to each group." (See page 1 of the Cluster section of the SYSTAT manual.)

Why Use Excel?

I write books and people buy them, thanks be. But I'm also a consultant and I like my clients to have an understanding of what I've done with the numbers they've handed me. I think that's one of the main reasons that I'm still in this dodge after 20 years.

I don't like to hand clients a pile of R printouts, whether literally or electronically. Nothing against R. It's a fine set of statistical procedures even if its documentation is impenetrable and its results look like they were laid out by archaic FORTRAN. I often use R to benchmark work that I've done in Excel.

SAS, SPSS, Stata, and similar packages are much better documented than is R, and the analytic results are laid out in a much more straightforward fashion. They are costly, though. And, like R, they take a fair amount of study to learn the proper way to navigate the user interface and to handle the command syntax correctly.

In contrast, most of my clients are perfectly comfortable in the familiar Excel environment and appreciate how easy it is to view a set of numbers in an Excel chart. And of course you'd be hard put to find a Windows box in a corporate or educational environment that *doesn't* already have some version of Excel up and running.

But is Excel capable of handling the complicated data reduction methods required by analytics in general and decision analytics in particular? Obviously, I believe it is. It's true that Excel is a general numeric analysis package, not built from the ground up to offer specialized statistical functionality. There's no WILKS() worksheet function.

Excel does offer an MDETERM() worksheet function, and if you point it at a Within matrix and a Total matrix then you've got your Wilks' lambda. Suppose that you're a budding analyst. Or suppose that you're a corporate suit who wants to know why someone thinks that Wilks' lambda says to stay out of a given line of business. I contend that either way you're much better off knowing *why* it's telling you something than just knowing what the numeric value is.

And Excel, used properly, can position you to know those things. Sometimes all you need is the built-in worksheet functions; it's entirely possible to do a multivariate analysis of variance directly on the worksheet, without resorting to any add-ins. I think it's a good idea to do that once or twice because it helps to cement the concepts in place.

But sometimes you need an assist from a tool such as Excel's Solver, an add-in that comes with the Excel application software. Chapter 2 shows you how to use Solver to help you complete a logistic regression (and by the way, the purely statistical packages use the same optimization algorithms—they're just tucked out of the way so you don't see them).

And there are some processes, such as finding the eigenvalues of a large correlation matrix, that are just so complex and loop-dependent that it's crazy to try to do them without coded procedures. But you'll find those procedures, coded in VBA and some open for your inspection, in the Excel files available with this book.

To underscore my point: In early 2013 I was approached to help a company build a model that would evaluate prospective investments. The client had almost 100,000 records to use in developing the model. The nature of the data was such that a logistic regression analysis was called for, and the client supplied the data in a text file that Excel could read easily. Using Excel, I tried running a logistic regression on that data set and my formulas resulted in arithmetic underflows.

Then, using R, I put the data through a logistic regression routine that's part of R's library. I got underflows again. Too many cases, and intermediate results too small for either Excel or R to handle accurately.

Now, this didn't pose any real problem. I wanted to save some of the data for cross-validation purposes, so I ran a random half of the data set through R's logistic regression routine, got my results, and validated them on the remaining half of the data. Then I confirmed the results using Excel. The client got both the R and the Excel results, of course, but I noticed that subsequent work that the client did with the model took place in Excel, where the results of the formulas were much more transparent.

Now, this homely little story is not only anecdotal, it's also a sample of 1. Nevertheless, it's true, and it's typical of my own experience with using Excel as an analytical engine. If you try out the methods I describe in this book, I'm confident you'll come to the same conclusion.

Enough said. I suggest that you pour yourself a serving of your beverage of choice, fire up the laptop, and move on to Chapter 1, "Components of Decision Analytics."

Components of Decision Analytics

Regardless of what line of work we're in, we make decisions about people, medical treatments, marketing programs, soil amendments, and so on. If we're to make informed, sensible decisions, we need to understand how to find clusters of people who are likely or unlikely to succeed in a job; how to classify medications according to their efficacy; how to classify mass mailings according to their likelihood of driving revenue; how to divide fertilizers into those that will work well with our crops and those that won't.

The key is to find ways of classifying into categories that make sense and that stand up in more than just one sample. Decision analytics comprises several types of analysis that help you make that sort of classification. The techniques have been around for decades, but it's only with the emergence of the term *analytics* that the ways that those techniques can work together have gained real currency.

This initial chapter provides a brief overview of each of the techniques discussed in the book's remaining chapters, along with an introduction to the conditions that might guide you toward selecting a particular technique.

Classifying According to Existing Categories

Several techniques used in decision analytics are intended for sets of data where you already know the correct classification of the records. The idea of classifying records into known categories might seem pointless at first, but bear in mind that this is usually a preliminary analysis. You typically intend to apply what you learn from such a pilot study to *other* records—and you don't yet know which categories those other records belong to.

Using a Two-Step Approach

A classification procedure that informs your decision making often involves two steps. For example, suppose you develop a new antibiotic that shows promise of preventing or curing new bacterial infections that have so far proven drug-resistant. You test your antibiotic in a double-blind experiment that employs random selection and assignment, with a comparison arm getting a traditional antibiotic and an experimental arm getting your new medication. You get mixed results: Your medication stops the infection in about one third of the patients in the experimental arm, but it's relatively ineffective in the remaining patients.

You would like to determine whether there are any patient characteristics among those who received your new medication that tend either to enable or to block its effects. You know your classification categories—those in whom the infection was stopped, and those in whom the infection was unaffected. You can now test whether other patient characteristics, such as age, sex, infection history, blood tests and so on, can reliably distinguish the two classification categories. Several types of analysis, each discussed in this book, are available to help you make those tests: Multivariate analysis of variance and discriminant function analysis are two such analyses. If those latter tests are successful, you can classify future patients into a group that's likely to be helped by your medication and a group that's unlikely to be helped.

Notice the sequence in the previous example. You start with a group whose category memberships are known—those who received your medication and were helped and those who weren't. Pending a successful test of existing patient characteristics and their response to your medication, you might now be in a position to classify new patients into a group that your medication is likely to help, and a group that isn't. Health care providers can now make more informed decisions about prescribing your medication.

Multiple Regression and Decision Analytics

The previous section discusses the issue of classifying and decision making purely from the standpoint of design. Let's take another look from the point of view of analysis rather than design—and, not incidentally, in terms of multiple regression, which employs ideas that underlie many of the more advanced techniques described in this book.

You're probably familiar to some degree with the technique of multiple regression. That technique seeks to develop an equation that looks something like this one:

$$Y = a_1X_1 + a_2X_2 + b$$

In that equation, Y is a variable such as weight that you'd like to predict. X_1 is a variable such as height, and X_2 is another variable such as age. You'd like to use your knowledge of people's heights and ages to predict their weight.

You locate a sample of, say, 50 people, weigh them, measure each person's height, and record their ages. Then you push that data through an application that calculates multiple regression statistics and in that way learn the values of the remaining three items in the equation:

- a_1, a coefficient you multiply by a person's height
- a_2, a coefficient you multiply by a person's age
- b, a constant that you add to adjust the scale of the results

You can now find another person whose weight you *don't* know. Get his height and age and plug them into your multiple regression equation. If your sample of 50 people is reasonably representative, and if height and age are reliably related to weight, you can expect to predict this new person's weight with fair accuracy.

You have established the numeric relationships between two predictor variables, height and age, and a predicted variable, weight. You did so using a sample in which weight—which you want to predict—is known. You expect to use that information with people whose weight you don't know.

At root, those concepts are the same as the ones that underlie several of the decision analytics techniques that this book discusses. You start out with a sample of records (for example, people, plants, or objects) whose categories you already know (for example, their recent purchase behaviors with respect to your products, whether they produce crops in relatively arid conditions, whether they shatter when you subject them to abnormal temperature ranges). You take the necessary measures on those records and run the numbers through one or more of the techniques described in this book.

Then you apply the resulting equations to a new sample of people (or plants or objects) whose purchasing behavior, or ability to produce crops, or resistance to unusual temperatures is unknown. If your original sample was a representative one, and if there are useful relationships between the variables you measured and the ones you want to predict, you're in business. You can decide whether John Jones is likely or unlikely to buy your product, whether your new breed of corn will flourish or wither if it's planted just east of Tucson, or whether pistons made from a new alloy will shatter in high temperature driving.

I slipped something in on you in the last two paragraphs. The first example in this section concerns the prediction of a continuous variable, weight. Ordinary, least-squares multiple regression is well suited to that sort of situation. But the example in the previous section uses categories, nominal classifications, as a predicted variable: cures infection versus doesn't cure it. As the values of a *predicted variable*, categories present problems that multiple regression has difficulty overcoming. When the *predictor* variables are categories, there's no problem. In fact, the traditional approach to analysis of variance (ANOVA) and the regression approach to ANOVA are both designed specifically to handle that sort of situation. The problem arises when it's the predicted variable rather than the predictor variables that is measured on a nominal rather than a continuous scale.

But that's precisely the sort of situation you're confronted with when you have to make a choice between one of two or more alternatives. Will this new product succeed or fail? Will this new medicine prolong longevity or shorten it due to side effects? Based solely on their voting records, which political party did these two congressional representatives from the nineteenth century belong to?

So, to answer that sort of question, you need analysis techniques—decision analytics—designed specifically for situations in which the outcome or predicted variable is measured on a nominal scale, in terms of categories. That, of course, is the focus of this book: analysis techniques that enable you to use numeric variables to classify records into groups, and thereby make decisions about the records on the basis of the group you project them into. To anticipate some of the examples I use in subsequent chapters:

- How can you classify potential borrowers into those who are likely to repay loans in accordance with the loan schedules, and those who are unlikely to do so?

- How can you accurately classify apparently identical plants and animals into different species according to physical characteristics such as petal width or length of femur?

- Which people in this database are so likely to purchase our resort properties in the Bahamas that we should fly them there and house them for a weeklong sales pitch?

Access to a Reference Sample

In the examples I just cited, it's best if you have a reference sample: a sample of records that are representative of the records that you want to classify and that are already correctly classified. (Such samples are often termed *supervised* or *training samples*.) The second example outlined in this chapter, regarding weight, height, and age, discussed the development of an equation to predict weight using a sample in which weight was known. Later on you could use the equation with people whose weight is not known.

Similarly, if your purpose is to classify loan applicants into Approved versus Declined, it's best if you can start with a representative reference sample of applicants, perhaps culled from your company's historical records, along with variables such as default status, income, credit rating, and state of residence. You could develop an equation that classifies applicants into your Approved and Declined categories.

Multiple regression is not an ideal technique for this sort of decision analysis because, as I noted earlier, the predicted variable is not a continuous one such as weight but is a dichotomy. However, multiple regression shares many concepts and treatments with techniques that in fact are suited to classifying records into categories. So you're ahead of the game if you've had occasion to study or use multiple regression in the past. If not, don't be concerned; this book doesn't assume that you're a multiple regression maven.

Multiple regression does require that you have access to a reference sample, one in which the variable that is eventually to be predicted is known. That information is used to develop the prediction equation, which in turn is used with data sets in which the predicted variable is as yet unknown. Other analytic techniques, designed for use with categorical outcome variables, and which also must make use of reference samples, include those I discuss in the next few sections.

Multivariate Analysis of Variance

Multivariate analysis of variance, or MANOVA, extends the purpose of ordinary ANOVA to multiple dependent variables. (Statistical jargon tends to use the term *multivariate* only when there is more than one *predicted* or *outcome* or *dependent* variable; however, even this distinction breaks down when you consider discriminant analysis.) Using ordinary univariate ANOVA, you might investigate whether people who pay back loans according to the agreed terms have, on average at the time the loan is made, different credit ratings than people who subsequently default. (I review the concepts and procedures used in ANOVA in Chapter 3, "Univariate Analysis of Variance (ANOVA).") Here, the predictor variable is whether the borrower pays back the loan, and the predicted variable is the borrower's credit rating.

But you might be interested in more than just those people's credit ratings. Do the two groups differ in average age of the borrower? In the size of the loans they apply for? In the average term of the loan? If you want to answer all those questions, not just one, you typically start out with MANOVA, the multivariate version of ANOVA. Notice that if you want MANOVA to analyze group differences in average credit ratings, average age of borrower, average size of loan, and average term of loan, you need to work with multiple predicted variables, not solely the single predicted variable you would analyze using univariate ANOVA.

MANOVA is not a classification procedure in the sense I used the phrase earlier. You do not employ MANOVA to help determine whether some combination of credit rating, borrower's age, size of loan, and term of loan accurately classifies applicants according to whether they can be expected to repay the loan or default. Instead, MANOVA helps you decide whether those who repay their loans differ from those who don't on any one of, or a combination of, the outcome variables—credit rating, age, and so on.

You don't use one univariate ANOVA after another to make those inferences because the outcome variables are likely correlated with one another. Those correlations have an effect, which cannot be quantified, on the probability estimate of each univariate ANOVA. In other words, you might think that each of your univariate F-tests is operating at an alpha level of .05. But because of the correlations the F-tests are not independent of one another and the actual alpha level for one test might be .12, for another test .08, and so on. MANOVA helps to protect you against this kind of problem by taking all the outcome variables into account simultaneously. See Chapter 4, "Multivariate Analysis of Variance (MANOVA)," for a discussion of the methods used in MANOVA.

It surprises some multivariate analysts to learn that you can carry out an entire MANOVA using Excel's worksheet functions only. But it's true that by deploying Excel's matrix functions properly—MDETERM(), MINVERSE(), MMULT(), TRANSPOSE() and so on—you can go from raw data to a complete MANOVA including Wilks' Lambda and a multivariate F-test in just a few steps. Nevertheless, among the files you can download from the publisher's website is a MANOVA workbook with subroutines that automate the process for you. Apart from learning what's involved, there's little point to doing it by hand if you can turn things over to code.

But MANOVA, despite its advantages in this sort of situation, still doesn't classify records for you. The reason I've gone on about MANOVA is explained in the next section.

Discriminant Function Analysis

Discriminant function analysis is a technique developed by Sir Ronald Fisher during the 1930s. It is sometimes referred to as *linear discriminant analysis* or *LDA*, or as *multiple discriminant analysis*, both in writings and in the names conferred by statistical applications such as R. Like MANOVA, discriminant analysis is considered a true multivariate technique because its approach is to simultaneously analyze multiple continuous variables, even though they are treated as predictors rather than predicted or outcome variables.

Discriminant analysis is typically used as a followup to a MANOVA. If the MANOVA returns a multivariate F-ratio that is not significant at the alpha level selected by the researcher, there is no point to proceeding further. If the categories do not differ significantly as to their mean values on any of the continuous variables, then the reverse is also true. The continuous variables cannot reliably classify the records into the categories of interest.

But if the MANOVA returns a significant multivariate F-ratio, it makes sense to continue with a discriminant analysis, which, in effect, turns the MANOVA around. Instead of asking whether the categories differ in their mean values of the continuous variables, as does MANOVA, discriminant analysis asks how the continuous variables combine to separate the records into different categories.

The viewpoint adopted by discriminant analysis brings about two important outcomes:

- It enables you to look more closely than does MANOVA at how the continuous variables work together to distinguish the category membership.

- It provides you with an equation called a discriminant function that, when used like a multiple regression equation, assigns individual records to categories such as Repays versus Defaults or Buys versus Doesn't Buy.

Chapter 5, "Discriminant Function Analysis: The Basics," and Chapter 6, "Discriminant Function Analysis: Further Issues," show you how to obtain the discriminant function, and what use you can make of it, using Excel as the platform. An associated Excel workbook automates a discriminant analysis using the results of a preliminary MANOVA.

Both MANOVA and discriminant analysis are legitimately thought of as multivariate techniques, particularly when you consider that they look at the same phenomena, but from different ends of the telescope. They are also *parametric* techniques: Their statistical tests make use of theoretical distributions such as the F-ratio and Wilks' lambda. Therefore these parametric techniques are able to return to you information about, say, the likelihood of getting an F-ratio as large as the one you observed in your sample if the population means were actually identical.

Those parametric properties invest the tests with *statistical power*. Compared to other, nonparametric tests, techniques such as discriminant analysis are better (sometimes much better) able to inform you that an outcome is a reliable one. With a reliable finding, you have every right to expect that you would get the same results from a replication sample, constructed similarly.

But that added statistical power comes with a cost: You have to make some assumptions (which of course you can test). In the case of MANOVA and discriminant analysis, for example, you assume that the distribution of the continuous variables is "multivariate normal." That assumption implies that you should check scattercharts of each pair of continuous variables, across all your groups, looking for nonlinear relationships between the variables. You should also arrange for histograms of each variable, again by group, to see whether the variable's distribution appears skewed.

> **NOTE**
>
> Excel can make your life a little easier here, although admittedly not by much. It's easy enough to create a scatterchart in Excel. (Begin by going to the Insert tab on the Ribbon in Excel 2007 or 2010 or 2013. Click the Chart Wizard button in an earlier version.) But if you have 3 categories and 7 continuous variables, that's $3 \times 7 \times 6$ or a tedious 126 scattercharts to create. Pivot charts would make things a little quicker, but pivot charts do not offer a scatterchart type.
>
> Excel has a worksheet function, SKEW(), which returns the skewness of a distribution of values. The function does not return perhaps the most popular version of skewness, the average cubed z-score. Instead, SKEW() uses this formula:
>
> $$N\sum_{i=1}^{N} z^3 / (N-1)(N-2)$$
>
> With a small number of records, Excel's value of skewness can be easily half again as large as the average cubed z-score (which of course does not depend on the number of records). Still, using SKEW() is undoubtedly faster than creating histograms. (The Data Analysis add-in has a Histograms tool that can speed the process considerably.)

As another example, MANOVA assumes that the variance-covariance matrix is equivalent in the different categories. All that means is that if you assembled a matrix of your variables, showing each variable's variance and its covariance with the other continuous variables in your design, the values in that matrix would be equivalent for the Repayers and for the Defaulters, for the Buyers and the Non-Buyers. Notice that I used the word "equivalent," not "equal." The issue is whether the variance-covariance matrices are equal in the population, not necessarily in the sample (where they'll never be equal). Again, you can test whether your data meets this assumption. Bartlett's test is the usual method and the MANOVA workbook, which you can download from the publisher's website, carries that test out for you.

If these assumptions are met, you'll have a more powerful test available than if they are not met. When the assumptions are not met, you can fall back on what's typically a somewhat less powerful technique: logistic regression.

Logistic Regression

Logistic regression differs from ordinary least squares regression in a fundamental way. Least squares regression depends on correlations, which in turn depend on the calculation of the sums of squared deviations, and regression works to minimize those sums—hence the term "least squares."

In contrast, logistic regression depends not on correlations but on odds ratios (or, less formally, odds). The process of logistic regression is not a straightforward computation as it is in simple or multiple regression. Logistic regression uses *maximum likelihood* techniques to arrive at the coefficients for its equation: for example, the values for a_1 and a_2 that I mentioned at the beginning of this chapter. Conceptually there's nothing magical about maximum likelihood. It's a matter of trial and error: the educated and automated process of trying out different values for the coefficients until they provide an optimal result. I discuss how to convert the probabilities to odds, the odds to a special formulation called the *logit*, how to get your maximum likelihood estimates using Excel's Solver—and how to find your way back to probabilities, in Chapter 2, "Logistic Regression."

Largely because the logistic regression process does *not* rely on reference distributions such as the F distribution to help evaluate the sums of squares, logistic regression cannot be considered a parametric test. One important consequence is that logistic regression does not involve the assumptions that other techniques such as MANOVA and discriminant analysis employ. That means you can use logistic regression with some data sets when you might not be able to use parametric tests.

For example, in logistic regression there is no assumption that the continuous variables are normally distributed. There is no assumption that the continuous variables are related in a linear rather than curvilinear fashion. There is no assumption that their variances and covariances are equivalent across groups.

So, logistic regression positions you to classify cases using continuous variables that might well fail to behave as required by MANOVA and discriminant analysis. It extends the number of data sets that you can classify.

But the same tradeoff is in play. Although you can get away with violations in logistic regression that might cause grief in MANOVA, nothing's free. You pay for discarding assumptions with a loss of statistical power. Logistic regression simply is not as sensitive to small changes in the data set as is discriminant analysis.

Classifying According to Naturally Occurring Clusters

In contrast to the techniques that I've briefly outlined in the preceding sections, the second set of analytic techniques that this book discusses does not necessarily start out with reference samples that include actual category membership. Instead, it's hoped that the categories (often termed *clusters* in these methods) will emerge from combinations of the measured variables, combinations established and assessed by the software you use.

Principal Components Analysis

The book moves back to genuinely multivariate analysis in Chapter 7, "Principal Components Analysis." This approach dates back to the beginning of the twentieth century and is therefore the oldest of the analytic techniques discussed in this book. Principal components analysis is the precursor to factor analysis, both historically and procedurally. Factor analysis began to gain currency in the 1930s, roughly 25 years after Karl Pearson was doing early work on principal components. And factor analysis nearly always starts with a principal components analysis, although the numeric inputs might be slightly different and the purposes of the two techniques aren't quite the same.

The idea behind principal components analysis is that it's possible to combine several measured variables into a single principal component (or, equivalently, many measured variables into just a few principal components) without losing a significant amount of meaningful information. The result is a much simpler data set that the researcher can investigate more easily. The same is true for factor analysis, but there the emphasis is on understanding how a factor, or component, which is not directly observable or measurable is expressed in variables that, in contrast, can be measured.

So far as I can tell, principal components analysis was used in just this way until the mid-1960s, when researchers in various fields began to notice that principal components analysis might also be useful for the purpose of classification. It can happen—and Chapter 7 details a couple of examples—that when you extract a few principal components from a larger number of measured variables, the records cluster together in the space that's defined by the principal components. Along with the Excel workbook for Chapter 7 you'll find a file named Factor.xls, which runs a principal components analysis for you and performs a Varimax rotation of the components' axes.

If those clusters make sense, you might well be onto a finding that's really compelling. But great care is needed: Methods that work with data that includes no information about actual membership are particularly susceptible to nonsense results. And when the composition of the clusters conforms to what you expect, it's even more important to have another data sample at hand so that you can validate your results.

If the first analysis results in ridiculous cluster assignments, you're probably not tempted to think that you're on to something. If the cluster assignments make sense, it's incumbent on you to replicate the finding. (You don't want to claim that you've achieved cold fusion on your kitchen table if you can't do it more than once.)

But principal components analysis has another role to play in the classification of records. Among the characteristics of the components you extract from a raw data set are the following:

■ The components are uncorrelated. This characteristic has several advantages. One relatively minor advantage is that the components are orthogonal—their axes are at right angles to one another, which can make the interpretation less ambiguous.

■ Another, more important advantage is that because two uncorrelated components cannot share variance, it's possible to set aside as irrelevant components that are extracted later in the process. Components have characteristics called *eigenvalues* that can tell you how much of the overall variance in the data set each component accounts for.

You can often remove components with low eigenvalues from subsequent analysis. Doing so tends to discard junk variation: measurement error, sampling error, variation that's specific to a particular variable and therefore contrary to the notion of a "component."

All this is consistent with the basic notion of principal components: to find combinations of variables that bring important, meaningful variation along with them and that leave irrelevant, misleading variation behind. You also wind up with (usually) many fewer components than there were measured variables, and that eases the task of making sense of the results.

When you get rid of irrelevant, nuisance variation, you can work instead with relatively clean components. That can make the groups subsequently derived by cluster analysis much clearer.

Unfortunately, even if the groups are clear, well separated, and distinct, it doesn't necessarily follow that they mean anything. Again, the better the results look at first, the more important it is to replicate them, validate them, and verify them.

Among the techniques that are particularly improved by the use of principal components instead of the raw data are those that are collectively termed *cluster analysis*.

Cluster Analysis

Cluster analysis is distinguished from other approaches to classification by the fact that it does not require you to know up front what category—that is, what cluster—each record in your data set belongs to. True, principal components analysis doesn't either, but although it's useful as a tool in classification, it's not intended as a classification technique.

> **NOTE** There are, however, certain equivalencies in the math that underlies principal components analysis and cluster analysis. It appears that the approach taken by principal components analysis is considerably closer to that taken by cluster analysis than had been previously recognized.

The two different branches of cluster analysis, the linkage methods and the centroid-based methods, are both designed to cause clusters to emerge from the variables (or, as I indicated in the previous section, the principal components) that you supply.

Methods such as discriminant analysis and logistic regression require you to supply a reference sample, one that separates a sample of records into the categories you're interested in. You develop your classification equation using that data set. Later on you apply the equation to records that are as yet unclassified.

Cluster analysis works differently. The algorithms look for records that are similar to one another, and assign (and reassign) those records to the same clusters. Typically, the algorithms keep plugging away until no records are reassigned during an iteration through the loop.

One problem that arises early when you're deciding on a clustering method is the question of what constitutes similarity. There are various ways to define similarity, and perhaps the most popular is by way of a distance measure: how far a given record is from another record, or from the center of a cluster.

> **NOTE** Cluster analysis, along with MANOVA and discriminant analysis, provides for the use of multiple continuous variables in cluster or category formation. With multiple continuous variables, the center of a cluster is not a simple mean value, but a vector of averages. That vector is called a *centroid*, a term that you'll come across often in this book.

It complicates matters that there are several types of distance. Ordinary Euclidean distance is one: The width of this sepal is 3.5 centimeters, and the width of that sepal is 3.75 centimeters. For various reasons, the Euclidean distance is usually squared: The squared Euclidean distance between the width of the two sepals is $(3.75 - 3.5)^2$. After some further calculations, though, some analyses take the square root of the results to return to a simple Euclidean metric.

Another type of distance measure is the familiar Pearson correlation (although the larger the correlation, the closer the records). Using Pearson correlation as a distance measure forces the standardization of the measures, and so the effect of the scale of the original measurement is removed.

Yet another measure is Mahalanobis' D^2, which incorporates the variables' covariances into the squared Euclidean distance, so that the variables are not necessarily and automatically regarded as orthogonal to one another.

Measures of similarity are not limited to distances, though. Agreement measures are sometimes used: "Both these people have studied calculus." But the math involved in handling agreement measures is not as straightforward as it is for distance measures.

Furthermore, with agreement measures you have to watch what you're using to indicate similarity. If two people both own 1920 Duesenberg autos, that's likely a more meaningful index of similarity than if two people *don't* own Duesenbergs.

Because squared Euclidean distances represent something of a standard method of measurement in cluster analysis, I stick with them as measures of similarity in this book's examples (see Chapter 8, "Cluster Analysis: The Basics," and Chapter 9, "Cluster Analysis: Further Issues").

The two branches of cluster analysis that I mentioned earlier, linkage methods and centroid-based methods, frequently return different results. Because cluster analysis is at root an exploratory method, one that seeks to establish undefined clusters, you might want to consider running both methods to determine which, if either, results in clusters that make sense to you.

The linkage methods work from the ground up, starting with the two records that have the smallest distance between them and calling those two records a cluster. Then the record with the smallest distance to that cluster's centroid is found, and that distance is compared to the smallest distance between that record and another single record. If the distance to the existing cluster is smaller, the third record is assigned to that cluster. But if the distance to another individual record is smaller, a new cluster is created. (Several different definitions of "smallest" distance exist in the linkage methods, including single linkage, complete linkage, and average linkage.)

The most popular of the centroid-based methods is *k-means*, where "k" simply refers to the number of continuous variables involved. K-means is more of a top-down approach than are the linkage methods. Further, you are expected to specify the number of clusters to establish. The centroids of each cluster are established randomly at the outset, and the process continues by assigning and reassigning individual records to their nearest cluster, updating the centroid values accordingly, until a journey through the loop causes no records to be reassigned to a different cluster.

The Excel workbooks available for download from the publisher's website include a workbook with VBA code that performs k-means analysis for you.

Some Terminology Problems

The first main section of this chapter focuses on situations in which you start out knowing which categories some of your records belong to, and you want to know how to classify other records whose categories aren't yet known. The second main section introduces other techniques that ignore known classifications at first. They seek instead to determine whether classifications emerge from how individual records cluster together due to their similarities on measured, continuous variables. Those techniques include principal component analysis (PCA) and cluster analysis.

Before moving on to Chapter 2, "Logistic Regression," I want to address some problems with terminology that characterize inferential statistics in general but multivariate statistics in particular, because of the way that variables can switch roles before you're through with them. These problems can create particular confusion in the exploratory context that often characterizes decision analytics.

The Design Sets the Terms

For a variety of reasons, it's important to distinguish between an analytic technique (such as univariate ANOVA) and your reason for using it. Suppose you have three treatments you want to test: a new drug, a traditional drug and a placebo. You plan to test whether the treatments have different effects on adult females' cholesterol levels. You intend to randomly sample your subjects from a population of women whose cholesterol levels are abnormally high, and to randomly assign them to one of your three treatments.

In this context it's typical and meaningful to refer to the cholesterol measures as a *dependent variable*. Your hypothesis is that the subjects' cholesterol levels *depend* on the treatment to which they are assigned. There is a *causal relationship* between the dependent variable and the treatment.

For some reason that's apparently lost to history, the three treatments you have in mind, taken together, are termed an *independent variable*. There's nothing independent about it. As the experimenter, you decide what values it takes on (here, new drug, traditional drug, and placebo). You decide (here, randomly) who to assign to which drug. The only rationale for terming it an independent variable seems to be to distinguish it from a dependent variable.

Still, that's a relatively benign problem. Statistical jargon has many more misleading terms than "independent variable." But it's necessary to remember that *independent variable* and *dependent variable* belong to your design, not to the statistical procedure. As you conceive of and carry out your experiment, the differences in average cholesterol level among your three treatment groups depend on the three treatments, not on extraneous sources of variation such as subject self-selection or regression toward the mean. Over time, the terms have come to connote the nature of the design: an independent variable, which is under the experimenter's control, and a dependent variable, which responds in a cause-and-effect fashion to differences in the independent variable.

Now suppose that you decide not to use traditional ANOVA math on your data. The design and management of your experiment is the same as before. But instead of accumulating squared deviations between and within groups, you use one of the available coding methods to represent group membership and pump your data through a multiple regression application.

The results—the sums of squares, the F-ratio, the p value—remain the same as with the traditional ANOVA. More important to this discussion, it's still appropriate to use the terms *dependent variable* and *independent variable*. Your experimental design has not changed—just the way that you do the arithmetic. The differences in the group means on the dependent variable are still caused by the differential effects of the treatments and, to a degree that's under your control, to the effects of chance.

Causation Versus Prediction

Now, completely alter the rationale for and the design of the research. Instead of researching the causal and differential effects of drugs on cholesterol levels, you're interested in determining whether a relationship exists between the Dow Jones Industrial Average (DJIA) and other indexes of market valuation, such as the advance-decline (A/D) ratio and the total volume on the New York Stock Exchange. The researcher could easily consult any of hundreds of online sources of historical information regarding the DJIA and associated statistics, such as trading volume and A/D ratios, to pick up tens of thousands of data points.

This is different. Here, the researcher is not in a position to manipulate the values of one or more independent variables, as is the case in a true experiment. The researcher cannot by fiat state that, "The advance-decline ratio shall be 1.5 on September 30," and observe a resulting change in the DJIA as though there were a causal relationship. Nor is the researcher able to randomly select and assign subjects to one group or another: Membership in the companies that make up the DJIA is largely fixed and certainly beyond the researcher's control.

There's nothing intrinsically wrong with this sort of situation, although it's often referred to, a little insultingly, as a "grab sample." It's well suited to *making predictions*, just not to *explaining causation*. The researcher can't directly manipulate the actual values of the predictor variables, but instead can ask, "What value of the DJIA would we expect to see if the trading volume increased by 10%?"

It's best to avoid terms such as *independent variable* and *dependent variable* with data acquired in this way. They imply that the researcher controls the independent variables, and that there is a causal relationship between an independent variable and the dependent variable. The relationship might indeed be causal, but the researcher is not in a position to control an independent variable so as to demonstrate the causality.

To acknowledge that "independent" and "dependent" might not be accurate terms without a randomized study with direct manipulation of an independent variable, many writers have adopted the terms *predictor variable* to refer, for example, to A/D ratios and trading volume, and *predicted variable* to refer to the variable they want to predict, such as the DJIA. (You also see terms such as *outcome* and *criterion* in place of *dependent* or *predicted*, but they just tend to beg the question.)

Why the Terms Matter

Two fundamental reasons explain why I have spent so much space here on what must seem the pedantry of terminology.

One reason is that most of the techniques of decision analytics are used in an exploratory way. You're looking for combinations of numerically measured variables that, taken together, might explain differences between categories. It's typical to use data that already exists, often in companies' operational databases, to search for those relationships and formulate hypotheses accordingly. Only then might you set up a true experiment in which you randomly select and assign subjects to groups and manipulate directly the nature of treatments applied to each group. In this way you hope to confirm your hypotheses, and only then it might be appropriate to imply causation using terms such as *independent* and *dependent*.

The second reason is that in at least a major subset of decision analytics work, the variables change horses midstream. As described in previous sections of this chapter on MANOVA and discriminant analysis, you might start out with two or more groups that act as predictor variables and two or more continuous variables that act as predicted variables. MANOVA asks whether any groups differ significantly on one or more predicted variables or on some combination of the predicted variables.

If you get a significant result from the MANOVA, you generally proceed to discriminant analysis, where you seek to determine which continuous variables, alone or in combination, distinguish the groups. In effect, you turn the design end for end. The categories that were the predictors in the MANOVA now constitute the predicted variable in the discriminant analysis. The continuous variables that were the predicted variables in the MANOVA are now the predictor variables in the discriminant analysis.

The situation is clearly impossible if you begin by calling the categories an independent variable in a MANOVA and wind up calling them a dependent variable in a discriminant analysis. It's just a little confusing, not impossible, if you think of the categories as predictors in the MANOVA and as predicted variables in the subsequent discriminant analysis.

Therefore, I have tried in this book to use *predictor variable* and *predicted variable* unless the context makes it clear that an example assumes a true randomized experiment.

Okay, let's move on to the meat of decision analytics, starting with logistic regression.

Logistic Regression

One of the tools of decision analytics is called *logistic regression*. This method actually isn't any sort of regression at all: It uses maximum likelihood estimates (which are optimized probabilities, as you'll see later in this chapter) instead of correlations to arrive at its solutions. The use of the word *regression* appears to be due to the similarity of the equations that result. For example, in ordinary, least squares multiple regression you might arrive at an equation that looks like this:

Income = b_1 × Age + b_2 × Education + *Intercept*

whereas logistic regression might be used for a different problem and might result in an equation that looks like this:

Probability of Payback = b_1 × CreditRating + b_2 × Age + *Intercept*

Apart from the differences in the names of the variables, these two equations appear similar. Each one estimates a value by multiplying a coefficient (the *b* values) times a variable and adding a constant called the *intercept*. So the ways the equations are structured look similar, and that seems to have led to the use of the term *regression* for both. But the differences in the derivations of the equations are profound.

This chapter discusses the derivation of the logistic regression equation and the reasons that it differs from ordinary least squares regression. Another book of mine, *Predictive Analytics: Microsoft Excel* (Que Publishing), devotes two full chapters to logistic regression. I spend only one chapter on it in this book, mainly to offer you a basis for contrasting logistic regression with two other important methods of classification, *discriminant function analysis* and *cluster analysis*. Although this chapter shows you how to carry out a logistic regression analysis using Excel, there's a good bit more to it than one chapter can cover.

The Rationale for Logistic Regression

Ordinary, least squares regression assumes and enforces a linear relationship between two variables. You might use simple regression to estimate a person's income from the number of years that he or she attended school. In that case, one of the assumptions you make is that in the population you want to investigate, there's a straight line that describes the relationship between income and years of education. Figure 2.1 shows an example.

Figure 2.1
This is why it's called *linear* regression.

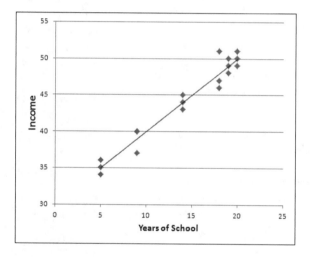

Notice in Figure 2.1 that a straight line describes the relationship between the two charted variables. Yes, most of the actual observations stray from that line, some by an eyelash and some by a greater margin. By and large, though, the relationship is linear. At any given point, if you go up by one year on the Years of School axis you go up by $1,000 on the Income axis.

Contrast that outcome with the one shown in Figure 2.2.

The relationship shown in Figure 2.2 does not involve a straight line. The amount of an increase in Income depends not only on Age but on the location on the horizontal axis of the Age value. Toward the middle of the axis, an increase of one year in Age is associated with an increase of $1,000 in Income. At the tails, though, getting one year older implies an additional $500, not $1,000.

(We usually term this sort of relationship *curvilinear*, reserving the term *linear* for relationships that are straight-line, or nearly so.)

Figure 2.2
This sort of relationship is usually termed *curvilinear*.

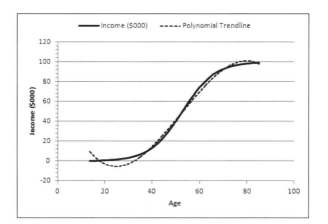

Least squares regression is perfectly capable of dealing with curvilinear relationships, although it takes a little extra handling. If the curve has just one bend, a quadratic component should suffice. With two bends (as shown in Figure 2.2, one at each end) in the curve, you might want to try fitting a cubic component. So your regression equation might be something such as this:

$$y = 79.846 - 7.6732x + 0.2026x^2 - 0.0013x^3$$

This equation is shown graphically in Figure 2.2 as the dashed line.

Although adding the squared and the cubed components to the equation helps, it's clearly not ideal. For example, the errors of estimate are larger at the tails of the distribution than toward its center. Notice how the differences between the plotted income (solid line) and the estimated income (dotted line) are much greater in the left hand tail than in the middle of the distribution.

Furthermore, the trendline would continue turning upward at the left end and downward at the right end if you extend the range of Age beyond the values shown in the chart. That would happen even though the actual probabilities flatten out at each end. Then, the curvilinear regression line would be telling you that the closer that Age comes to zero, the greater the Income. It would also tell you that the higher the Age, the lower the Income.

Suppose that instead of investigating the relationship between age and income, you were interested in the relationship between income and the probability of repaying a loan (to anticipate an example from later in this chapter). The curved trendline in Figure 2.3 is a much better representation of the reality of the situation than is the straight line.

Figure 2.3
Linear regression can mislead you when the angle of the slope varies at different locations on the horizontal axis.

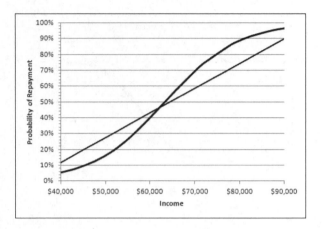

The Scaling Problem

The question of the accuracy of the regression line is not the only issue, though. There is also the problem of maximum values and minimum values. Suppose that you are using least squares regression to estimate a probability such as the likelihood of borrowers paying off loans within some specified period. You might set up an analysis like the one shown in Figure 2.4.

Figure 2.4
Least squares regression can cause impossible estimates such as probabilities that are less than zero and greater than 1.

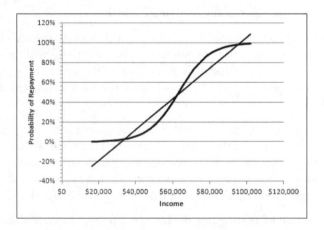

In Figure 2.4, as in Figure 2.3, the probability that borrowers will repay loans appears on the vertical axis and the borrowers' income on the horizontal axis. This situation shows one of the problems that can come up in purely linear regression. The predictor variable—here, Income—must be allowed to vary from zero (or in some cases, from a negative amount) to well into the hundreds of thousands.

But the predicted variable—here, probability of repayment—often must stay within certain limits. When the predicted variable represents a probability, it's normally required that it stay within a 0% to 100% range. Negative probabilities aren't allowed. Probabilities greater than 100% aren't helpful when you're trying to determine the interest rate that you will offer a potential borrower.

So ordinary least squares regression confronts you with a couple of scaling problems at the tails of the regression lines. Linear regression can take you into the uncharted territory of negative probabilities and of probabilities that exceed 100%. Curvilinear regression can create headaches by pointing the regression line in the wrong direction after a bend has taken place.

About Underlying Assumptions

If you began to study quantitative analysis at roughly the time that I did—by which I mean sometime during the twentieth century—you probably encountered dire warnings about assumptions that are made in regression analysis, in the analysis of variance, and similar methods.

Many students got the idea that all those assumptions put you into such a straitjacket that there wasn't much point to doing the analysis at all. In fact, an entire branch of statistical analysis, *nonparametrics*, was nurtured by worries about the effects of violating those assumptions. That's just wrong.

> **NOTE** Many nonparametric methods are now all but abandoned due to the so-called "robustness studies" of the 1960s and '70s, which showed that parametric techniques are frequently robust with respect to the violation of their assumptions. (But many of those methods are still with us, frequently with good reason.)

In particular, you can certainly carry out regression analysis (for example) even if some of the underlying assumptions are violated. But there are cases, such as those that are this chapter's topic, in which ignoring the assumptions can take you to misleading conclusions.

I don't want you to forget about those assumptions, but I do think that you should apply them judiciously. Some situations can be handled much more effectively if you ask yourself how well they meet an assumption. And there are plenty of situations in which it doesn't make any difference whether you ignore those assumptions. The next few sections discuss the assumptions, their violation, and the possible results.

Equal Spread

One problem with least squares regression analysis comes about when you consider the problem of equal variances, sometimes termed *homoscedasticity*. The problem becomes acute when you are working with dichotomies such as Buys versus Doesn't Buy, or nominal variables with categories such as Toyota versus Ford versus General Motors.

When you analyze an outcome variable that takes on many different numeric values, it can be a good idea to check whether your data conforms to the assumption of equal variances.

Suppose that you're investigating the relationship of age to weight in adolescent males—say, between 12 and 18 years of age. The assumption of equal variances holds that you expect the variability in weight to be the same in 13-year-olds as in 12-year-olds, the same in 14-years-olds as in 13-year-olds, and so on.

What if that assumption is violated? What if the variability in weight among 17-year-olds is much less than the variability among 12-year-olds? Even if that's so, you don't need to worry that the planets will leave their orbits. You can still calculate a correlation coefficient between age and weight. You can still calculate a regression coefficient and intercept, and use an F-test to check the reliability of whatever finding you arrive at.

The worst case would be that if you used the regression equation to predict the weight of 12-year-olds (whose variability you find to be higher), your predictions would not be as accurate as they would be for 17-year-olds (whose variability you find to be lower). Figure 2.5 shows how this could come about.

Figure 2.5
The variability among the younger subjects is clearly greater than among the older.

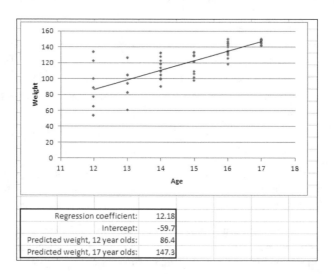

Notice that the spread of weights for younger subjects on the vertical axis in Figure 2.5 is visibly greater than the spread of weights among older subjects. If you run a regression analysis of weight on age for this data set, you get the coefficient and intercept shown in cells G17 and G18. Applying those figures to a new subject whose age is 12 results in a predicted weight of 86.4, and for a 17-year-old the prediction would be 147.3.

If you selected another ten 12-year-olds and applied the regression equation, you would predict that each of them would weigh 86.4 pounds. And if these additional ten 12-year-olds actually displayed the same degree of variability as those in your original sample (which you can see on the chart in Figure 2.5), your estimates would be off by as much as 40 to 50 pounds. Notice that your original sample includes two 12-year-olds who weigh 134 pounds, and one who weighs only 53 pounds.

But if you applied the same regression equation to ten new 17-year-olds, your errors of estimate would be much smaller. Because the variability in weight among 17-year-olds is low compared to 12-year-olds, your estimate of 147.3 for 17-year-olds is unlikely to be off by more than 7 or 8 pounds. The weights of your original sample of 17-year-olds range from 141 to 150.

So the accuracy of your prediction depends on the age of those whose weight you're predicting. That's inconvenient. And a statistic such as the standard error of estimate (which is the standard deviation of the differences between your predictions and the actual values) will be a less accurate gauge of your equation's usefulness for younger ages than for older ages.

But violating the assumption of equal variances doesn't invalidate your analysis. You can still make a reasonably accurate estimate of the weight of older adolescents based on their ages.

Keep in mind also that the assumption of equal variances pertains to the population that your sample comes from. Samples always involve some degree of error, and the smaller your sample the more error you expect. With samples as small as those depicted in Figure 2.5 you expect that some error finds its way into the analysis. The variance of the weights of 12-year-olds might in fact be very close to that of 17-year-olds in the population. But with only 12 to 16 observations in each age group you expect to see differences in variability that wouldn't appear if you had, say, 200 observations in each group.

However, in the example used in this section, the differences in variability are relatively benign. The situation is different when you're dealing with a dichotomy, or any categorical variable such as product brand.

Equal Variances with Dichotomies

Suppose that you want to predict the probability of the purchase of a product, using as a predictor the number of similar products a shopper has bought. With a dichotomous dependent variable such as *buys—doesn't buy*, the variance is calculated as pq, where p is a probability and q is $(1 - p)$. Therefore, if the probability p is 10% that a shopper who has already bought five similar products will make another purchase, then the probability q that he won't make the purchase is 90%.

In that case, the variance of the probability that the shopper will purchase is $(0.1)(0.9)$, or 0.09. What of shoppers who have bought just one similar product? Or ten similar products? There are just two possibilities:

■ The shoppers who have already purchased larger or smaller numbers of similar products have different probabilities of buying the product in question. In that case their values of p differ, and therefore so do their values of q. Then the variance pq must differ according to the probability of purchasing, and you can't meet the assumption of equal variances.

■ All the shoppers have the same probability of purchasing, regardless of the number of similar products they have bought in the past. Then p is the same for all shoppers, and so is pq, the variance of the probabilities. This situation meets the assumption of equal variances. But if all shoppers have the same probability of buying, what's the point of analyzing the relationship at all? Only one probability of purchase exists, and it does not vary with the number of prior purchases.

In sum, when your predicted variable is a dichotomy, the equal variances problem becomes thornier than when the predicted variable is measured on a continuous scale. You can arrive at equal variances at different values of the predictor variable only when the probability of a predicted value is identical across all values of the predictor. A situation that's manageable when the predicted value is measured on a continuous scale becomes impossible to handle when the outcome is a dichotomy.

Equal Spread and the Range

Don't be misled, by the way, by the appearance of an XY (Scatter) chart of two variables such as age and weight. That sort of chart is extremely useful for several reasons, but it can suggest that there's less variability in the tails of the distribution than in the center, and that's not necessarily so. See Figure 2.6.

Figure 2.6
The variability toward the center of the distribution is apparently greater than at its tails.

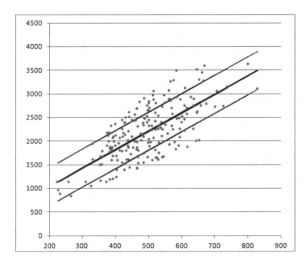

One of the problems with the range as a measure of the degree of variability in a set of normally distributed values is that the range is sensitive to the number of values involved.

Suppose that you have at hand the weight of 10 men. The variable Weight is distributed normally and the *population* of adult males has relatively few instances of weights less than 100 pounds, and relatively few more than 200 pounds. It is therefore unlikely that your *sample* of 10 men includes any that are lower than 100 pounds or greater than 200. The range of weights in your sample is likely to be smaller than 100 pounds (that is, 200 pounds minus 100 pounds).

But it's a different matter if you have a sample of 100 men rather than 10. With a much larger sample it is much more likely that you have at least one person who weighs more than 200 pounds, or at least one who weighs less than 100 pounds. It is now quite likely that the calculated range of weights in your sample is more than 100.

So the range is affected by the sample size, and that makes the range undesirable as a means of gauging the variability in a population on the basis of a sample.

The standard deviation—or, in the context of errors of prediction, the standard error of estimate—is a different matter. It is largely independent of the sample size.

When you see a chart such as the one shown in Figure 2.6, your eye is drawn to the relatively narrow ends of the cigar shaped scatterplot and its relatively thick center. It therefore appears as though the variability is low at the ends and high at the center. But that's an illusion induced by the fact that you're looking at ranges, not standard deviations.

A much better gauge is to select some subset of the observations: say, those with values from 200 to 350 on the horizontal axis. Determine how many of those observations are within one standard error of estimate of the regression line. You'll find that roughly 68% of the observations lie between one standard error below and one standard error above the regression line. This will be true regardless of the number of observations included in the subset you chose. It will be true if the relationship is linear and if the two original variables are themselves normally distributed.

> **NOTE** The upper and lower diagonal lines in Figure 2.6 are located one standard error of estimate above and below the regression line. Recall that the standard error of estimate is *defined* as the standard deviation of the residuals: that is, the differences between the estimated values and the observed values. It is usually *calculated* as the square root of the ratio of the residual sum of squares to the degrees of freedom for the full regression.

The Distribution of the Residuals

Another assumption that's made in least squares regression is that the residuals are normally distributed at each value of the predictor variable.

When you estimate the values of a predicted variable using a regression equation, you often have the subjects' actual values on the predicted variable as well as their values on the predictor variable. No regression equation predicts perfectly unless the relationship between the predictor variable and the predicted variable is trivial (for example, using degrees Fahrenheit to predict degrees Celsius). Therefore, the weight you predict for Sam based on his age is unlikely to be a perfect match for his actual weight. The same is true for Ed and Ben and Hal.

Calculating the Residuals

If you subtract a subject's actual weight from his predicted weight the result is called a *residual* (another term for the same result is *error*). Ordinary least squares analysis assumes that these residuals are distributed as a normal distribution for each value of the predictor. So if you're predicting weight from age, and if Sam and Ed and Ben and Hal are each 15 years old, least squares analysis assumes that the four residuals would resemble a normal distribution if they were plotted on a chart.

Of course with just four observations it can be difficult to decide whether they are normally distributed. But many years of experience, as well as the outcomes of the robustness studies mentioned earlier in this chapter, provide good evidence that the assumption of normally distributed residuals doesn't matter all that much—provided that the departure from normality isn't too severe. Furthermore, even if it is severe, the only aspect of regression analysis in question would be the inferential tests, usually F-tests of the overall regression equation and t-tests of the individual regression coefficients.

However, when your predicted variable is a dichotomy or is measured on a categorical scale, the departure from normality is bound to be severe, as the next section demonstrates.

The Residuals of a Dichotomy

Perhaps you're interested in predicting the likelihood that homebuyers will make purchases, when the predictor variable is income and the predicted variable is either a 1 (purchased) or a 0 (didn't purchase). If you regress purchase behavior onto income you get a result that looks much like the chart in Figure 2.7.

Figure 2.7
This layout is typical of regressing a dichotomy onto an interval variable.

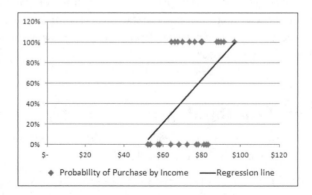

You could predict, before you even saw the data, that charting a dichotomy against an interval variable would look something like the situation in Figure 2.7. A variety of values stretches across the horizontal axis. But because the vertical axis displays a variable that can take on only two values, you wind up with two horizontal data series, one at 0% and one at 100%. Every observation has either a 0% or 100% value on the variable that's to be predicted.

But what you're really concerned about is whether the *residuals* are normally distributed. You can get the residuals by subtracting the actual outcome (0 or 1) from the predicted outcome (which is distributed in a fashion similar to the distribution of the predictor variable). Figure 2.8 shows how the residuals are distributed across the predicted values.

Figure 2.8
These residuals are not distributed normally.

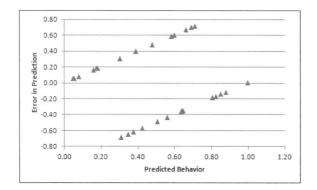

The residuals shown in Figure 2.8 are the result of subtracting a 1 versus 0 dichotomy (the observed behavior) from a continuous variable (the predicted values). You will always get a distribution of residuals against predicted values similar to the one in Figure 2.8 when you use least squares regression to predict a dichotomy from a continuous variable.

This sort of distribution violates an assumption that underlies the use of least squares regression, that residuals are normally distributed at any given point or points for the predicted values. An outcome such as the one shown in Figure 2.8 is a strong clue that least squares regression is the wrong approach for that data set.

Using Logistic Regression

As you've seen earlier in this chapter, several problems arise when you consider using least squares analysis on an outcome variable that's a dichotomy, measured as a probability. You can quantify a variable such as *Buys/Doesn't Buy* by counting the number of shoppers who buy and those who don't, as well as some predictor variable that interests you, such as age. Then you can try to predict the probability that 20-year-olds will buy, 21-year-olds, 22-year-olds, and so on.

This chapter has discussed the problems with equal variances, normal distributions, and the scale of the predicted variable, that plague least squares regression when the predicted value is measured as a probability, and particularly as a probability in a dichotomy. There are three steps you can take, though, that largely eliminate these problems.

Using Odds Rather Than Probabilities

Odds are closely related to probabilities—in fact, they are a ratio of probabilities, and you often hear of analyzing "odds ratios" instead of simply "odds." If the probability that a major league ballplayer will get a hit on his next at bat is 0.333, then the odds that he'll get a hit are

0.333/0.666

or 0.5, often expressed as "two to one against." The odds in this case are the ratio of the probability of a hit to the probability of not getting a hit. For every three at bats, you have some reason to think that the batter will get one hit and make two outs, for a batting average of 0.333 and odds of two to one against.

It's just as easy to convert odds to probabilities as it is to go from probabilities to odds. If you know the odds are 0.5, two to one against, the formula is

0.5/(1 + 0.5)

or 0.333. More generally, if p is the probability of an event, then the associated odds are calculated with this formula:

p/(1 + p)

Why might it be more useful to work with odds than with probabilities? Recall from this chapter's section "The Scaling Problem" that you don't want to place arbitrary limits on your predictor variable: For example, you don't want to limit the income level that you use as a predictor to, say, $100,000. But a regression equation based on least squares can easily project a probability greater than 100% that someone will purchase, if that someone's income is high enough. We don't regard probabilities greater than 100% as quantitatively meaningful.

There are ways that odds behave differently than probabilities. Figures 2.9 and 2.10 have two further examples.

In Figure 2.9, the relationship between the predictor, Income, and the predicted variable, Probability of Sale, is such that if the Income is less than $40,000 or greater than $85,000, the Probability of Sale is less than 0% or greater than 100%. Both predictions are, of course, meaningless. The problem is that while a probability must fall between 0% and 100%, the straight regression line forces the prediction too low or too high if Income is outside the $40,000 to $85,000 range.

Figure 2.9
An unrestricted predictor variable can easily take predicted probabilities outside the range of 0 to 1.

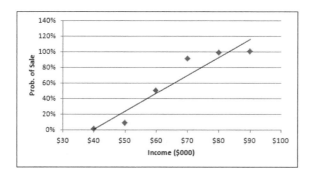

Figure 2.10
Odds ratios can meaningfully fall outside the range 0 to 1.

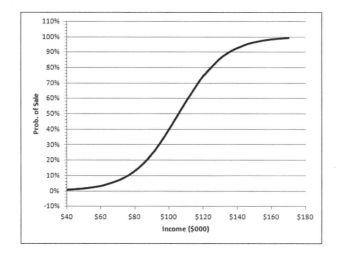

Figure 2.10 shows how logistic regression can avoid the problems caused by a straight regression line. Later in this chapter you see how it comes about, but a brief explanation of the results in Figure 2.10 is that the *odds*, rather than the probability, of a purchase are estimated using Income as the predictor. Odds are not restricted to a particular range in the way that probabilities are. After you have estimated the odds, converting from odds to probabilities gets you the curved line shown in Figure 2.10. Notice that the curved line does not fall below 0% at the low end of Income, nor does it exceed 100% at Income's upper end.

Using Log Odds

Perhaps you have wondered where the term *logistic* regression comes from. The answer is that in the process of carrying out a logistic regression analysis, you convert odds to the logarithm, or *log*, of the odds.

You might recall from trigonometry that a logarithm is an exponent—a *power*—that you use to raise a base number so that the result is another number whose value you want to hold onto, but to use only indirectly.

For example, what's called the *natural log* of the number 10 is about 2.3. When you're working with the natural logs, the *base* is 2.718. If you raise the base of 2.718 to the 2.3rd power, the result is 10:

2.718 ^ 2.3 = 10

There are various reasons that it's often more convenient to work with logarithms than with the numbers that they represent. In the preceding example, there might be a reason that you would prefer to work with the logarithm 2.3 rather than with the number 10. In Excel, you use the LN() function to get the natural log:

LN(10) = 2.3

When and if the time comes to convert the logarithm back to the number it represents, you take what's called the *antilog* of the logarithm. In Excel, the EXP() function returns the antilog:

EXP(2.3) = 10

In the context of logistic regression, you use the log of the odds rather than the odds directly because an odds ratio cannot be a negative number—but its log *can* be negative. The log of the odds is convenient because the logistic regression can be permitted to estimate a negative value (such as the fantasy –10% probability) without resulting in an impossible and uninterpretable outcome. Logistic regression estimates the *log* of the odds.

> **NOTE** The log of the odds is termed the *logit*. The standard pronunciation is "law-git" with a hard "g" as in *graft*. But you also hear "low-git" with a soft "g" as in *magic*.

There's no problem if the estimated logit is a negative number, because you subsequently use the antilog to convert the logit back to odds, which therefore turns positive. Later yet you convert the odds back to a probability, which is then between 0% and 100%, just where it should be.

Using Maximum Likelihood Instead of Least Squares

The third major way in which logistic regression parts company with least squares regression is its use of maximum likelihood techniques. Although least squares is tantamount to maximum likelihood under certain conditions, the maximum likelihood techniques used in logistic regression typically depend on the trial-and-error methods like those used by Excel's Solver add-in.

Logistic regression seeks to construct an equation that looks similar to a least squares regression equation: That is, the equation includes an intercept term and a coefficient for each predictor variable involved.

A criterion is established. The criterion, usually termed the *log likelihood*, is the sum of the logarithms of the predicted values. Excel's Solver, or some other optimization tool, is used to try different values of the equation's intercept and coefficients until the log likelihood is maximized. At that point, the optimal values for the intercept and the coefficients have been found: The differences between the predictions and the actual values (usually 0 and 1) are then at a minimum, and the likelihood of an accurate estimate is maximized. Logistic regression seeks to maximize a likelihood, whereas least-squares regression seeks to minimize the squared deviations of the predicted from the actual values. In many ways the distinction between *maximum* likelihood and *least* squares is merely semantic, but it's in our jargon now and we have to make the best of it.

With those three issues in mind—odds ratios, the logarithms of the odds ratios (termed *logits*), and maximum likelihood estimation—it's time to take a look at an actual logistic regression analysis.

Maximizing the Log Likelihood

You are running an online loan business and you'd like to come up with some rational decision rules concerning whether to make loans to applicants. You have some historical information to work with, and you can count on getting accurate information from new applicants regarding their annual income, state of residence, and (of course) the amount of the loan for which they're applying.

Income is an important predictor of an applicant's ability to repay a loan, for obvious reasons. And you can't predict a probability of repayment unless you know how much the applicant wants to borrow. State of residence isn't as obvious. Different states have different laws and regulations regarding how a creditor may go about collecting a bad debt: Some states make it relatively difficult for a creditor to collect. So you decide to include a variable, State, that takes the value 1 if the applicant's state makes it more difficult for a creditor to successfully sue to recover a loan amount, and the value 2 otherwise.

You also want to know whether the proposed loan amount bears a relationship to the likelihood of repayment. You suspect that other things being equal, the larger the loan the less likely that it will be repaid.

Setting Up the Data

Part of your small sample of historical data appears in Figure 2.11.

Your objective is to determine whether there's a useful relationship between three predictor variables and the probability that a borrower will repay the loan. It's useful, as shown in column A of Figure 2.11, to represent that probability as either 0 or 1. Using the available historical data, each of the borrowers either repaid the loan (1) or didn't (0). On a going-forward basis, you don't expect to predict either a 0 or a 1 in all cases, or even most of them. But later on you can adopt decision rules such as "Approve the loan if the projected probability of repayment is greater than 80%."

Figure 2.11
A genuine business deci-
sion should be supported
by much more data than
is used in this example.

	A	B	C	D
1			Coefficients	
2	Intercept	Income	Loan Amt	State
3	1.0000	0.0000	0.0000	0.0000
4				
5	Payback (0 = No, 1 = Yes)	Income ($000)	Loan Amount ($000)	State
6	1	155.790	4.934	2
7	1	178.685	4.954	2
8	0	84.801	5.467	2
9	0	134.144	5.715	1
10	0	151.509	5.751	1
11	1	144.062	5.930	2
12	0	133.540	5.957	1
13	0	159.768	5.992	1
14	1	178.298	6.183	2
15	1	132.660	6.342	1
16	0	104.618	6.444	2
17	0	136.788	6.465	1
18	0	103.064	6.555	1
19	0	85.570	6.671	1

Setting Up the Logistic Regression Equation

To assess the relationship, if any, between the probability of repayment and the three predictor variables you have at hand, logistic regression requires that you construct an equation
that looks much like a standard multiple regression equation:

$$\text{Probability} = \text{Intercept} + B_1X_1 + B_2X_2 + B_3X_3$$

where:

- Intercept is a constant value.
- B_1, B_2, and B_3 are coefficients that multiply the predictor variables.
- X_1, X_2, and X_3 are (in this case) the three predictor variables: Income, Loan Amount,
  and State.

The difference between an equation developed by least squares regression techniques and
one developed by logistic regression is based on the way the intercept and the coefficients
are derived.

In least squares regression, the traditional approach involves matrix algebra, creating SSCP
(sum of squares and cross product) matrices, then transposing, inverting, and multiplying
them to arrive at the intercept and coefficients.

> **NOTE**
> More recent techniques involve "decomposition" approaches that avoid the problems with multicol-
> linearity and singular matrices that occasionally crop up with the traditional techniques.

In contrast, logistic regression uses an optimization routine such as Excel's Solver. A criterion, similar in effect to least squares R^2, is established. Then the user points Solver at a set of coefficients, each set to a starting value, and tells Solver to adjust the coefficients and the intercept so that the criterion is maximized. Solver tries out different values for the coefficients and intercept until its internal rules decide that the criterion value can't be improved on.

It's most straightforward to start with some named cells that will hold the coefficients. In Figure 2.11, those cells are in the range A3:D3. Using Excel 2007 or later, the user takes these steps:

1. Select the cell that's to be named.
2. Click the Formulas tab on the Ribbon.
3. Click Define Name in the Defined Names area.
4. Type the name to be used in the Name box.
5. Accept or change the name's Scope.
6. Click OK.

For Figure 2.11 (and subsequent figures based on the same worksheet), I named the four cells as follows:

- Cell A3: Intercept
- Cell B3: IncomeCoef
- Cell C3: LoanCoef
- Cell D3: StateCoef

> **TIP**
> Because I often want to run similar logistic regression analyses on different worksheets, but with the same underlying data set, I prefer to set the scope of the names to the worksheet on which they're defined (rather than to the workbook). That way I can use the same cell names repeatedly and allow them to take on, and retain, different values depending on the worksheet where they are defined.

Notice in Figure 2.11 that I supplied starting values for the intercept and coefficients, in A3:D3. It doesn't matter much which starting values you choose. But if you select 1 for the intercept and 0 for each coefficient you might give Solver a small head start on arriving at the optimal values. Not incidentally, by supplying a 0 as the coefficient for each variable, you in effect remove that variable from the equation. The variable re-enters the equation when Solver tries a nonzero value for that coefficient.

The next step is to set up the range of *logits*, which are the result of the logistic regression equation. See Figure 2.12.

Figure 2.12
The logits are analogous to the predicted values you would get from a least squares regression equation.

| E6 | ▼ | (| ƒx | =Intercept+IncomeCoef*B6+LoanCoef*C6+StateCoef*D6 |

◢	A	B	C	D	E	F	G
1			Coefficients				
2	Intercept	Income	Loan Amt	State			
3	1.0000	0.0000	0.0000	0.0000			
4							
5	Payback (0 = No, 1 = Yes)	Income ($000)	Loan Amount ($000)	State	Logit	Odds	Probability that Payback = 0
6	1	155.790	4.934	2	1.0000	2.7183	0.7311
7	1	178.685	4.954	2	1.0000	2.7183	0.7311
8	0	84.801	5.467	2	1.0000	2.7183	0.7311
9	0	134.144	5.715	1	1.0000	2.7183	0.7311
10	0	151.509	5.751	1	1.0000	2.7183	0.7311
11	1	144.062	5.930	2	1.0000	2.7183	0.7311
12	0	133.540	5.957	1	1.0000	2.7183	0.7311
13	0	159.768	5.992	1	1.0000	2.7183	0.7311
14	1	178.298	6.183	2	1.0000	2.7183	0.7311
15	1	132.660	6.342	1	1.0000	2.7183	0.7311
16	0	104.618	6.444	2	1.0000	2.7183	0.7311
17	0	136.788	6.465	1	1.0000	2.7183	0.7311
18	0	103.064	6.555	1	1.0000	2.7183	0.7311
19	0	85.570	6.671	1	1.0000	2.7183	0.7311

The formula for the first logit, shown in cell E6 in Figure 2.12, is

=Intercept+IncomeCoef*B6+LoanCoef*C6+StateCoef*D6

Notice how the formula mirrors the pattern shown earlier for a multiple regression equation:

Probability = Intercept + B_1X_1 + B_2X_2 + B_3X_3

where the Bs are coefficients and the Xs are the predictor variables.

When you establish a cell or range name in Excel, the default is to make the reference absolute. For example, the default address for the name Intercept is $A$3. (You can change the default to make it relative, such as A3, or mixed, such as $A3, and there are some situations in which it pays to do so.) But with an absolute reference, you can copy and paste the formula in E6 down through the end of the historical data set, so that its final instance would be

=Intercept+IncomeCoef*B41+LoanCoef*C41+StateCoef*D41

Getting the Odds

With the initial values of the logits in hand, you can now calculate the odds. Recall from the section "Using Log Odds" that the logit is the log of the odds. You can now continue working backward and use the logit to determine the odds that a given applicant in your data history would pay back the loan, given the values on the predictor variables.

To get the odds from the logit, use Excel's antilog function EXP(). In cell F6 of Figure 2.12, the formula is

=EXP(E6)

Again, you can copy and paste that formula into F7:F41.

> **TIP** You already have the logits in E6:E41. Given that, a quicker way to populate F7:F41 is to double-click the fill handle for cell F6. When a cell, F6 in this example, is selected, you see a small black square on its lower-right corner. That's the cell's *fill handle*. If you double-click it, the contents of the selected cell are copied and pasted into a range that extends as far as an adjacent filled range—here, E6:E41—extends. You could drag the fill handle instead, and without an adjacent filled range you have to either drag or copy and paste. But I've always found that dragging a fill handle has a disconcerting habit of running away with itself and before I can make it stop, it's filled something ridiculous like F7:F200000.

Notice in Figure 2.12 that the logits are all identical (at 1) and the odds are also identical (at 2.71828). This is because I have initialized the intercept to 1.0 and the coefficients to 0.0. When the coefficients are all zero, none of the three predictor variables has an effect on the logit, and therefore only the intercept contributes to the logit's value. The base of the natural logarithms is 2.718, and so the antilog of 1 (the starting value that I've used for the intercept) is 2.718.

Getting the Probabilities

It's as simple to get the probabilities from the odds as it is to get the odds from the logits. Here's the formula in cell G6:

=F6/(1+F6)

The formula conforms to the pattern mentioned in the "Using Odds Rather Than Probabilities" section. Divide the odds by 1 plus the odds.

Just enter the formula in G6 and then use the fill handle to copy and paste it through the remainder of the cases.

It's useful at this point to step back a moment from the tedious matter of entering the formulas to look at where you are at present. You entered a formula that will shortly return logits in column E. You used Excel's antilog function to convert the results of those formulas to odds, in column F. And you entered a formula to convert the odds to probabilities, in column G.

The reasons to use logits and their antilogs, the odds, are that by doing so you can let the values of the predictor variables extend as far as you want, both above and below zero, and allow the logits and odds to vary in response. The logits can become very large or very small—including negative values—and when you subsequently convert back to probabilities, via the odds, you won't wind up with a probability greater than 100% or less than 0% that an applicant will repay the loan.

The probability that you get is the one you'll see in column G: It's the probability that an applicant with a given income and loan amount, who lives in a given type of state, will repay the loan. That might turn out to be useful information if the logistic regression equation turns out to be a good predictor of repayment behavior.

But it's not a good way to assess the predictive validity of the logistic regression equation. To do that, you want a slightly different but closely related probability: To assess the equation, you want to measure the probability that the equation has made the correct prediction. I cover that in the next section.

Calculating the Log Likelihood

The logical basis for the steps I describe in this section will have to wait for a later section, "The Rationale for Log Likelihood." As a practical matter it's not feasible to discuss that basis without keeping the actual results in view. To get the actual results it's necessary to get the maximum likelihood intercept and coefficients. So, this section describes what to do, and I describe shortly why you want to do it.

Figure 2.13 shows the results of the logistic regression analysis after Solver has optimized the intercept and the coefficients.

Figure 2.13
The intercept and the coefficients have been optimized when the log likelihood in cell H2 has been brought as close to 0 as possible.

H2		fx	=SUM(I6:I41)					

	A	B	C	D	E	F	G	H	I
1			Coefficients						
2	Intercept	Income	Loan Amt	State		Sum Log Likelihood		-11.2830	
3	18.0875	-0.1118	0.4805	-3.5709					
4									
5	Payback (0 = No, 1 = Yes)	Income ($000)	Loan Amount ($000)	State	Logit	Odds	Probability that Payback = 0	Prob. of correct classification	Log Likelihood
6	1	155.790	4.934	2	-4.1035	0.0165	0.0162	0.9838	-0.0164
7	1	178.685	4.954	2	-6.6535	0.0013	0.0013	0.9987	-0.0013
8	0	84.801	5.467	2	4.0904	59.7641	0.9835	0.9835	-0.0166
9	0	134.144	5.715	1	2.2630	9.6116	0.9058	0.9058	-0.0990
10	0	151.509	5.751	1	0.3387	1.4031	0.5839	0.5839	-0.5381
11	1	144.062	5.930	2	-2.3134	0.0989	0.0900	0.9100	-0.0943
12	0	133.540	5.957	1	2.4468	11.5510	0.9203	0.9203	-0.0830
13	0	159.768	5.992	1	-0.4690	0.6256	0.3848	0.3848	-0.9549
14	1	178.298	6.183	2	-6.0199	0.0024	0.0024	0.9976	-0.0024
15	1	132.660	6.342	1	2.7303	15.3376	0.9388	0.0612	-2.7935
16	0	104.618	6.444	2	2.3443	10.4259	0.9125	0.9125	-0.0916
17	0	136.788	6.465	1	2.3278	10.2551	0.9112	0.9112	-0.0930
18	0	103.064	6.555	1	6.1418	464.8981	0.9979	0.9979	-0.0021
19	0	85.570	6.671	1	8.1539	3476.7871	0.9997	0.9997	-0.0003

To bring about the results shown in Figure 2.13, take these steps:

1. Enter this formula in cell H6:

   =IF(A6=0,G6,1-G6)

2. Enter this formula in cell I6:

   =LN(H6)

3. Select the range H6:I6. Use the fill handle for cell I6 to copy and paste H6:I6 into H7:I41. The values in Column H are now the predicted probabilities of the actual behavior (represented by 0s or 1s in Column A), rather than the probability of failure to repay shown in Column G. The values in I6:I41 of course are the logarithms of the probabilities in Column H.

4. Ensure that the formula in cell H2 is

   =SUM(I6:I41)

   so that H2 represents the sum of the logs, in Column I, of the probabilities in Column H.

With those formulas in place, it's time to deploy Solver. You use Solver to maximize the value in H2, the sum of the log likelihoods, by finding the optimum values for the intercept and coefficients in the range A2:D2.

Finding and Installing Solver

In Excel 2007 or later, click the Ribbon's Data tab. If you see Solver in the Data tab's Analysis area, you're ready to go. (In a version prior to Excel 2007, look for Solver in the Tools menu.)

If you don't see Solver in the Analysis area, or if you don't see the Analysis area at all, you need to make Solver available to Excel. Click the Ribbon's File tab, click Options in the navigation bar, and then click Add-Ins in the navigation bar. Make sure that Excel Add-Ins is selected in the Manage drop-down box at the bottom of the window and click Go. You see an Add-Ins dialog box. (If you're using Excel 2003 or earlier, you can find the Add-Ins dialog box by clicking Add-Ins on the Tools menu.)

If you see Solver in the Add-Ins dialog box, fill its check box and click OK. You should now find Solver in the Analysis area of the Data tab or, prior to Excel 2007, in the Tools menu.

If you don't find Solver in the Add-Ins dialog box, you have to return to the Office installation routine and install Solver from the disc or from the set of installation files that you downloaded.

Running Solver

To run Solver and optimize the intercept and coefficients, take these steps:

1. Select cell H2. This is the cell that Solver uses as its criterion.

2. Click Solver in the Analysis area of the Data tab (or in earlier versions on the Tools menu). The Solver Parameters dialog box shown in Figure 2.14 appears.

3. If you started by selecting cell H2, its address appears in the Set Objective box. Click the Max button: You want Solver to maximize the value in cell H2.

Figure 2.14
The appearance of the
dialog box varies with
the Excel version, but
the basic functionality is
available in all versions.

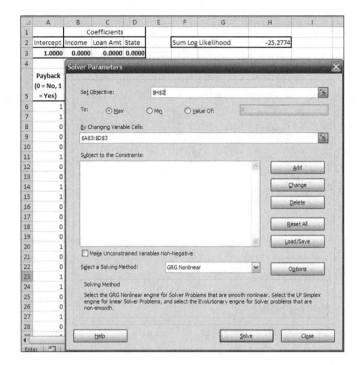

4. Click in the By Changing Variable Cells box and drag through A3:D3 (or otherwise enter the address). Solver will change the values in these cells as it seeks to maximize the value in cell H2.

5. Choose GRG Nonlinear from the Select a Solving Method drop-down list.

6. Click the Options button. In the Options dialog box and on its GRG Nonlinear tab, click the Central button under Derivatives. Also, if it's available in your version of Excel, make sure that the Require Bounds on Variables checkbox is cleared.

7. Click OK to return to the Solver Parameters dialog box, and then click Solve to start the Solver.

Solver responds by trying out different values for the intercept and the coefficients in the range A3:D3. When Solver decides that it cannot improve the criterion cell that you specified in the Set Objective box (cell H2 in this example), Solver displays a message that it has found a solution. Make sure that the Keep Solver Solution option button is selected and then click OK to dismiss Solver and return to the worksheet. The results appear in Figure 2.15.

At this point, Solver has identified the values of the intercept and the coefficients that result in the value in cell H2, the total log likelihood, to be maximized. Now that the actual results are in Figure 2.15, it's time to get a better sense of where they come from and what they mean.

Figure 2.15
The maximum likelihood outcome has been reached.

| H2 | ▼ | | fx | =SUM(I6:I41) | | | | | |

	A	B	C	D	E	F	G	H	I
1			Coefficients						
2	Intercept	Income	Loan Amt	State		Sum Log Likelihood		-11.2830	
3	18.0875	-0.1118	0.4805	-3.5709					
4									
5	Payback (0 = No, 1 = Yes)	Income ($000)	Loan Amount ($000)	State	Logit	Odds	Probability that Payback = 0	Prob. of correct classification	Log Likelihood
6	1	155.790	4.934	2	-4.1035	0.0165	0.0162	0.9838	-0.0164
7	1	178.685	4.954	2	-6.6535	0.0013	0.0013	0.9987	-0.0013
8	0	84.801	5.467	2	4.0904	59.7641	0.9835	0.9835	-0.0166
9	0	134.144	5.715	1	2.2630	9.6116	0.9058	0.9058	-0.0990
10	0	151.509	5.751	1	0.3387	1.4031	0.5839	0.5839	-0.5381
11	1	144.062	5.930	2	-2.3134	0.0989	0.0900	0.9100	-0.0943
12	0	133.540	5.957	1	2.4468	11.5510	0.9203	0.9203	-0.0830
13	0	159.768	5.992	1	-0.4690	0.6256	0.3848	0.3848	-0.9549
14	1	178.298	6.183	2	-6.0199	0.0024	0.0024	0.9976	-0.0024
15	1	132.660	6.342	1	2.7303	15.3376	0.9388	0.0612	-2.7935
16	0	104.618	6.444	2	2.3443	10.4259	0.9125	0.9125	-0.0916
17	0	136.788	6.465	1	2.3278	10.2551	0.9112	0.9112	-0.0930
18	0	103.064	6.555	1	6.1418	464.8981	0.9979	0.9979	-0.0021
19	0	85.570	6.671	1	8.1539	3476.7871	0.9997	0.9997	-0.0003

The Rationale for Log Likelihood

Return to column G in Figure 2.15. It contains the calculated probabilities that each borrower will *not* repay a loan of a given Amount, given that the borrower has a given Income and lives in one of two different types of State. That's the probability returned by the logistic regression equation, via the logits that the equation calculates directly in Column E and then converts first to odds in Column F and finally to a probability in Column G. Although the observed behavior shown as 1 or 0 in Column A is binary—the loan was either repaid or it wasn't—the predicted probabilities take on a different value for each borrower, because each borrower has a different set of values for the predictor variables, Income, Loan Amount, and State.

The probabilities in Column G can help you decide whether a borrower is likely to repay a loan, when the same variables, coefficients, and intercept are applied to a new set of applicants. That's an important purpose for the probabilities in Column G, but it doesn't directly address the issue of the accuracy of the logistic regression equation. *Before* you apply the equation to a new set of applicants, you'd like some idea of whether the equation will tend to advise you to loan money to people you shouldn't, to withhold loans from people who are very likely to pay it back, to make good choices, or some random mix of those possibilities.

The best way to assess the quality of the equation (and this applies to any equation, whether it comes from logistic regression, least squares analysis, or the entrails of a sheep) is to have lots and lots of actual cases, not just the ridiculously inadequate 36 in this chapter's example. Tens of thousands isn't too many.

Take a random sample that consists of half of your available cases. Run your analysis on that random sample. Take the resulting equation and apply it to the remaining half of your original cases, and determine how well the equation works on a sample of cases that was not used to derive the equation in the first place.

This process is called *cross-validation*, and it's easily the best way to evaluate the quality of the analysis you've done: in particular, how useful the equation is in estimating an outcome such as the repay versus doesn't repay behavior in this example.

You don't always have the luxury of tens of thousands of records, though, so you often want to resort to a different sort of criterion. In logistic regression, one method is termed *log likelihood*. It's conceptually similar to the use of R^2 in multiple regression analysis; there, you'd like to derive an equation that has the maximum possible R^2 value.

You might recall that R^2 measures the proportion of variability in the predicted measure that's associated with variability in the predictor variables: It's a measure of shared variance. You'd like to maximize R^2 in a multiple regression, and the log likelihood in a logistic regression, because doing so in either case returns the best combination of predictor variables given the observations you have at hand. But R^2 and log likelihood represent different concepts.

The Probability of a Correct Classification

Have another look at the formula in cell H6 of Figure 2.15. It is

=IF(A6=0,G6,1–G6)

The actual value in cell A6 is 1, so in this case the borrower actually paid off the loan. Bear in mind that the equation returns a probability that the borrower *will not* repay the loan. The value in cell G6 is 0.0162, so the equation predicted that the borrower would have only a 1.6% probability of defaulting.

In cell H8, the formula is

=IF(A8=0,G8,1–G8)

The value in cell A8 is 0, so the borrower actually defaulted. The value in cell G8 is 0.9835, so the equation predicted that the borrower had a 98% probability of defaulting. Cell H8 notices that the borrower actually defaulted (A8 equals 0) and so it returns the calculated value in cell G8, 0.9835.

The formulas in Column H put the predictions on a common footing: Regardless of whether the borrower paid off, Column H tells us the predicted probability of the borrower's actual behavior, whether that behavior is repayment or default—not simply, as in Column G, the predicted probability of defaulting on the loan.

The borrower in Row 6 paid the loan off (there's a 1 in A6). The equation predicts that this borrower's probability of default is 0.0162, so the predicted probability of repayment is 1 – 0.0162, or 0.9838. That's the value you see in cell H6 by virtue of the IF function. It's the probability that the borrower repaid, and that's in fact what happened.

On the other hand, the borrower in Row 8 defaulted. The predicted probability of default in Column G is 0.9835. The IF formula in cell H8 says that if the borrower defaulted (0 in Column A), then return the predicted probability of default in Column G. As you see, the equation predicted that the probability of default for this borrower is 0.9835, and the borrower did default.

For reasons I discuss shortly, it's helpful to take the logarithms of the probabilities in Column H and find the sum of those logarithms (that's the purpose of cell H2, which you used Solver to maximize). By working with the probabilities in Column H, you can address the question of the logistic regression's accuracy in the estimation of borrowers' actual behavior. Although it's conceptually related, it's a fundamentally different issue than the estimation of the borrowers' propensity to default, as calculated in Column G.

Using the Log Likelihood

Suppose you had an equation such as the one that's been developed in this chapter, but that it predicted perfectly whether a borrower would repay the loan or would default. In that case, every record would have a 1.0 in Column H. There would be just two possibilities:

- If the borrower defaults then the equations in both Column G and Column H would return a value of 1.0 as the probability of a default.

- If a borrower repays the loan then the equation would return a value of 0.0 in Column G as the probability of a default, and the equation in Column H would return a value of 1.0.

In both cases, the results in Column H would be telling you that your equation predicted the outcome with perfect accuracy. The probability would be 1.0, or 100%, that the equation correctly classified the applicant as one who would repay or one who would default.

If the behavior of each applicant were independent of the behavior of each other applicant, you could take the product of the probabilities in Column H to calculate an overall probability that the equation would correctly classify any given applicant.

INDEPENDENCE OF OBSERVATIONS

That assumption of independence is an important one. As I suggested elsewhere in this chapter, you can safely ignore some assumptions about a population's distributional characteristics, and you need to pay attention to some assumptions only in certain circumstances. But the assumption of the independence of observations is crucial in just about any statistical analysis that you want to use as a basis for generalizing from a sample to a population. In terms of the example used in this chapter: If the probability that John will default has no effect on the probability that Jane will default, then you have two independent observations.

Furthermore, you can multiply the two probabilities together and arrive at a *joint probability* that both events will occur. This is exactly like finding the probability of, say, two heads in two flips of a fair coin.

> But if the probability that John will default somehow exerts an influence on whether Jane will default, you have a problem. How strong is the influence? How often does it take place? What's the direction of the causation?
>
> In some analyses, such as a dependent groups t-test or an analysis of covariance, dependency is expected—even helpful and planned for. But those analyses deal with dependence between values of variables *for the same observational units*: The size of the loan that John applies for depends to some degree on his income.
>
> The problem of non-independence is at its most acute when you have dependence between values of variables *for different observational units*: Jane's probability of default depends to some degree on John's income.

Given that your individual observations are independent of one another, it's possible in theory to assess the overall accuracy of your logistic regression equation by getting the *continued product* of all the individual probabilities as calculated in Column H of Figure 2.15. But as a practical matter there's a problem with doing that.

> **NOTE**
> A *continued product* is simply the result of multiplying a series of numbers together. The continued product of 3, 7, and 11 is 231. The operator that represents the continued product is symbolized as Π, much as the operator that symbolizes summation over a series of values is symbolized as Σ.

All is well if you have nothing but 1.0 in Column H. Even if you have 40,000 observations, Excel has no difficulty in multiplying 1.0 by itself 40,000 times and returning the result of 1.0.

But it's a fantasy to think that any logistic regression equation—or a least squares equation, for that matter—will return nothing but values of 1.0 as the probability of predicting the outcome values exactly. If that does happen with real-world data, either there's an error in a formula somewhere or you're predicting something trivial such as people's height in centimeters from their height in inches.

No, you will always get a set of values that range from 0.0 to 1.0. Those values represent the values of a dichotomous variable that are predicted by your equation.

The problem has to do with getting the continued product of those numbers. The continued product of a series of fractional values can get extremely small, so small that you eventually encounter what's called *arithmetic underflow*. The number is too small for a computer to store it accurately.

For example, on the computer I'm using to write this chapter, Excel 2010 is capable of accurately computing the product of 703 numbers that were returned by the RAND() function. Include a 704th number in the continued product, though, and Excel 2010 cannot successfully and accurately store the result on this computer. You will usually want many more than 700 observations to obtain a logistic regression equation that you will regard as reliable: one that you can successfully deploy with a different set of observations. (I should add that the problem is not limited to analyses that you run in Excel. Other applications are also subject to underflow and overflow. The problem crops up less often in specifically statistical applications, but it's still there.)

Once again, though, logarithms provide an assist. The usual way to get the continued product in logistic regression, whether you're using Excel, R, or SAS, is by way of the logarithms of the probabilities. Those logarithms are shown in Column I of Figure 2.15, repeated here for convenience as Figure 2.16.

Figure 2.16
Column I contains the natural logarithms of the probabilities in Column H.

H2	▾	fx	=SUM(I6:I41)						
	A	B	C	D	E	F	G	H	I
1			Coefficients						
2	Intercept	Income	Loan Amt	State		Sum Log Likelihood		-11.2830	
3		18.0875	-0.1118	0.4805	-3.5709				
4									
5	Payback (0 = No, 1 = Yes)	Income ($000)	Loan Amount ($000)	State	Logit	Odds	Probability that Payback = 0	Prob. of correct classification	Log Likelihood
6	1	155.790	4.934	2	-4.1035	0.0165	0.0162	0.9838	-0.0164
7	1	178.685	4.954	2	-6.6535	0.0013	0.0013	0.9987	-0.0013
8	0	84.801	5.467	2	4.0904	59.7641	0.9835	0.9835	-0.0166
9	0	134.144	5.715	1	2.2630	9.6116	0.9058	0.9058	-0.0990
10	0	151.509	5.751	1	0.3387	1.4031	0.5839	0.5839	-0.5381
11	1	144.062	5.930	2	-2.3134	0.0989	0.0900	0.9100	-0.0943
12	0	133.540	5.957	1	2.4468	11.5510	0.9203	0.9203	-0.0830
13	0	159.768	5.992	1	-0.4690	0.6256	0.3848	0.3848	-0.9549
14	1	178.298	6.183	2	-6.0199	0.0024	0.0024	0.9976	-0.0024
15	1	132.660	6.342	1	2.7303	15.3376	0.9388	0.0612	-2.7935
16	0	104.618	6.444	2	2.3443	10.4259	0.9125	0.9125	-0.0916
17	0	136.788	6.465	1	2.3278	10.2551	0.9112	0.9112	-0.0930
18	0	103.064	6.555	1	6.1418	464.8981	0.9979	0.9979	-0.0021
19	0	85.570	6.671	1	8.1539	3476.7871	0.9997	0.9997	-0.0003

One property of logarithms is that their sum equals the logarithm of the product of the numbers on which they're based. Therefore,

$$LN(.2) + LN(.4) + LN(.7) = -2.8824$$

and

$$LN(.2 \times .4 \times .7) = -2.8824$$

That means you don't have to get the continued product of hundreds or thousands of probabilities. Instead you can take the (natural) logarithm of each probability and calculate their sum. Doing so, even with 40,000 probabilities, largely mitigates the problem of arithmetic underflow. (Furthermore, it's usual to report the result as the sum of the logarithms, which is termed the *log likelihood*.)

It's also true that the logarithm of any number greater than 0 and less than 1 is negative. (It's true whether you're using natural logs, or base 10 logs, or base 2 logs, or any other base.) So because you're dealing with probabilities, the logarithms of those probabilities must all be negative, and their sum must be a negative number.

Once again, suppose that the calculated probabilities are all 1.0, so that the continued product equals 1.0 and the equation predicts perfectly. Then their logarithms are all 0.0, and the logarithms sum to 0.0.

If the calculated probabilities are all very close to 1.0 (say, 0.9999) then their continued product is fairly close to 1.0. The predictions are not perfect but approach perfection quite closely. Their logarithms are each –.0001, and across, say, 1,000 observations the logarithms sum to –.1.

If the calculated probabilities are all roughly .5, so the predictions are fairly haphazard, the sum of their logarithms over 1,000 cases would be about –700.

So, the better the predictions, the closer the probabilities are to 1.0, and the closer the sum of the logarithms is to 0.0. The logarithms of probabilities are always negative numbers, but the closer a probability is to 1.0, the closer its logarithm is to 0.0. *This is the reason that you instructed Solver to adjust the intercept and coefficients in such a way as to maximize the value in cell H2.*

Cell H2 contains the sum of the logarithms and as a practical matter will always be a negative number. You want Solver to optimize the prediction, and that happens when the sum of the logarithms, the log likelihood, approaches 0.0 as closely as possible. You get Solver to do that by specifying that it is to maximize the Objective cell. When the Objective cell starts out with a negative value such as –50, to maximize it means to move it toward zero, not toward –100.

> **NOTE** In some versions of Excel prior to 2010, Solver termed the Objective cell as the Target cell, and you might see that terminology on the Solver's dialog box.

The Statistical Significance of the Log Likelihood

Although cross-validation with large numbers of cases, as described previously, is probably the most useful and intuitively satisfying route to validating a logistic regression equation, you don't always have a large number of cases to work with. That's especially true if you bear in mind that you would probably want to use half of the cases to derive the equation and the other half to validate it.

A different approach is to use statistical inference. The log likelihood value, which Solver maximized to arrive at the optimum values for the intercept and the coefficients, can be converted to a chi-square. That chi-square has a particular number of degrees of freedom, largely defined by the number of variables in the equation.

The log likelihood, as you've seen, must always be a negative value. On the other hand, a chi-square is the square of a z-score:

$$z = \frac{(X - \mu)}{\sigma}$$

2

Whenever X is smaller than μ, the z-score is negative. But chi-square is the square of z, so it must be positive regardless of the value of X.

To treat the log likelihood as a chi-square value, then, you need to transform it. You can't sensibly ask where in the distribution of positive chi-square values you'll find a negative log likelihood value. The standard way to make that transformation is to multiply the log likelihood by –2. Doing so converts the negative log likelihood to a positive number and increases its variance: It can then be treated as a chi-square variable with a given number of degrees of freedom. And in that case, you can use Excel's CHISQ.DIST.RT() function to tell you the probability of getting a chi-square as large as the one you obtained from your sample, assuming that the coefficients in your equation fail to increase its accuracy when applied to the population.

> **NOTE** The term *Deviance* (or *D*) is often used to refer to the converted log likelihood. You might also see it termed −2LL. The term *deviance* refers to the deviation between the probabilities that the equation predicts and the actual 0s and 1s that represent the dichotomy you're studying.

To test whether the regression equation's coefficients add materially to the predictive ability of the equation, you can run Solver twice: once to calculate the log likelihood for the full equation, just as shown in Figures 2.15 and 2.16.

Then you run Solver again, but this time you omit the coefficients from the regression equation: In effect, you ask Solver to come up with the best log likelihood based solely on the intercept. To do so, the two general steps are

1. Set the regression coefficients to 0 and the intercept to 1.
2. Run Solver to maximize the log likelihood but *remove* the coefficients from the list of variable cells in Solver's dialog box.

These two instances of Solver results give you two log likelihoods: one with the intercept and all the coefficients, and one with the intercept only. You then convert the log likelihoods to Deviance estimates, find the difference between the two Deviances, and use Excel's CHISQ.DIST.RT() function to test the statistical significance of the difference.

At any rate, that's the 30,000 foot view of the process (which is termed the *models comparison approach* and which is used in other contexts such as multiple regression analysis). The next section describes the steps in more detail.

Setting Up the Reduced Model

The first task is to get the log likelihood when no coefficients are involved, just the intercept. To do so, take the following steps. They are based on the location of data as shown in Figure 2.16.

1. Set the intercept in cell A3 to 1.0.

2. Set the coefficients in the range B3:D3 to 0.

3. Start Solver by clicking the Solver button in the Analysis area of the Ribbon's Data tab.

4. Continue to have Solver maximize the value in cell H2.

5. Modify the list of variable cells by changing A3:D3 to A3 only. You don't want Solver to touch the coefficients in B3:D3 for this run.

6. Click Solve.

The results appear in Figure 2.17.

Figure 2.17
The log likelihood based on the intercept alone is considerably farther from zero than that shown in Figure 2.16.

	H2	▾	●	f_x	=SUM(I6:I41)				
	A	B	C	D	E	F	G	H	I
1			Coefficients						
2	Intercept	Income	Loan Amt	State		Sum Log Likelihood		-24.0569	
3	0.4520	0.0000	0.0000	0.0000					
4									
5	Payback (0 = No, 1 = Yes)	Income ($000)	Loan Amount ($000)	State	Logit	Odds	Probability that Payback = 0	Prob. of correct classification	Log Likelihood
6	1	155.790	4.934	2	0.4520	1.5714	0.6111	0.3889	-0.9445
7	1	178.685	4.954	2	0.4520	1.5714	0.6111	0.3889	-0.9445
8	0	84.801	5.467	2	0.4520	1.5714	0.6111	0.6111	-0.4925
9	0	134.144	5.715	1	0.4520	1.5714	0.6111	0.6111	-0.4925
10	0	151.509	5.751	1	0.4520	1.5714	0.6111	0.6111	-0.4925
11	1	144.062	5.930	2	0.4520	1.5714	0.6111	0.3889	-0.9445
12	0	133.540	5.957	1	0.4520	1.5714	0.6111	0.6111	-0.4925
13	0	159.768	5.992	1	0.4520	1.5714	0.6111	0.6111	-0.4925
14	1	178.298	6.183	2	0.4520	1.5714	0.6111	0.3889	-0.9445
15	1	132.660	6.342	1	0.4520	1.5714	0.6111	0.3889	-0.9445
16	0	104.618	6.444	2	0.4520	1.5714	0.6111	0.6111	-0.4925
17	0	136.788	6.465	1	0.4520	1.5714	0.6111	0.6111	-0.4925
18	0	103.064	6.555	1	0.4520	1.5714	0.6111	0.6111	-0.4925
19	0	85.570	6.671	1	0.4520	1.5714	0.6111	0.6111	-0.4925

When Solver has finished, store the result that was reached for the log likelihood in some cell. Be sure to store it as a value, not as the formula in cell H2.

> **TIP** If you're still with me, you surely know this. Nevertheless, in Excel the way to store a formula as the value it returns is to copy the cell with the formula, select a different (and normally a blank) cell, and paste it with the keyboard sequence Alt+E+S+V. Or, click the Paste button on the Home tab, choose Paste Special, click the Values button, and then click OK.

Label the pasted value so that you know later on what it represents.

Setting Up the Full Model

Take the six steps outlined in the preceding section, *except* in step 5 call for Solver to use the range A3:D3 as the variable cells: Thus, you're asking Solver to put the intercept and all three variable coefficients into the equation.

When Solver has finished, copy and paste the log likelihood from cell H2 (again, as a value rather than as a formula) into a blank cell. If you are following these instructions using the data supplied in the downloadable workbook for this chapter, your results should be the same as appear in cells B2 and B3 of Figure 2.18.

Figure 2.18
The significance of the difference between the two Deviance values is what you'll be testing.

	A	B	C
			C7 =CHISQ.DIST.RT(C5,C6)
1		Log Likelihood	Deviance
2	Intercept Only	-24.057	48.114
3	Full Model	-11.283	22.566
4			
5	Difference		25.548
6	Degrees of Freedom		3
7	Probability		0.000012

You still need to convert the two log likelihoods to Deviance, or chi-square values. As described earlier, simply multiply each by –2 to get the values in cells C2 and C3 of Figure 2.18.

The difference between the two Deviance values, shown in cell C5 of Figure 2.18, is one measure of the increment in the log likelihood you get by adding the variables Income, Loan Amount, and State to the logistic regression equation. You can test the statistical significance of the increment by comparing it to the chi-square distribution. In Figure 2.18, that's done in cells C6 and C7.

Cell C6 contains the degrees of freedom for the chi-square test in cell C7. You might see sources of information on logistic regression refer to this value not as *degrees of freedom* but as *constraints*. The coefficients in the intercept-only model are *constrained* to equal 0. The model that includes the intercept and all three coefficients is unconstrained—all three coefficients are free to vary as Solver searches for the values that maximize the log likelihood. The number of constraints, or degrees of freedom, for the chi-square test of the deviance statistic is the number of constrained variables in one model less the number of constrained variables in the other model.

Regardless of the terminology, then, you can treat the number of unconstrained coefficients in the full model (3) less the number of unconstrained coefficients in the intercept-only model (0) as the degrees of freedom for a chi-square test.

That test is carried out in cell C7 of Figure 2.18 with this formula:

=CHISQ.DIST.RT(C5,C6)

The formula makes use of the CHISQ.DIST.RT() function to evaluate the chi-square value in C5 in the chi-square distribution with 3 (cell C6) degrees of freedom. The function returns the area in that distribution that lies to the *right* (the RT portion of the function name) tail of the distribution. It is the probability of obtaining a value at least as large as that in cell C5—the increment in the deviance value—if that increment were due to simple sampling error when the three predictor variables have no effect in the population from which the sample was taken.

In this case, only one one-hundred-thousandth of the distribution lies to the right of a value of 25.548, and the probability of obtaining a chi-square of 25.548 with 3 degrees of freedom is 1 in 100,000.

There are several reasons that you should take the latter statement with a grain of salt. One is that it is difficult to measure such an extreme value with much confidence in the accuracy of the measurement. As a personal and subjective matter, I find myself much more comfortable limiting myself to statements such as "extremely unlikely." As I noted earlier in this chapter, a cross-validation is a much more satisfying, even more defensible, method of assessing how useful the predictors are in classifying your cases.

It's also wise to keep in mind that this sort of statistical test is open to question when the data come from a convenience sample instead of from an experimental context with random selection and random assignment. Issues such as the directionality of the causation (if any) and Simpson's Paradox can confound the interpretation of the results. When it's at all possible, arrange for thousands of observations and prefer a cross-validation to a statistical test that's unsupported by a true experimental design.

Univariate Analysis of Variance (ANOVA)

3

One of the important approaches to classifying observations is *discriminant function analysis*. Chapter 5, "Discriminant Function Analysis: The Basics," and Chapter 6," Discriminant Function Analysis: Further Issues," in this book explore discriminant function analysis in considerable detail, but there's some groundwork to lay before getting into those matters.

Some of that groundwork concerns multivariate analysis of variance, or MANOVA. The acronym MANOVA itself is symptomatic of the sad state of affairs regarding statistical terminology. Anyone might think that the word *multivariate* refers to the multiple independent or predictor variables that are often used in regression analysis. So if you read that Smith et al. had run a multiple regression analysis that predicted income from a combination of years of education, age, and sex, you might think that Smith et al. had performed a multivariate analysis.

But conventionally the term *multivariate analysis* refers not to the presence of multiple independent or predictor variables, but to the presence of multiple *dependent* variables. Suppose that Smith & Co. had decided instead to investigate the differential effects of corporate policies that permit, or prohibit, employees' working from home. If the dependent variables in such a study were a measure of productivity and a measure of absenteeism, you could accurately term it a multivariate study. A statistical analysis of the results might involve a MANOVA: a multivariate analysis of variance.

Chapter 4 covers MANOVA. Before getting into MANOVA it's helpful to review the case in which there's just one dependent variable: the so-called *univariate* case, or a simple analysis of variance (*ANOVA*). This chapter reviews the basics of ANOVA as to both theory and computation.

But this chapter is *only* a review. If you have not studied the analysis of variance in the past, I recommend that you begin with a more thorough introduction to the topic; one good place to go is *Statistical Analysis: Microsoft Excel 2010* by Conrad Carlberg and published in 2011 by Que Publishing.

The Logic of ANOVA

Despite the implications of the term *analysis of variance*, you use ANOVA to make inferences about the means—the average values—of two or more populations. If you follow the logic of the analysis, you see how comparing two sources of variation in an outcome measure can help you determine the likelihood that different populations have different means.

The term *variance* itself has a variety of meanings. In accounting, for example, it's often used to identify the difference between a budgeted amount and an actual expenditure. In statistical analysis, though, "variance" means a measure of the variability in the values of a variable.

The meaning of variance is not as straightforward and intuitive as other measures of variability such as the range. In fact, the variance is defined as the average squared deviation of each observation in a set from the mean value of the set:

$$s^2 = \sum_{i=1}^{N} (X_i - \bar{X})^2 / N$$

where:

- s^2 is the variance of the set.
- N is the number of observations in the set.
- X_i is the i-th observation in the set.
- $\bar{X}$ is the mean of the set of observations.

In words, subtract the mean from each number, square the result, add up the squares, and divide by the number of observations.

> **NOTE** That's the formula for the variance of a population. It's a little different if you want to estimate the variance of the population based on a sample. Then, you divide by N − 1 instead of by N.

Using Variance

The variance (the average squared deviation from the mean) is not as rich in intuitive meaning as the range (the largest observation minus the smallest). But the variance has many useful qualities, both as a statistic and as a concept, so it's a good idea to acquaint yourself with it in as many contexts as possible. The more you do that, the more familiar the concept becomes.

One of those contexts is the analysis of variance, which depends on analyzing the variance of a set of scores in order to make inferences about the means of population values.

Suppose you have observations for three random samples of people: those with college degrees, those with high school diplomas only, and those who left high school before graduating. You know which group each person belongs to as well as his or her annual income. Your hypothesis is that the college graduates have the highest annual income, and that those who left high school without graduating have the lowest.

It's easy to determine which sample has the largest average income and which has the smallest. But that's not really interesting information. You would far prefer to decide whether the populations that those samples represent have different average incomes. Does the population of college graduates have a higher average income than the population of high school graduates? And of the three populations, do those who left high school early have the lowest average income?

The route to answering those questions goes through analyzing the variance of the incomes.

Partitioning Variance

You saw earlier that the variance of a group of observations depends on the squared differences between each observation's value and the group's mean value. One of the ways that you deal with variance in an ANOVA is to calculate the variance of each group; in the present example, that's these three variances:

- The variance of the income of the sample of college graduates
- The variance of the income of the sample of high school graduates
- The variance of the income of the sample of high school dropouts

Figure 3.1 shows a couple of ways that you can go about calculating those variances using Excel.

Cells B14:D14 in Figure 3.1 each show an estimate of a population variance given the data available from the sample; for example, we would estimate that the variance of income in the population of college graduates is just under 302 million. The variance estimates in row 14 are made by dividing the sum of the squared deviations (provided by the DEVSQ() function) by $N - 1$, or 9.

Cells B15:D15 provide precisely the same information as you see in row 14, but they use the VAR.S() function. The VAR.P() function would return the variance of the same set of 10 numbers, but then we would be treating those 10 numbers as though they constituted a full population.

Figure 3.1
Either VAR.S() or DEVSQ()
gets you to the variance.

	B17		f_x	=AVERAGE(B3:B12)	
	A	B		C	D
1					
2		College		High School	No Diploma
3		$ 30,055	$	25,423	$ 31,239
4		$ 36,674	$	73,394	$ 12,675
5		$ 52,793	$	35,739	$ 10,521
6		$ 86,054	$	62,352	$ 14,218
7		$ 49,727	$	66,792	$ 29,985
8		$ 71,118	$	18,272	$ 13,132
9		$ 43,544	$	40,996	$ 38,198
10		$ 66,496	$	51,061	$ 35,497
11		$ 46,710	$	16,565	$ 16,545
12		$ 39,384	$	18,307	$ 16,249
13					
14	DEVSQ()/(N-1)	301,730,025		463,392,652	112,679,499
15	VAR.S()	301,730,025		463,392,652	112,679,499
16					
17	Average Income	$ 52,256	$	40,890	$ 21,826

I provided both calculations, DEVSQ()/(N – 1) and VAR.S(), in Figure 3.1 simply as a reminder that

- The variance is the result of dividing the sum of the squared deviations by (N – 1) using a sample, or by N using a population.

- You can get the variance more directly in Excel by using the VAR.S() function using a sample, or VAR.P() if your data actually are a population.

Expected Values of Variances (Within Groups)

Let's step back a moment to the original purpose of this example, to determine the likelihood that three populations of people—college graduates, high school graduates, and those who did not graduate from high school—have different average incomes. Whether they do or not, we can be sure that the individuals in each population have different income levels. It's not true that everyone with a college degree (or high school diploma, or no schooling beyond grade school) has the same income as everyone else in that population. Incomes vary and therefore have a variance.

Each variance that's shown in Figure 3.1 is an estimate of the variance in the population. In this case there are three different estimates, and they're very different from one another. The largest estimate, in cells C14 and C15, is more than four times greater than the smallest estimate, in cells D14 and D15.

But we assume that the variances in the population are equal. We assume that the differences we see in the sample variances are due to simple sampling error: That with (in this case) only 10 observations in each sample, we're going to get some actual data that inflates the result over what it actually is in the population (or, equivalently, is an underestimate of the population value).

We can get a somewhat more accurate estimate of the actual population variance by simply averaging the three sample variances. Taking their average gives us our best estimate of the variance in the population.

NOTE This is true when all the samples have the same number of observations. Things are trivially more complicated when the N's are unequal.

It's important to notice here that the average of the sample variances is independent of any difference in the sample means (or in the population means, for that matter). All we're doing is measuring the variability of 10 individual scores around the mean of the College sample, of another 10 scores around the mean of the High School sample, and of another 10 scores around the mean of the No Diploma sample—and then averaging those three variance measures. It doesn't matter whether the three sample (or population) means are identical or even farther apart than they are in Figure 3.1 (see Figure 3.2).

Figure 3.2
The means are much farther apart, but the variances are the same as in Figure 3.1.

	B17	▾	f_x =AVERAGE(B3:B12)	
	A	B	C	D
1				
2		College	High School	No Diploma
3		$ 80,055	$ 50,423	$ 31,239
4		$ 86,674	$ 98,394	$ 12,675
5		$ 102,793	$ 60,739	$ 10,521
6		$ 136,054	$ 87,352	$ 14,218
7		$ 99,727	$ 91,792	$ 29,985
8		$ 121,118	$ 43,272	$ 13,132
9		$ 93,544	$ 65,996	$ 38,198
10		$ 116,496	$ 76,061	$ 35,497
11		$ 96,710	$ 41,565	$ 16,545
12		$ 89,384	$ 43,307	$ 16,249
13				
14	DEVSQ()/(N-1)	301,730,025	463,392,652	112,679,499
15	VAR.S()	301,730,025	463,392,652	112,679,499
16				
17	Average Income	$ 102,256	$ 65,890	$ 21,826
18				

So, regardless of any difference in the mean values, we have the same estimate of the variance in the population: the average of the three sample variances.

This value, the average of the sample variances, is our best estimate of what's called the *expected value of the mean square within groups*.

- *Expected value*: This means that if we were to repeat the experiment many times, we expect the average of the repeated results would equal the value in the population from which we took the sample.

- *Mean square*: This is simply another term for *variance*. Recall that to calculate the variance, you divide the sum of the squared deviations by the number of observations.

That's the average squared deviation, or the *mean square*. (Yes, these are samples and so you divide by N – 1 instead of by N, but tradition has it that we're to call it a mean square.)

■ *Within groups*: We calculate the variability within each group rather than across all the groups at once. The reason for this becomes apparent shortly.

The mean square within is the average of variances of equal-size groups. That value is an estimate of the population variance. The expected value of the mean square *within groups* is the population variance:

$$E\left(MS_W \right) = \sigma^2$$

where E represents *expected value*.

Expected Values of Variances (Between Groups)

There's another way to estimate the population variance. Instead of looking at, and averaging, the variances within each sample, you can get an estimate of the population variance by working with the *variance of the group means*.

The expected value of the mean square *within groups* is the population variance. But the expected value of the mean square between groups is the population variance plus something more:

$$E(MS_B) = \sigma^2 + n\sum(\mu_j - \mu)^2 / (J-1)$$

where:

■ n is the number of observations per group.

■ J is the number of groups.

■ μ_j is the mean of group j.

■ μ is the grand mean.

The derivation of the formula for the long-term, expected value of the mean squares between groups is not especially difficult, but it is quite lengthy. You can find it in the Excel workbook associated with this chapter, on the Que Publishing website at quepublishing.com/title/9780789751683.

A more intuitive way to think of the mean square between groups is as follows. Suppose that there are two farms, McDonald's farm and Maggie's farm. McDonald applies a new kind of fertilizer to the plots on his farm. Maggie, more skeptical, sticks with the fertilizer that she's been using for years. The results, measured by yield per plot, are shown in Figure 3.3.

Figure 3.3
It doesn't look as though the new fertilizer has had much effect on the plot yields.

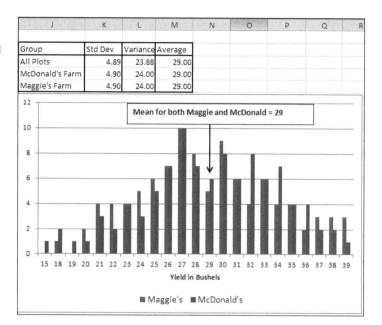

Group	Std Dev	Variance	Average
All Plots	4.89	23.88	29.00
McDonald's Farm	4.90	24.00	29.00
Maggie's Farm	4.90	24.00	29.00

According to Figure 3.3, the average yield of 29 bushels is the same at both McDonald's farm and Maggie's. Furthermore, the variance of plot yield at each farm is identical: 24 at McDonald's farm and 24 at Maggie's. On the basis of these two samples it looks like the population of plots that get the new fertilizer would have the same average yield as the population of plots that use the old kind.

What about the nearly identical variances? The variability of the plot yields at Maggie's farm, 24, is calculated by getting the squared differences of each plot's yield from the mean of her yields, which is 29. The same is true of the variability of the yields at McDonald's farm: His mean yield is also 29, and his individual yields bear the same sum of squared deviations from the mean as Maggie's.

In fact, because both samples have the same mean value of 29, we know that the overall variance will be close to the two individual variances. If you calculate the overall variance—the variability of each plot yield from the grand mean—you get virtually the same result, because the mean for Maggie's farm, the mean for McDonald's farm, and the grand mean are identical: 29 bushels. Therefore the sum of the squared deviations is the same regardless of whether you subtract a farm's mean or the grand mean from each plot value. Figure 3.3 shows that the overall variance is 23.88. (The overall variance is slightly smaller than either farm variance because the denominator, $(N-1)$, is 199 overall, but $(N-1)$ is 99 at each farm.)

Figure 3.4 shows a different outcome, where McDonald's new fertilizer has a dramatic effect on the crop yields.

In Figure 3.4, the mean yield for McDonald's farm is higher by ten bushels than for Maggie's farm. The farm variances are the same, 24 in each case. But the overall variance has increased from 23.88 to 49. The reason is that the increase in yield on McDonald's farm—coupled with the absence of an increase on Maggie's farm—causes many of the plot yields at *both* farms to be farther from the grand mean than is the case in Figure 3.3.

Figure 3.4
Here the fertilizer seems to have boosted McDonald's plot yields by 10 bushels per plot.

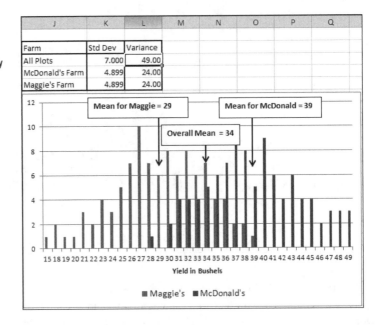

Because the variance within each farm remains the same, the increase in the overall variance is due to the increase in the plot yields at McDonald's farm. That increase pulls the individual plot yields farther apart from one another and therefore farther apart from the overall average.

This suggests that we can make an inference about whether the average yields are different in the populations of farms that get these two different fertilizers. We can make that inference by examining the relationship between two variances:

■ *Within groups:* The variance of the yields within each farm. This measure reflects the variability of each plot yield from the average yield of its farm. Any difference between the average yields of the two farms is irrelevant to the variance within groups.

■ *Between groups:* The variance of the yields taking the difference between the farms' averages into account.

The prior section discussed the expected value of the mean square within groups: the long-term average of the variance within each group if we ran the same experiment many times over. That long-term average is expected to equal the variance of the plot yields in the population of plots that we're sampling from. Again, the expected value of the mean square within groups is as follows:

$$E(MS_W) = \sigma^2$$

and in contrast, the mean square between groups is as follows:

$$E(MS_B) = \sigma^2 + n\sum(\mu_j - \mu)^2 / (J-1)$$

So $E(MS_W)$ is expected to equal $E(MS_B)$ if there are no differences in the group means, which would be reflected in the second term of the expected value of the mean square between. If there are no differences in the group means, the differences between the group means and the grand mean are zero, and so are the squared differences.

But if there are differences in the average values of the populations, there will tend to be differences between the means of the sampled groups and the grand mean. In turn, the squared differences will be positive and the second factor in the expected value of the mean square between, which is as follows:

$$n\sum(\mu_j - \mu)^2 / (J-1)$$

will increase the value of the mean square between over and above the value of the mean square within.

If you form this ratio:

$$E(MS_B) / E(MS_W)$$

its value is 1.0 when the mean square between is the same as the mean square within. It will become greater and greater than 1.0 as the differences between the group means and the grand mean increase. This is called the *F-ratio*.

The F-Ratio

An F-ratio is the ratio of two variances. As such, it can be used to test whether any two variances are different—for example, the variance of the heights of 15-year-old boys versus the variance of the heights of 15-year-old girls. When the F-ratio is used in the analysis of variance, however, it is the ratio of the variance (usually called the mean square) between groups to the variance (or mean square) within groups.

> **NOTE** The statistician George Snedecor named the F distribution (which represents the sampling distribution of the F-ratio) after Sir Ronald Fisher, who was responsible for many of the fundamental advances in statistical theory made during the early part of the twentieth century.

Generally, the larger the ratio of mean square between (MS_B) to mean square within (MS_W), the more confident you can be that a genuine difference exists between the means of the populations from which you have taken your samples.

But the characteristics of the F distribution are well known, and so you can do better than simply becoming more confident. Under the assumption that the population's group means are identical (the *null hypothesis*) you can determine the probability that an experiment would return an F-ratio of, say, 1.5 when equal population means would lead you to expect an F-ratio of 1.0.

The distribution of the F-ratio depends on the following:

■ The degrees of freedom $(J - 1)$ of the MS_B

■ The degrees of freedom $(N - J)$ of the MS_W

■ Whether all the population means are identical

Figure 3.5 shows the distribution of F-ratios for 3 and 156 degrees of freedom when the population means are all equal.

Figure 3.5
The distribution of F-ratios when the population means are identical is called a *central* F distribution.

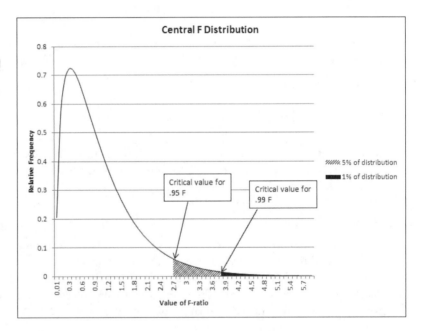

Suppose that you take many, many samples from populations whose means are equal. For each set of four samples, with 40 observations each, you calculate an MS_B and an MS_W, form an F-ratio, and chart the result. After you've done that thousands of times the distribution of the F-ratios would look much like the one shown in Figure 3.5.

Because the population means are equal, the mean of the F distribution is 1.0 as the degrees of freedom for MS_W approaches infinity: The larger the number of observations, the more accurately you can estimate the population means via the sample means. Still, sampling error causes you to get some F-ratios much larger than 1.0 even when the population means are all equal. You expect to get some F-ratios smaller than 1.0. In fact, the distribution of the F-ratios from many repeated instances of the same experiment resembles the curve in Figure 3.5 very closely.

And we know the characteristics of the curve well enough to state that even when the population means are equal, we would get an F-ratio larger than 2.7 only 5% of the time. We would get an F-ratio larger than 3.8 only 1% of the time. These unusually large F-ratios would be due to inevitable sampling error, not to genuine differences in the mean values of the populations.

Excel provides various functions that help you evaluate F-ratios. For example, this formula:

=F.DIST.RT(2.66,3,156)

returns 0.05 or 5%. The function and its arguments are as follows:

- F.DIST notifies Excel that you're interested in the F distribution.
- .RT calls for the *right* tail of the F distribution.
- 2.66 is the value of a particular F-ratio.
- 3 is (J – 1), the number of groups minus 1, the degrees of freedom for MS_B.
- 156 is (N – J), the number of observations minus the number of groups, the degrees of freedom for MS_W.

Again, with those values, Excel tells you that the right tail of a central F distribution with 3 and 156 degrees of freedom, to the right of an F-ratio of 2.66, contains 5% of the area under the curve.

Similarly, this formula:

=F.DIST.RT(2.12,3,156)

returns 0.1 or 10%. Ten percent of the area under the curve is found to the right of an F-ratio of 2.12, given that the population means are equal and that you're working with 160 observations in four groups.

At some point you get an F-ratio that's so large you're not willing to believe that it came about from errors in sampling from populations that have the same means—in other words, you find it more sensible to believe that the larger MS_B is due to real differences between population means, not simply to sampling error. You need a decision rule to make that judgment objectively, though.

In the present example, you might promise before looking at the data that you'll decide the population means are different if you get an F-ratio of 2.66 or greater. As we just saw, you'll get an F-ratio at least that large, with 3 and 156 degrees of freedom, 5% of the time when the population means are identical.

In the jargon of statistics, you have *set alpha* to 5%. You will make a *Type I error* 5% of the time; that's how often you'll erroneously reject the null hypothesis. In 5% of the imaginary repetitions of the same experiment, you would decide that population means differ, when in fact they don't.

I just presented the logic of what's called the *F-test* backward—that is, I presented the values of F-ratios and showed you how to determine how often those ratios (and larger ratios) would occur when the population means are identical. In fact, you normally decide on an alpha level—the percent of the time that you're willing to make the mistake of erroneously rejecting the null hypothesis. Then you determine what the minimum value of the F-ratio must be for you to reject it.

That latter value, the minimum result that will cause you to reject the null hypothesis, is termed the *critical value*.

To determine the critical value using Excel, trot out the F.INV.RT() function instead of the F.DIST.RT() function. Here's an example:

    =F.INV.RT(0.05,3,156)

returns 2.66. The function itself and its arguments are as follows:

- F.INV notifies Excel that you're interested in the *inverse* of the F distribution. You supply the probability and Excel returns the associated F value. (In contrast, using F.DIST, you supply the F value and Excel returns the probability.)
- .RT calls for the *right* tail of the F distribution.
- 0.05 is the probability that you'll make a Type I error and erroneously reject the null hypothesis. (This probability is also called *alpha*.)
- 3 is $(J - 1)$, the number of groups minus 1, the degrees of freedom for MS_B.
- 156 is $(N - J)$, the number of observations minus the number of groups, the degrees of freedom for MS_B.

So you obtain 2.66 as the critical value. If your experiment involves four groups, with 40 observations per group, and you want to limit the probability that you will reject a true null hypothesis to 5%, then the critical value for the F-ratio is 2.66.

The Noncentral F Distribution

The discussion in the prior section assumed that there is no difference in the means of the populations that you take your samples from. When you form an F-ratio based on those samples you compare it to a central F distribution, one that assumes that there are no differences in the population means.

But in reality there might be differences in the means of the populations. If so, the second term in this equation is greater than zero and causes the mean square between groups to exceed the mean square within groups:

$$E(MS_B) = \sigma^2 + n\sum(\mu_j - \mu)^2 / (J-1)$$

If that's the reality of the situation, we're no longer dealing with a central F distribution but a *noncentral* F distribution. The effect is to stretch the F distribution out to the right: The mean of the F distribution is no longer 1.0 but some larger value that depends on the size of the differences between the population means. The size of those differences is called the *noncentrality parameter*, and it's symbolized as λ, lambda.

Figure 3.6 shows several F distributions, each based on a different value of the noncentrality parameter.

Figure 3.6
The distribution of F-ratios when the population means are different is called a *noncentral* F distribution.

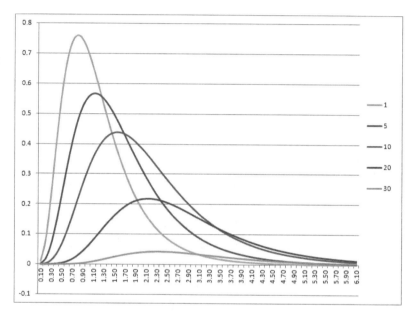

When the population means are different, you're working with a noncentral F distribution, and the likelihood of getting an F-ratio that's substantially larger than 1.0 increases in comparison to that ratio's likelihood in the central F distribution.

The greater the noncentrality parameter, the larger the differences between the population means, and the more likely you are to obtain an F-ratio that's larger than the critical value you establish to reject the null hypothesis of no differences among the population means.

This effect is directly analogous to the situation in a t-test, where the farther apart two sample means are, the more likely you are to correctly decide that the population means differ. In either case, t-tests or F-tests, the issue is one of *statistical power*: the sensitivity of the statistical test to differences between sample means.

You can visualize this effect most clearly by viewing two F distributions simultaneously, one a central F and one a noncentral F, such that both distributions are based on the same number of degrees of freedom. Figure 3.7 provides an example, with a central and a noncentral F distribution, based on 3 degrees of freedom for MS_B and 21 degrees of freedom for MS_W.

Figure 3.7
An F-ratio that exceeds the critical value is more likely to come from the noncentral F distribution than from the central F distribution.

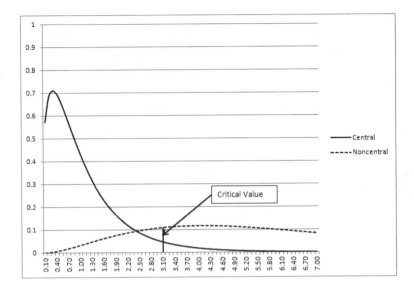

Single Factor ANOVA

The first main section of this chapter distills a considerable amount of statistical and distributional information into just a few pages. At this point it usually helps to walk through an ANOVA to make the concepts more concrete.

In this section I describe an experiment and discuss some of the assumptions and decisions that the experimenter might make. You then see how the resulting data is analyzed using Excel, and the conclusions that the experimenter reaches.

Suppose that a medical researcher wants to compare the effects of three treatments on the low density lipoproteins (LDL, the so-called "bad cholesterol") in three groups of heart patients. The researcher wants to administer either a statin or a statin in combination with niacin to two of the three groups. The third group will be treated by means of a low fat, low calorie diet in an attempt to lower the patients' amount of abdominal fat.

The researcher randomly selects 72 patients from a hospital's post-cardiac unit and randomly assigns each patient to one of the three groups (with, of course, the patient's informed consent as well as the concurrence of the doctors involved). The random selection and assignment is part of the so-called "gold standard" of research and helps to ensure that the three groups start out on an equal footing. Nonrandom assignment, or the use of existing and intact groups, could easily result in one group starting the experiment with a substantial advantage in LDL levels, compared to the other two groups.

Adopting an Error Rate

The researcher decides to adopt a Type I error rate, also termed an alpha level, of 0.001. By doing so, the researcher determines that only once in 1,000 times that this experiment might be run would the null hypothesis of no difference in the population means be rejected, when there actually were no differences.

This is a fairly stringent criterion, and in addition to the protection against rejecting a true null hypothesis, it also makes it more difficult to reject the null hypothesis when it's *false*. The researcher has decided that it would be more costly to decide that one treatment is better than the others (when it's not) than to decide that the treatments are equally effective (when they're not). The researcher does not want to recommend a change in treatment when that change might do no good.

Adopting this alpha level means that the critical value of the F-test will have to exceed 7.65 if the researcher is to reject the null hypothesis of no differences between the three populations from which the samples are taken (the population of heart patients who take statins alone, the population that takes statins and niacin in combination, and the population that treats LDL levels with diet alone).

The researcher determines the critical value of 7.65 by using Excel's F.INV.RT() function, as follows:

   =F.INV.RT(0.001,2,69)

which returns 7.65 (actually, 7.647869). At the end of the experiment, if the resulting F-ratio is less than 7.65, the researcher will continue to regard the null hypothesis of no difference in the population mean as tenable.

If the F-ratio turns out to be larger than 7.65, the researcher will reject the null hypothesis and conclude that there is at least one population mean that's different from the other two. The researcher might then use a *multiple comparison procedure* to determine where the significant difference lies. (Multiple comparison procedures are not discussed in this book. Two such procedures are discussed in some detail in *Statistical Analysis: Microsoft Excel 2010*.)

Note that the design described here would never actually be followed in a medical experiment—in particular, the sample sizes are far too small for anything other than a preliminary pilot study. The size of samples does exert some influence on controlling the role of chance in deciding whether a null hypothesis is true or false; this is a matter of what's termed *internal validity*.

But with sample sizes of 24 per group, the experiment's *external validity* or *generalizability* is seriously limited. External validity refers to the researcher's ability to generalize the experimental findings to other members of the same populations. It's difficult to imagine that a finding based on an average value from 24 people could generalize convincingly to the tens of millions of people who might need to establish better control over their cholesterol levels.

Computing the Statistics

Figure 3.8 shows the LDL cholesterol levels of each patient at the end of the experiment, along with some preliminary statistical calculations.

Figure 3.8
The calculations are simplified when each group contains the same number of observations.

	A	B	C	D	E	F	G	H
	F9				*fx* =AVERAGE(F7:H7)			
1	Statin	Niacin & Statin	Diet			Statin	Niacin & Statin	Diet
2	113	110	113					
3	108	108	108		Average	111.38	110.75	112.63
4	114	114	116		Sum of Squares	115.63	114.50	145.63
5	110	110	112		n	24	24	24
6	110	110	112		SS/(n-1)	5.03	4.98	6.33
7	113	114	114		Variance	5.03	4.98	6.33
8	113	111	114					
9	114	114	115		Mean square within	5.45		
10	108	109	109		Mean square between	21.875		
11	109	110	110					
12	109	109	110					
13	113	113	114					
14	111	109	112					
15	113	110	114					
16	114	115	117					
17	110	109	111					
18	110	108	111					
19	113	112	114					
20	110	109	112					
21	109	109	110					
22	108	109	110					
23	113	110	113					
24	113	111	114					
25	115	115	118					

The preliminary calculations that appear in Figure 3.8 are all based on Excel's worksheet functions. The group means are in F3:H3 and are calculated using Excel's AVERAGE() function. For example, the formula in cell F3 is

=AVERAGE(A2:A25)

The sums of squares are in cells F4:H4 and are calculated using Excel's DEVSQ() function, which returns the sum of the squared deviations of a series of values from their mean. The formula in cell F4 is

=DEVSQ(A2:A25)

The sample sizes appear in cells F5:H5, and each sample contains 24 observations. No worksheet functions are used to obtain these values.

The variance of each group appears in cells F6:H6. The estimate of the population variance is returned by dividing the group's sum of squares by its degrees of freedom. The degrees of freedom for a group in an analysis of variance is the group sample size minus 1. So, in this case, the degrees of freedom for each group is 23. The formula used to calculate the variance in cell F6 is

=F4/(F5–1)

Another way to get the estimate of the population variance from sample observations is by way of Excel's VAR.S() worksheet function. That has also been done in Figure 3.8, in cells

F7:H7. I supplied both methods simply to demonstrate that they are equivalent. Cell F7 contains this formula:

=VAR.S(A2:A25)

Obviously it's easier to use the VAR.S() function than the combination of DEVSQ() with a count of each group's degrees of freedom. But down the road it's useful to bear in mind that the group variance is the ratio of its sum of squares to its degrees of freedom.

With groups of equal sample sizes, as in this example, it's easy to calculate the mean square within for the ANOVA. Just take the average of the group variances.

I've put off discussing the term *mean square between* until this point because it's much easier to buy into it in the context of the calculations than in the context of its theory. Bear in mind that the idea behind the F-test in the analysis of variance is to compare two estimates of the variance in the population:

- One based on the natural variation characteristic of individual observations—the mean square within
- One based on the natural variation among individuals, plus any variation induced by differences in the means of the groups that the individuals belong to—the mean square between

3

If there's no additional variation induced by differences in group means, we expect the two estimates themselves to be negligibly different.

Here's where the terminology can get somewhat confusing. The term "mean square *between*" suggests that the variance being estimated is the variability of the group means, the differences *between* the average values of each group. But in fact the mean square between is expected to estimate the individual variation plus any added variation due to mean differences.

The rationale for the term *mean square between* becomes clearer when you consider the way that it's calculated. Suppose that you calculate the standard deviation of the group means. In the example shown in Figure 3.8, that would be the standard deviation of 111.38, 110.75, and 112.63, or 0.955. That statistic is termed the *standard error of the mean*, and it's an important concept in both descriptive and inferential statistics.

You can calculate the standard error of the mean on an Excel worksheet using Excel's STDEV.S() function. On the worksheet shown in Figure 3.8, for example, you might use this formula:

=STDEV.S(F3:H3)

(You would use STDEV.S() instead of STDEV.P() because you're estimating a population standard deviation on the basis of a sample.)

But another formula for the standard error of the mean does not involve the means of the groups. The definitional formula for the standard error of the mean is as follows:

$$\sigma_{\bar{X}} = \sigma_X / \sqrt{n}$$

where:

- $\sigma_{\bar{X}}$ is the standard error of the mean (notice the $\bar{X}$, pronounced "x-bar," in the subscript).
- σ_X is the standard deviation of the individual observations in a sample.
- n is the size of that sample.

So, on the basis of a single sample, you can use the sample standard deviation s_X and the sample size n to estimate the standard error of the mean: the standard deviation of the means of many samples that are similarly taken.

The derivation of this formula is not difficult, and you can find it in the next section of this chapter.

If you square both sides of the formula, you get the *variance error of the mean*:

$$\sigma_{\bar{X}}^2 = \sigma_X^2 / n$$

And by rearranging the equation you get the *mean square between*:

$$\sigma_X^2 = n\sigma_{\bar{X}}^2$$

That is, the *mean square between* is not the variance of the means—the variance error of the mean $\sigma_{\bar{X}}^2$—but rather it is the population variance σ_X^2 as estimated via the variance error of the mean.

The variance error of the mean is the square of the standard error of the mean, just as the variance of a set of scores is the square of the standard deviation of those scores. The next section provides the derivation of the standard error of the mean, and thus the derivation of the variance error of the mean—also known as the mean square between, your second estimate of the population variance.

Deriving the Standard Error of the Mean

Suppose that you take many samples from a population and calculate the mean of each sample. In that case you can calculate the variance of all those means.

If each sample consists of exactly two observations, x_1 and x_2, the mean of the observations is $(x_1 + x_2)/2$. So the variance of many sample means, each based on two observations, can be written as follows:

$$\sigma_{\bar{X}}^2 = \sigma_{(x_1+x_2)/2}^2$$

To get the mean of two observations you can divide their sum by 2 or multiply their sum by 0.5. When you multiply a variable by a constant, the resulting variance is the original variance times the square of the constant. For example, suppose you multiply the two values x_1 and x_2 by the constant c. Then the sum of the squared deviations, SS, for x_1 and x_2 is

$$SS_{cX} = \sum_{i=1}^{n} (cX_i - c\bar{X})^2$$

$$SS_{cX} = \sum_{i=1}^{n} [c(X_i - \bar{X})]^2$$

$$SS_{cX} = \sum_{i=1}^{n} c^2 (X_i - \bar{X})^2$$

$$SS_{cX} = c^2 \sum_{i=1}^{n} (X_i - \bar{X})^2$$

and if you divide by the degrees of freedom:

$$\frac{SS_{cX}}{n-1} = c^2 \sum_{i=1}^{n} (X_i - \bar{X})^2 / (n-1)$$

Therefore:

$$s_{cX}^2 = c^2 s_X^2$$

In words, when you multiply each value in a set of values by a constant, the variance of the new set is the square of the constant times the variance of the original set.

In terms of the derivation of the standard error of the mean, we're dividing the two observations in each sample by 2, or multiplying by 0.5, to get their mean. Therefore, to get the variance of those means across many samples:

$$s_{(X_1+X_2)/2}^2 = 0.5^2 \times s_{(X_1+X_2)}^2$$

So:

$$s_{\bar{X}}^2 = 0.5^2 \times s_{(X_1+X_2)}^2$$

When two variables, such as X_1 and X_2 here, are independent of one another, the variance of their sum is equal to the sum of their variances:

$$s_{(X_1+X_2)}^2 = s_{X_1}^2 + s_{X_2}^2$$

We can use that fact in the prior formula:

$$s_{\bar{X}}^2 = 0.5^2 \times (s_{X_1}^2 + s_{X_2}^2)$$

We have imagined drawing many samples of size 2, X_1 and X_2, from a population. The variance of the first member in each of many samples, $s_{X_1}^2$, equals the variance of the population from which the samples are drawn, σ_X^2. The variance of the second member of all those samples also equals σ_X^2. Therefore:

$$\sigma_{\bar{X}}^2 = 0.5^2 \times (\sigma_X^2 + \sigma_X^2)$$

$$\sigma_{\bar{X}}^2 = 0.5^2 \times 2\sigma_X^2$$

$$\sigma_{\bar{X}}^2 = \sigma_X^2 / 2$$

In general, when you substitute n for the example's sample size, you get the following:

$$\sigma_{\bar{X}}^2 = \sigma_X^2 / n$$

In words, the variance of the means of samples from a population is equal to the variance of the population divided by the sample size.

I want to stress this: The symbol $\sigma_{\bar{X}}$ is the standard error of the mean. You *estimate* the standard error of the mean by dividing the sample variance by the sample size and taking the square root of the result. It is *defined* as the standard deviation of means, which are calculated on repeated samples from a population.

The next section discusses Excel's Data Analysis add-in, a set of statistical tools that includes a single-factor ANOVA tool. You'll be able to compare the results of using Excel's worksheet functions to complete a single-factor ANOVA with the results of using the add-in's ANOVA tool on the same data set.

Using the Data Analysis Add-In

For many years, the Excel installation files have included an add-in that performs several statistical analyses. In older Excel versions, the documentation refers to it as the Analysis ToolPak. This book terms it the Data Analysis add-in, because that's the label you see in the Ribbon after the add-in has been installed in more recent versions. Some of the tools in the Data Analysis add-in are useful, but their reach is limited. I explain more about that later in this section.

The Data Analysis add-in might already be available to you. With Excel 2007 or 2010, click the Ribbon's Data tab and look for Data Analysis in the Analysis group. In Excel 2003 or earlier, look for Data Analysis in the Tools menu. If you find Data Analysis you're all set.

Installing the Data Analysis Add-In

If you don't see Data Analysis, you need to make it available to Excel, and you might even have to install it from the installation disc or the downloaded installation utility.

The Data Analysis add-in might have been installed on your working disk but not yet made available to Excel. If you don't see Data Analysis in the Analysis group on the Data tab, take these steps:

1. In Office 2010, click the File tab and click Options in its navigation bar. In Office 2007, click the Office button and click the Excel Options button at the bottom of the menu.

2. The Excel Options window opens. Click Add-Ins in its navigation bar.

3. If necessary, select Excel Add-Ins in the Manage drop-down and then click Go.

4. The Add-Ins dialog box appears. If you see Analysis ToolPak listed, be sure its check box is filled. (*Analysis ToolPak* is an old term for this add-in.) Click OK.

You should now find Data Analysis in the Analysis group on the Data tab.

Things are a little quicker in versions of Excel prior to 2007. Choose Add-Ins from the Tools menu. Look for Analysis ToolPak in the Add-Ins dialog box, and fill its check box if you see it. Click OK. You should now find Data Analysis in the Tools menu.

If you do not find Analysis ToolPak in the Add-Ins dialog box, regardless of the version of Excel you're using, you need to modify the installation. You can do this if you have access to the installation disc or downloaded installation file. It's usually best to start from the Control Panel. Choose Add or Remove Software, or Programs and Features, depending on the version of Windows that you're running. Choose to change the installation of Office.

When you get to the Excel portion of the installation, click Excel's expand box (the one with a plus sign inside a box). You see another expand box beside Add-Ins. Click it to display Analysis ToolPak. Use its drop-down to select Run From My Computer, and then Continue and OK your way back to Excel.

Now continue with step 1 in the preceding list.

Using the ANOVA: Single Factor Tool

The data shown in Figure 3.8 is repeated for convenience in Figure 3.9.

The data layout shown in Figure 3.9 works well for most of the tools in the Data Analysis add-in, including the ANOVA: Single Factor tool. To get the dialog box that's also shown in Figure 3.9, take these steps:

1. Click the Ribbon's Data tab.

2. Click Data Analysis in the Data tab's Analysis group. A list box with the names of the various tools available to you appears.

3. Click the ANOVA: Single Factor tool and then click OK.

Figure 3.9
The data set is laid out as an Excel list or table: Records in rows, variables in columns, with variable names in the first row.

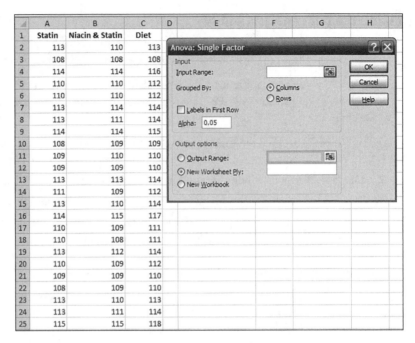

The dialog box shown in Figure 3.9 appears. Complete the entries in the dialog box using these steps (which assume that your data is laid out as in the figure):

1. Click in the Input Range box.

2. Using your mouse pointer, drag through the range A1:C25. Notice that this range includes the variable names in the first row.

3. Make sure that the Grouped By Columns option button is selected.

4. Make sure that the Labels in First Row check box is selected.

5. The prior section in this chapter specified that the researcher wanted to use 0.001 as the alpha level—the likelihood that a true null hypothesis would be rejected. Enter the value 0.001 in the Alpha box.

6. Click the Output Range option button and then click in the range edit box to its right. (Be sure to see the Note immediately following this list.)

7. With your cursor in the range edit box, click some cell in the active worksheet to identify the upper-left cell of the range where you want the ANOVA output to start. Be sure that there's no data to the right of and below that cell that you cannot afford to lose.

8. Click OK.

After clicking OK, the results shown in Figure 3.10 appear.

Figure 3.10
The ANOVA: Single Factor tool produces only the values in E1:I7 and E10:K15.

	E	F	G	H	I	J	K	L
1	Anova: Single Factor							
2								
3	SUMMARY							
4	*Groups*	*Count*	*Sum*	*Average*	*Variance*			
5	Statin	24	2673	111.375	5.027		Std Err of the Mean	0.955
6	Niacin & Statin	24	2658	110.75	4.978		Var Err of the Mean	0.911
7	Diet	24	2703	112.625	6.332		Mean Square Between	21.875
8								
9								
10	ANOVA							
11	*Source of Variation*	*SS*	*df*	*MS*	*F*	*P-value*	*F crit*	
12	Between Groups	43.75	2	21.875	4.017	0.022375	7.64786854	
13	Within Groups	375.75	69	5.446				
14								
15	Total	419.5	71					
16								
17	=DEVSQ(H5:H7)*24	43.75						
18	=DEVSQ(A2:A25)+DEVSQ(B2:B25)	375.75						
19	+DEVSQ(C2:C25)							
20	=DEVSQ(A2:C25)	419.5						

Understanding the ANOVA Output

A walkthrough of the ANOVA: Single Factor output begins with the descriptive statistics. In Figure 3.10, the counts, sums, averages, and variances for each group appear in the range E4:I7. Notice that the names of the groups appear in E5:E7. The names would not appear if you had not included them in the input range for the analysis (A1:C25) or if you had not selected the Labels in First Row check box of the tool's dialog box (refer to Figure 3.9).

Using the Descriptive Statistics

The descriptive statistics are useful for a variety of reasons. They help you summarize the results of the experiment, where the most interesting issue is usually whether the sample means differ and if so by what degree. Other reasons to examine the descriptive statistics involve the relationship between the sample variances and the sample counts.

Not as in this example, when you have unequal sample counts and unequal variances, the probabilities associated with the F-ratios can get distorted. You might think that you're working with an alpha level of 0.01, but the relationship between the unequal counts and the unequal variances can actually change the nominal alpha level from 0.01 to 0.03. A different pattern in that relationship can change the nominal alpha level from 0.01 to 0.005. This is termed the *Behrens-Fisher problem* and is discussed in some detail in *Statistical Analysis: Microsoft Excel 2010*, Chapter 10.

Using the Inferential Statistics

The portion of the output that helps you make inferences about the populations from which the samples are drawn is in E11:K15 in Figure 3.10. The ANOVA table shown there follows standard layout conventions, with a different row for each source of variation (between groups and within groups). The columns in the ANOVA table are described in the following sections.

Source of Variation

A single factor analysis of variance has only two sources of variation: between groups and within groups. Other types of ANOVA have additional sources of variation.

For example, suppose that in this chapter's example the researcher had decided to employ patient's sex as an additional factor. Then there would have been two additional sources of variation. There would be no "between groups" source; it would be replaced by a Treatment source and a Sex source. Further, because a given treatment might have a different effect for men than for women, another source of variation would be the interaction of treatment and sex.

This Data Analysis add-in offers two ANOVA tools for two-factor designs. One tool—Two Factor with Replication—provides a standard two-factor analysis for designs with equal group sizes only. The other tool—Two Factor without Replication—actually assumes a repeated measures design in which the person or object being observed is the second factor. The repeated measures ANOVA makes certain restrictive assumptions, and most analysts today prefer to use a multivariate test, which does not make those assumptions, before adopting the univariate results.

SS (Sums of Squares)

There is a sum of squares associated with each source of variation. For the Between Groups source, the sum of squares is based on the total of the squared deviations of each group mean from the grand mean. The ANOVA tool returns the Sum of Squares Between in cell F12 of Figure 3.10. You can also find it in cell F17, where it is calculated as follows:

=DEVSQ(H5:H7)*24

That is, the sum of the squared deviations of each sample mean from the grand mean, multiplied by the number of observations in each sample.

For the Within Groups source, the sum of squares is the total of the sum of squared deviations of each observation from the mean of the sample it belongs to. The ANOVA tool places it in cell F13 in Figure 3.10. You can also find it in cell F18, where it is calculated as follows:

=DEVSQ(A2:A25)+DEVSQ(B2:B25)+DEVSQ(C2:C25)

The latter formula totals the sum of the squared deviations of each observation from the mean of the sample it belongs to.

The sum of squares reported by the ANOVA tool in cell F15 does not actually pertain to a source of variation—there is no "total" source. The value reported there, 419.5, is the sum of the squared deviations of each individual observation from the grand mean of all the observations. You could calculate using this formula:

=DEVSQ(A2:C25)

Notice that the Total Sum of Squares, 419.5, is the total of the Sum of Squares Between and the Sum of Squares Within. One of the purposes of the analysis of variance is to partition the total sum of squares into two or more components that do not overlap but are independent—that is, that they total to the sum of squares calculated via the individual observations' differences from the grand mean.

The fact that the sums of squares are independent means that the variability in the individual scores can be allocated unambiguously to either the effect of the sample's mean on its component scores, or to the ordinary variation of individual observations from one another.

This lack of ambiguity in allocating the variability is of fundamental importance in any statistical technique that depends on the general linear model, which includes simple t-tests, the analysis of variance, the analysis of covariance, multiple regression, and multivariate analysis of variance (which is discussed in Chapter 4).

When you are running an analysis of variance that employs two or more factors (for example, treatment and sex) and at the end of the experiment you find that you do not have an equal number of observations in each cell of the design, you usually have difficulty establishing that sort of unambiguous allocation of variance. Techniques for dealing with the ambiguity exist, principally by means of multiple regression.

However, unequal sample sizes in single factor ANOVAs do not create that sort of problem. (As noted earlier in this chapter, though, the combination of unequal sample sizes and unequal sample variances can cause problems with the nominal versus the actual alpha rates.)

df (Degrees of Freedom)

The degrees of freedom in a single factor ANOVA are always calculated as follows:

■ The Degrees of Freedom Between equals the number of samples minus 1, often symbolized as $(J - 1)$. Here, 3 samples minus 1 equals 2.

■ The Degrees of Freedom Within equals the total number of observations minus the number of samples, often symbolized as $(N - J)$. Here, 72 observations minus 3 samples equals 69.

The concept of degrees of freedom is an elusive one. You can find a discussion and demonstration of its effects in Chapters 2 and 3 of *Statistical Analysis: Microsoft Excel 2010*.

MS (Mean Squares)

The mean squares are calculated by dividing each sum of squares by its associated degrees of freedom. The result, although termed a *mean square*, is a measure of variance.

> **NOTE** The use of the term *mean square* has more to do with tradition than with accuracy. You divide the sum of squares for a source of variation by the number of values involved in the sum of squares, minus a value that depends on the source of variation. Therefore, it's not a true "mean square"—an average squared deviation would divide by the number of values involved, not by the number of values minus 1 or minus J. But by tradition it's termed a mean square.

You can see from the calculations shown in Figure 3.10 that the mean square within depends on two sources of information: the sum of squares of the deviations of individual observations from the mean of the sample they belong to, and the degrees of freedom within. The size of the differences between the group means does not enter the picture. In this example, by adding or subtracting a constant to each of a group's observations, the group means could be changed to 5, 115, and 10,900—and the individual observations around their respective means would still have an average variance of 5.44.

Furthermore, the calculation of the mean square between also depends on two sources of information: the sum of the squared deviations of the sample means from the grand mean and the degrees of freedom between. The mean square between is calculated without reference to the variability within the samples.

Therefore, we have two estimates of the population variance. We know that the two mean squares both estimate the population variance from an understanding of their expected values (discussed earlier in this chapter).

But one estimate is based on the group means and the other is based on the within-group variability. To the extent that the former exceeds the latter, we have a situation that suggests the populations underlying the samples have different means.

F (F-Ratio)

The F-ratio is the result of dividing MS_B by MS_W. Even if the population means all equal one another, you can get an F-ratio that's substantially larger than 1.0, simply due to sampling error. By referring to the distribution of F-ratios with different degrees of freedom, you can determine the probability of observing an F-ratio as large as the one you calculate even if the populations have the same mean values. (Refer, for example, to Figure 3.5.)

P-Value (Probability of F-Ratio)

The p-value is the probability of obtaining an F-ratio as large or larger than the one observed, assuming that the null hypothesis of no difference between group means is true.

Under the ground rules that have been followed for many years by inferential statistics, this probability must be equal to or smaller than the alpha level that the researcher establishes at the beginning of the experiment. In this example, the researcher decided on an alpha level of 0.001 early on, and in consequence cannot reject the null hypothesis. This is so even though the obtained p-value is fairly small, 0.022.

The researcher presumably had sound reasons for setting alpha to a stringent 0.001 level ("sound reasons" usually involve an assessment of the relative costs of incorrectly concluding that the populations means are identical, versus incorrectly concluding that they aren't). If the researcher decides to reject the null hypothesis after seeing that the p-value is fairly small—just not as small as originally hoped—then the ground rules are broken.

This is just one way to fudge the data. When researchers do that, consumers of the research can never be sure whether the researcher has published results because they were welcome, or whether other results were suppressed because they weren't.

F Crit (Critical Value)

Recall that you specified a particular alpha level on the ANOVA dialog box, shown in Figure 3.9. The effect of that alpha level on the output appears as the critical value for the F-ratio. The ANOVA tool combines the information about the degrees of freedom for the F-ratio's numerator and denominator with the alpha level you specify. The tool provides the minimum F-ratio needed to achieve that alpha level, given the numbers of degrees of freedom at hand.

In this example (as I mentioned earlier in this chapter) you would need an F-ratio of 7.65 to reject the null hypothesis at the 0.001 alpha level, given that you have 2 and 69 degrees of freedom. The actual F-ratio of 4.02 falls far short of the 7.65 criterion.

The Regression Approach

The analysis of variance, as outlined so far in this chapter, is one way to estimate the probability that different populations have different means. In the example used in this chapter, the ANOVA studied one outcome variable, LDL levels. The basis for a univariate ANOVA is what's called the *general linear model*. Here's a quick overview of the general linear model:

$$X_{ij} = \mu + \alpha_j + \varepsilon_{ij}$$

The above formula shows how the general linear model accounts for the value of an observation in a single factor, univariate analysis of variance. A given observation, X_{ij}, is the i-th person (or object, or some measurable entity) in the j-th group. Each value of the outcome variable is made up of three components:

- The grand mean of the population, symbolized by μ.
- The effect of being in group j. This effect, which might pull the members of that group above the grand mean μ or push them down below μ, is symbolized by α_j.
- The residual is symbolized by ε_{ij}. It is what's left over in person i's score after the grand mean and the effect of being in group j have been accounted for.

Suppose you own a gasoline-powered car, a subcompact, that gets 28 miles per gallon. If the average mpg of all gas powered cars is 20 mpg and all subcompacts is 32 mpg, then the general linear model would describe your car as follows:

$$20 + 12 - 4$$

The overall average is 20 mpg (μ). The effect of a car being a subcompact is to raise the expected mpg from 20 to 32, so the subcompact effect is +12 (α). And because your particular car gets 28 instead of 32 mpg, the effect of it being your car is –4 (ε).

The general approach taken by traditional analysis of variance is to divide the overall variability of all the cars into two components:

- A Within component—the variability of each car's (ε_{ij}) mileage around the mean of its group, such as subcompacts (group j).
- A Between component—the variability of each group's (α_j) mean around the grand mean (μ).

Prior sections in this chapter detailed the traditional approach to the ANOVA calculations. But there is another approach, a close cousin, to the calculations that has much to recommend it: multiple regression in conjunction with what's called *effect coding*.

I personally prefer that approach to the traditional calculations: I think it provides more insight into the data, it provides more information about the relationships, and it prepares the ground for more advanced analyses such as the analysis of covariance. It gives you ways of dealing sensibly with unbalanced designs, which have different sample sizes. Excel even has a native worksheet function, LINEST(), which runs the analysis for you so that you don't have to resort to the Data Analysis add-in or enter several different functions on the worksheet.

Using Effect Coding

In traditional ANOVA calculations you know which group an observation belongs to because it's labeled accordingly: for example, Statin versus Statin plus Niacin versus Diet, or Subcompact versus Full Size versus SUV.

Using effect coding (or one of the closely related coding schemes including dummy coding and orthogonal coding) you add numeric variables that define the group membership. Figure 3.11 shows the general idea.

Figure 3.11

Columns C and D contain what are called effect codes.

	A	B	C	D	E
1	Treatment Name	Treatment Code (Statin)	Treatment Code (Statin & Niacin)	LDL	
2	Statin	1	0	113	
3	Statin	1	0	108	
4	Statin	1	0	114	
5	Statin	1	0	110	
6	Statin	1	0	110	
7	Niacin & Statin	0	1	110	
8	Niacin & Statin	0	1	108	
9	Niacin & Statin	0	1	114	
10	Niacin & Statin	0	1	110	
11	Niacin & Statin	0	1	110	
12	Diet	-1	-1	113	
13	Diet	-1	-1	108	
14	Diet	-1	-1	116	
15	Diet	-1	-1	112	
16	Diet	-1	-1	112	
17					

The idea behind effect coding is to provide each observation a code (1, 0, or −1) that identifies the observation's membership in one of the groups. It takes as many new variables, or *vectors*, to completely define the membership as the original variable has degrees of freedom.

So, in Figure 3.11, two vectors are used because there are three groups (and therefore (J − 1) or two degrees of freedom). Using effect coding:

- All the members of one group are assigned a code of 1 on a variable.
- All the members of other groups are assigned a code of 0 on that variable, except the members of a final group.
- The members of a final group, who are assigned a code of −1 on that variable as well as any other coded variable.

So, in Figure 3.11, for column B, all the Statin members get a 1. The Statin + Niacin members get a 0. The Diet members get a −1 in column B.

For column C, all the Statin members get a 0. The Statin + Niacin members get a 1. The Diet members again get a −1.

There are three groups, but you need only two columns: The codes on those columns completely define the group membership of each observation. This approach enables the regression coefficients to reflect the numeric effect of being in a particular group—that is, the α's mentioned earlier.

With the effect codes established as in Figure 3.11, you can use the worksheet function LINEST() to get all the necessary statistics for an analysis of variance. Figure 3.12 shows the full data set used in Figures 3.8 through 3.10, with the associated group names and the resulting effect codes in columns B and C. (There are too many observations to show more than the first group in Figure 3.12, but the entire data set and accompanying analysis are in the downloadable workbook for this chapter.)

Figure 3.12

The range F2:H6 contains the results of using the LINEST() function on the data in B2:D73.

	F2				f_x {=LINEST(D2:D73,B2:C73,,TRUE)}							
	A	B	C	D E	F	G	H	I	J	K	L
1	Treatment Name	Treatment Code (Statin)	Treatment Code (Statin & Niacin)	LDL							
2	Statin	1	0	113	-0.833	-0.208	111.583				
3	Statin	1	0	108	0.389	0.39	0.28				
4	Statin	1	0	114	0.104	2.33	#N/A				
5	Statin	1	0	110	4.017	69	#N/A				
6	Statin	1	0	110	43.75	375.75	#N/A				
7	Statin	1	0	113							
8	Statin	1	0	113	Anova: Single Factor						
9	Statin	1	0	114							
10	Statin	1	0	108	SUMMARY						
11	Statin	1	0	109	Groups	Count	Sum	Average	Variance		
12	Statin	1	0	109	Statin	24	2673	111.375	5.027		111.375
13	Statin	1	0	113	Niacin & Statin	24	2658	110.75	4.978		110.75
14	Statin	1	0	111	Diet	24	2703	112.625	6.332		112.625
15	Statin	1	0	113						Grand Mean	111.583
16	Statin	1	0	114							
17	Statin	1	0	110	ANOVA						
18	Statin	1	0	110	Source of Variation	SS	df	MS	F	P-value	F crit
19	Statin	1	0	113	Between Group	43.75	2	21.875	4.017	0.022	7.648
20	Statin	1	0	110	Within Groups	375.75	69	5.446			
21	Statin	1	0	109							
22	Statin	1	0	108	Total	419.5	71				
23	Statin	1	0	113							
24	Statin	1	0	113							
25	Statin	1	0	115							
26	Niacin & St	0	1	110							
27	Niacin & St	0	1	108							

Figure 3.12 contains quite a bit of material to bring to your attention.

The LINEST() Formula

A formula that uses the LINEST() function must be array-entered if you are to get the full set of results. (If you're familiar with array formulas and the mechanics of using them, by all means skip ahead to the next section.)

To get the results shown in F2:H6 of Figure 3.12, begin by selecting that range of cells. Then type the following formula:

=LINEST(D2:D73,B2:C73,,TRUE)

but don't press Enter yet. After typing the formula so that you can see it in the Formula Bar, hold down Ctrl and Shift and then press Enter. This keyboard sequence tells Excel that you are entering an array formula, one whose results occupy the selected range of cells.

In response, Excel calculates the LINEST() statistics and displays them in the selected range of cells. When you look at an array formula after it has been entered, you see that the formula itself is surrounded by curly brackets—see the Formula Bar in Figure 3.12. By the way, leave it to Excel to supply the curly brackets. If you supply them you'll just confuse Excel.

The LINEST() Results

The LINEST() worksheet function returns an array of results, in five rows and a number of columns that depends on the number of predictors, or *x-values*, that you supply. The first two rows are directly concerned with the regression equation that quantifies how you can use the x-values to predict the outcome variable, or *y-values*.

The third through fifth rows, in the first two columns only, provide information about the expected accuracy of the regression equation. These rows also constitute an ANOVA which tells you whether the regression equation explains a reliable, replicable amount of the overall variance in the outcome variable.

The Regression Coefficients and Intercept

The first row of LINEST() results contains the regression equation's coefficients and intercept. You can use those values to predict a particular outcome value. For example, here's how you could predict the LDL value for the first person in the list (that is, the observation in row 2):

$$(-0.833 \times 0) + (-0.208 \times 1) + 111.583$$

or 111.375. The regression coefficient in cell F2 is multiplied by the effect code in cell C2. The regression coefficient in cell G2 is multiplied by the effect code in cell B2. Then the intercept, 111.583, is added. The result is, and always will be, the mean of the group to which the observation belongs. (It's a good exercise to convince yourself that the latter statement is true.) And the difference between an observation's actual value on the predicted variable is the residual: the ε_{ij} part of the equation for the general linear model:

$$X_{ij} = \mu + \alpha_j + \varepsilon_{ij}$$

> **NOTE**
>
> That regression equation might throw you at first. Notice that the first observation has a 1 in column B and a 0 in column C. So the first coefficient, reading left to right, found in column F is multiplied by the second effect code in column C; the second coefficient, in column G, is multiplied by the first effect code in column B.
>
> The reason is that LINEST() has always returned the regression coefficients in reverse. If there were three predictor variables, you would use the third coefficient on the first variable; the second coefficient on the second variable; and the third coefficient on the first variable. There's no good reason for it, but it's too late now.
>
> LINEST() always returns the intercept in the rightmost cell of the first row of its results.

Figure 3.12 also repeats the results of the Data Analysis add-in's Single Factor ANOVA tool from Figure 3.10. Cell L15 contains the grand mean, 111.583, calculated by taking the average of the group averages in I12:I14. Compare that value to the intercept returned by LINEST() in cell H2. *With effect coding, the regression equation's intercept equals the average of the group averages.* (When the sample sizes are equal, this value is the same as the average of the individual observations.)

Now notice the value in cell L12, 111.375. It is calculated using this formula:

    =H2+G2

The result of that formula, 111.375, is equal to the average value for the first group, shown in cell I12. The intercept plus the regression coefficient for the first group equals the average value for the first group. In other words, using effect coding, the regression coefficient equals the effect of being in the associated group. Here, the coefficient is –0.208, and the mean for the first group is 0.208 below the grand mean of 111.375.

The same is true for the mean of the second group. Notice the value in cell L13, 110.75. It is returned by this formula:

    =H2+F2

The result, 110.75, is equal to the mean of the second group, shown in cell I13. The effect of being in the second group is to reduce the average LDL value by 0.833, and the regression coefficient for the second group is –0.833.

And note that the mean of the third group, 112.625, shown in cell I14, also appears in cell L14, which contains this formula:

    =H2–(G2+F2)

In general, with effect coding:

- The regression equation's intercept is equal to the mean of the group means on the outcome measure; when the groups have equal numbers of observations, the mean of the group means is equal to the mean of the individual observations.

- A regression coefficient's value equals the effect of being in a particular group, vis-à-vis the intercept. The "particular group" is the group that's assigned the value 1 on the vector associated with the regression coefficient in question.

- The group that is assigned an effect code of –1 on all vectors obviously does not have an effect code of 1 on any vector. Therefore no regression coefficient directly represents the effect of being in that group. The effect is easily calculated as the negative of the sum of the other coefficients.

The second row of the LINEST() results always contains the standard errors of the regression coefficients (or, in the results' final column, of the intercept). You can use these standard errors to form a t-ratio:

t = (regression coefficient) / (standard error)

and in terms of the addresses of the first coefficient returned in Figure 3.12:

=F2/F3

You can test the result using Excel's T.DIST() function to determine whether the coefficient is significantly different from zero, in a statistical sense. If it is not, there are times that you might want to drop that variable from the regression equation, on the grounds that if in the population the coefficient is zero, then it adds no information to the results of the equation. But there are better ways to test this (the models comparison approach, for example), and there can be good reasons not to drop a variable that is judged not significantly different from zero. You can find more on this issue in the chapters on regression analysis in *Statistical Analysis: Microsoft Excel 2010*.

LINEST() Inferential Statistics

The inferential statistics that LINEST() provides appear in the third through fifth rows, first and second columns. Perhaps the most useful is R^2, which appears in the third row and first column. R^2 is the square of the multiple correlation: the correlation between the actually observed y-values and the y-values predicted by the regression equation.

It's generally true that the square of a correlation coefficient expresses the proportion of the variability in one variable that is shared by, or attributable to, or in common with, variability in the other variable. The same is true in multiple regression. The value of R^2 expresses the proportion of variability in the observed y-values that is shared with the best linear combination of the predictor variables, or x-values.

That best linear combination is the set of values predicted by means of the regression equation. Another way to think about R^2 is that it is closely related to the multiple correlation coefficient. The higher that coefficient, the closer the predicted values are to the actually observed values, and therefore the more accurate the regression equation.

In Figure 3.12, you find R^2 in cell F4, with a value of 0.104. So 10.4% of the variability in the observed levels of LDL is shared with the predicted levels. Put another way, the multiple correlation between the observed and predicted values is 0.33.

You can find the *standard error of estimate* in the third row, second column of the LINEST() results, or in cell G4 of Figure 3.12. The standard error of estimate is the standard deviation of the residual values, the differences between the observed and the predicted values.

Therefore, the smaller the standard error of estimate is, the more accurate the regression equation. The formula for the standard error of estimate is as follows:

$$SE_{Est} = \sqrt{SS_{res} / (N - k - 1)}$$

where:

- SS_{res} is the sum of squares residual, found in LINEST()'s fifth row, second column.
- N is the total number of observations (here, 72).
- k is the number of predictor variables (here, 2).

The values returned by LINEST() in its first three rows are not found in the standard ANOVA output. They are more closely related to regression analysis than they are to traditional ANOVA approaches. But the final four values, in the fourth and fifth rows, first and second columns of the LINEST() results, can be found in the usual ANOVA table. That table is repeated in the range F17:L22 of Figure 3.12.

LINEST() returns the F-ratio for the ANOVA in its fourth row, first column. In Figure 3.12, notice that the value in cell F5, 4.017, is identical to the F-ratio reported by the ANOVA tool in cell J19. Similarly, the degrees of freedom for the residual returned by LINEST() in cell G5, 69, is the same as the degrees of freedom for the mean square within, in cell H20.

Finally, LINEST() returns in its fifth row, first and second columns, the sum of squares for the regression and the sum of squares for the residual. Notice that these two sums of squares are identical to those returned by the ANOVA tool in cells G19 and G20. The terms are different, sum of squares regression instead of between, and sum of squares residual instead of within, but the concepts and the values themselves are identical.

Therefore, you have in the LINEST() results all the information needed to build the ANOVA table: sums of squares and degrees of freedom from which you can calculate mean squares. (You do have to calculate the degrees of freedom for the regression yourself, but it's always k – 1, the number of predictors minus 1.) You also have the F-ratio, which you can submit to F.DIST.RT() to get the probability associated with that F-ratio.

It's illuminating, by the way, to take the ratio of the sum of squares regression to the total sum of squares. In the layout of Figure 3.12, you could use this formula:

```
=F6/(F6+G6)
```

which returns the value 0.104. That's R^2 for this set of data. In other words, R^2, the proportion of variability in the predicted variable that it shares with the best linear combination of the predictor variables, is identical to the ratio of the sum of squares regression to the total sum of squares.

There are other interesting relationships between different results returned by the regression analysis, and I wish I had space here to discuss them. I don't, and it's time to move on to multivariate ANOVA. But if this sort of thing interests you at all then I urge you to dig further into it using a book that can afford the space needed. *Statistical Analysis: Microsoft Excel 2010* is one. Another one, a classic, is *Multiple Regression in Behavioral Research* by Kerlinger and Pedhazur (Holt, Rinehart and Winston, 1973).

3

Multivariate Analysis of Variance (MANOVA)

A *multivariate analysis of variance*, or MANOVA, is an analysis of variance with more than one dependent variable. Initially, the idea behind univariate ANOVA—ANOVA with one dependent variable only—is fairly straightforward. And the thinking behind multivariate ANOVA remains straightforward, but the steps needed to carry it out become complicated.

Fortunately, software relieves you of most of the complex baggage that comes along with this sort of analysis and frees you up to concentrate on its findings and its uses. It's important to keep in mind the reasons that one would want or need to resort to multivariate techniques. These reasons have to do with the additional problems you encounter when you have more than one dependent variable. The reasons also pertain to the opportunities to understand treatments and their interactions when you are measuring them with more than just one outcome measure.

A good place to start is with the fundamental problem that's addressed by multivariate ANOVA, the fact that outcome measures aren't independent of one another.

The Rationale for MANOVA

From one perspective, the difference between ANOVA and MANOVA is that you have two or more dependent variables. Just as in ANOVA, you have one set of observations that are divided, preferably by random selection and assignment, into two or more groups. Each group receives a treatment that's of interest to you, and one or more groups receive no treatment, or a placebo of some sort, or are treated in some traditional way that you want to contrast with newer methods.

So why not run two ANOVAs, with the accompanying F-tests, as described in Chapter 3, "Univariate Analysis of Variance (ANOVA)"? Your independent variable might be a marketing campaign that's delivered to, or withheld from, randomly selected visitors to a website; the dependent variables might be number of products purchased and number of dollars spent.

Or your treatment might be a new medication, contrasted with an existing medication and with a placebo. The dependent variables might be cholesterol levels as well as triglyceride measures.

What's the problem with running two ANOVAs, one that contrasts the effects of the two medications and the placebo on cholesterol, and one that contrasts their effects on triglycerides?

Correlated Variables

The difficulty is that the outcome measures are *correlated*. They are not independent of one another. You have two different measures taken on the same set of people or animals or plants or anything that can respond to a stimulus. It is therefore possible to calculate a correlation between the two measures; they are related to one another.

That fact has consequences for the probability statements that you can make about the resulting F-ratios. If you ignore the fact that the outcome measures are correlated, you miss the effects that the correlation—the degree of dependence between the measures—has on the likelihood of the F-ratios that you obtain.

Consider a coin flip. With a fair coin, the probability of getting a heads is the same as the probability of getting a tails on any given flip. And the events are independent of one another: That is, the probability of getting a heads on Flip 2 is 50% *regardless* of what the outcome was on Flip 1. The two events, two consecutive flips, are independent of one another.

Suppose that you conducted an experiment in which you flipped a fair coin twice, noting each outcome, and repeated that act 100 times. You would have 100 pairs of outcomes. If you assigned the value of 1 to a heads and 0 to a tails, then the correlation between 100 Flip 1's and 100 Flip 2's would be close to zero. And the long-run average of that correlation, if you repeated the experiment many times, would be exactly 0.0.

Now suppose that you have a coin that isn't fair: It has a memory. It remembers what the result of the prior flip was, and that memory makes the coin slightly more likely than a fair coin to repeat the result of the prior flip. Say, for example, that Flip 2 from that coin comes up the same as Flip 1 60% of the time.

In that case, the long-run correlation between Flip 1 and Flip 2 would be 0.20. The two events would be dependent, just like two dependent variables in a multivariate ANOVA. Furthermore, you couldn't depend on the coin's behavior considered in isolation. Flip 2 would no longer have a probability of 50% regardless of Flip 1. To state the probability of a heads on Flip 2 you would have to refer to Flip 1, to see what it had been—to see what effect the coin's memory of Flip 1 had on the result for Flip 2.

Correlated Variables in ANOVA

Two ANOVAs with a single dependent variable each would have an analogous effect on your marketing or your medical experiment. If two or more dependent variables are of interest to you, they are likely related, correlated: statistically, if not necessarily causally, dependent on one another.

You could of course decide to use two outcome measures that are not statistically dependent on one another—say, your blood pressure and the size of your neighbor's high school graduating class. But while two such measures would not be mutually dependent, they would not both be of interest to the experiment that you have in mind.

In sum: If the two dependent variables aren't both of interest then there's no point to analyzing them both. If they're both of interest, they may well be correlated (as are total cholesterol and triglyceride levels); then your two univariate ANOVAs are not normally independent of one another, and their results are therefore suspect.

But multivariate ANOVA can help solve the dependency problem. It does so by quantifying the relationship between the outcome variables. By taking the relationship into account, MANOVA provides you first with a multivariate test, much like a univariate F-test, to help you decide whether some combination of your outcome variables reliably distinguishes between different levels of your independent variables. And if they do, you can follow that initial multivariate test with univariate tests that take the outcome variables one at a time. Or you might well follow up with the sort of analysis discussed in Chapter 5, "Discriminant Function Analysis: The Basics," and Chapter 6, "Discriminant Function Analysis: Further Issues," which helps you understand how the dependent variables combine to create a successful discrimination between groups.

Even so, it's important to choose your dependent variables with an eye to their degree of correlation. Ideally, you'd like them to be moderately correlated, perhaps somewhere between 0.2 and 0.6.

Suppose that the dependent variables are known to correlate somewhere around 0.1, and therefore share only about 0.1^2 or 1% of their variability. Even if they were both of genuine research interest in an experiment, if they are not correlated in the population then there's no point to trotting out a multivariate analysis. You're back to the fair coin, and you might as well run a couple of univariate ANOVAs.

On the other hand, if the dependent variables are correlated too strongly, you can run into the same sort of problem that you sometimes encounter in ordinary least squares multiple regression: multicollinearity. In regression analysis, when predictors are too strongly correlated, it becomes difficult to disentangle their contributions to the variability of the outcome measure. In MANOVA, multicollinearity in the dependent variables can make it difficult to interpret how the centroids distinguish among the levels of the independent variables.

> **NOTE**
>
> *Centroids* are just the set of group means for each dependent variable. See the next section for more information about centroids in multivariate ANOVAs.

Visualizing Multivariate ANOVA

As you go through the material in this chapter, keep in mind that MANOVA is capable of dealing with many different dependent variables at once. However, the examples I discuss here are generally limited to two dependent variables. The principal reason is that it's much easier for both the reader and the author to view the effects of two dependent variables on a two-dimensional medium such as a page in a book or an Excel scatter chart on a computer screen, than to imagine a similar layout with three dependent variables.

That said, suppose you actually carried out a small experiment of the sort mentioned in the prior section, one with three treatment (two medications and a placebo) and two dependent variables (one measure of total cholesterol and another of triglyceride levels). If you were to run a standard univariate ANOVA using the total cholesterol as the outcome measure, adopting 0.05 as the alpha level, your results might appear as in Figure 4.1.

Figure 4.1

The standard ANOVA regards the group differences as nonsignificant at the 0.05 level.

A	B	C	D	E	F	G	H	I	J	K
Group	Triglyc-erides	Choles-terol		Treatment Vector 1	Treatment Vector 2					
1	150.07	198.12		1	0			Triglycerides		
1	151.01	198.12		1	0			-0.240	-0.604	152.272
1	152.06	197.11		1	0			0.377	0.377	0.266
1	152.06	196.07		1	0			0.308	1.031	#N/A
1	153.14	195.02		1	0		F Ratio:	2.668	12.000	#N/A
2	150.99	200.02		0	1			5.674	12.759	#N/A
2	150.99	199.00		0	1					
2	152.02	197.96		0	1		Prob. Of F:	0.110		
2	153.08	197.96		0	1					
2	153.08	196.90		0	1			Cholesterol		
3	151.90	200.00		-1	-1			0.367	-1.113	198.001
3	152.90	200.00		-1	-1			0.475	0.475	0.336
3	152.90	198.97		-1	-1			0.322	1.302	#N/A
3	153.94	197.92		-1	-1		F Ratio:	2.850	12.000	#N/A
3	153.94	196.85		-1	-1			9.657	20.332	#N/A
							Prob. Of F:	0.097		

Figure 4.1 shows the underlying data set in the range A1:C16. The three treatment groups are recorded in Column A, the Triglyceride levels in Column B, and the Cholesterol levels in Column C.

Columns E and F contain effect-coded vectors that represent group membership in a way that Excel's LINEST() worksheet function can deal with. Group 1 gets a 1 in the first vector and a 0 elsewhere. Group 2 gets a 1 in the second vector and a 0 elsewhere. Group 3 gets a –1 in both vectors.

Univariate ANOVA Results

With the data set up using coded vectors, you can run anything from a simple single-factor ANOVA to a complex, factorial analysis of covariance (ANCOVA) using the LINEST() function. In Figure 4.1, two ANOVAs appear, in the guise of LINEST() results, in I3:K7 (triglycerides) and in I12:K16 (cholesterol).

If you're at all familiar with LINEST()—and you should be if you intend to do any reasonably sophisticated statistical analysis in Excel—then you know that the F-ratio for the full regression appears in the fourth row, first column of LINEST()'s results. The F-ratio for a univariate ANOVA using triglyceride levels as the dependent variable is in cell I6. Cell J9 tests that F-ratio using the appropriate degrees of freedom and returns the information that the F-ratio is not significant at a 0.1 alpha level.

The F-ratio for a univariate ANOVA using cholesterol levels as the dependent variable is in cell I15. Cell J18 tests that F-ratio using the appropriate degrees of freedom and returns the information that the F-ratio is barely significant at the 0.1 alpha level.

Neither F-ratio would be grounds to reject a null hypothesis at the adopted 0.05 alpha level, and you would conclude that the treatments applied to the three groups made no difference to their mean triglyceride or cholesterol levels.

Multivariate ANOVA Results

Now suppose that you had also run a multivariate ANOVA on the same data set. Figure 4.2 shows the results you would get.

Figure 4.2
The multivariate ANOVA rejects the null hypothesis well beyond the nominal alpha level of 0.05.

C12	▾	f_x	=F.DIST.RT(B12,4,22)				

	A	B	C	D	E	F	G
1	Univariate F-ratios						
2	Dependent Variable	Source	SS	DF	Mean Square	F-Ratio	Prob of F
3	Triglycerides	Between	5.674	2	2.837	2.668	0.110
4		Within	12.759	12	1.063		
5	Cholesterol	Between	9.657	2	4.829	2.850	0.097
6		Within	20.332	12	1.694		
7							
8	Selected Multivariate Statistics						
9	Wilks Lambda =		0.119				
10							
11			F-ratio	Prob of F			
12			10.430	0.000			
13			(4 and 22 DF)				

First compare the univariate findings in Figure 4.2 with those in Figure 4.1. In Figure 4.2, the F-ratios in cells F3 and F5 are identical to those in Figure 4.1, and of course so are the associated p-values in cells G3 and G5. The univariate F-tests report no significant differences at the 0.05 alpha level.

Now look at the multivariate F-ratio in cell B12 of Figure 4.2. With 4 and 22 degrees of freedom, it's highly significant. (I explain how the multivariate F-ratio comes to have those degrees of freedom later in this chapter.) The multivariate F-test reports, then, that there's a difference somewhere associated with group membership. That difference is expressed in some combination of the two dependent variables, in a way that the univariate F-tests did not report.

This is a comparatively rare outcome for a MANOVA to have univariate F-tests that fail to meet the adopted alpha level when the multivariate F-test reports a significant outcome. Nevertheless I've spent some ink on it because the visual representation helps to lay the groundwork for a fuller understanding of multivariate ANOVA (see Figure 4.3).

Figure 4.3
Differences that aren't apparent on a single axis are obvious in the two-dimensional plane.

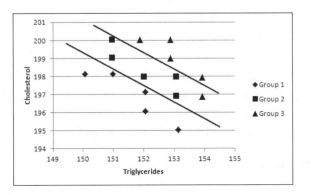

The chart in Figure 4.3 plots the 15 individuals in your study, with cholesterol levels on the vertical Y axis and triglyceride levels on the horizontal X axis. If you were to project each observation against either axis, you would find that the three groups overlap so much on both axes that you would conclude—looking one-dimensionally—that no difference exists between the groups on either measure.

And that's exactly the conclusion reached by the two univariate F-ratios.

But if you view the results in light of the two dimensions of the scatter chart in Figure 4.3, it's clear that the groups are separated. Of the 15 participants in your study, only one is misclassified according to the diagonal lines drawn onto the chart (that's the triangular marker with a value of about 154 on the X axis and 197 on the Y axis).

Figure 4.4 shows the confidence intervals for each group mean using a single axis: a bar chart for triglycerides and a column chart for cholesterol.

Figure 4.4
On a univariate basis you would conclude that the group means don't reliably differ from one another.

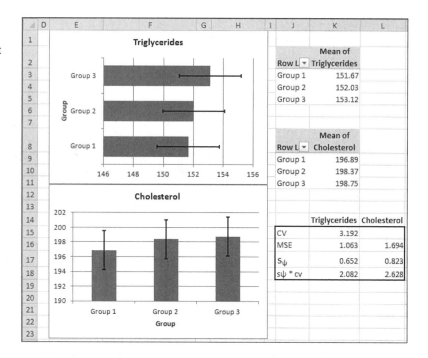

Taking one variable at a time, it's clear that you would conclude that no differences on either dependent variable exist between the groups. Notice how the error bars (the thinner bars centered on the mean of each group) span the mean of each of the other two groups. Were there a significant difference between any two of the group means, or even a more complex contrast such as the mean of two groups contrasted with the mean of the third, then the associated confidence intervals would not span the other means in the contrast.

> **NOTE** The error bars are based on the standard errors of contrasts calculated using the Scheffé procedure. The scope of the error bars is therefore relatively large.

Means and Centroids

In more formal terms, a univariate ANOVA examines differences in group *means* on one dependent variable. Samples are drawn from two or more populations and inferential statistics are calculated and analyzed. These statistics help determine the probability that one or more populations of the sampled populations are centered at different points on the continuum that's represented by the dependent variable.

By comparison, multivariate ANOVA examines differences in group *centroids* on more than one dependent variable. A centroid is a vector of group means. So, in the example this chapter has worked with so far, there are three centroids.

- Group 1: {151.67;196.89}
- Group 2: {152.03;198.37}
- Group 3: {153.12;198.75}

> **NOTE**
> The centroid vectors are usually construed to be column vectors, not row vectors. That is, each univariate mean value in a centroid occupies a different row in a single column. Excel's convention for representing different rows in an array, as in the preceding bullet list, is to separate them by semicolons. (Different columns in an array are separated by commas.) Therefore, the values in the centroids listed previously are separated by semicolons to indicate that each centroid is to be thought of as a column vector.

So the question that MANOVA addresses directly is whether any reliable difference exists between the centroids for the different groups or other linear combination of the dependent variables. It does *not* directly address whether any reliable differences exist between the means that comprise the centroids.

It's also possible to obtain a multivariate F-ratio that does not meet the alpha level that you've set, *and* in the same analysis to obtain univariate F-ratios that do meet your alpha level. This can come about for various reasons, but perhaps the most typical is that the dependent variables are correlated too strongly. Then, if one of them successfully distinguishes on a univariate basis between the levels of the independent variable, it's likely that all do.

However, there are undesirable consequences to strong correlations among the independent variables. Adding them into (say) the bivariate plane as in Figure 4.3, or a multivariate space with more than two dependent variables, won't help the centroids discriminate among the groups. Of course that's one of the primary reasons to run a MANOVA at all: to protect yourself against deciding differences exist on a given dependent variable when in fact they don't.

From ANOVA to MANOVA

Chapter 3 of this book reviews the basics of univariate ANOVA. It discusses how ANOVA's principal inferential statistic, the F-test, puts you in a position to decide whether differences between groups' mean values are real in the populations, or simply due to sampling error.

The F-test does so by forming the ratio of two estimates of the variance in the dependent variable: the variance estimate that's calculated using the differences *between* groups, divided by the variance estimate that's calculated using the differences *within* groups.

Notice that the F-ratio is based on variances, and variances are defined (and calculated) using the squared deviations of a single variable. Figure 4.5 recapitulates what's involved.

Figure 4.5

The sums of squares (and therefore the variances) are all based on the sum of squared deviations of one variable only.

	A	B	C	D	E	F	G	H	I	J
				D9		=DEVSQ(D2:D6)				
1		Group A	Group B	Group C						
2		100	151	118		ANOVA				
3		224	156	191		*Source of Variation*	*SS*	*df*	*MS*	*F*
4		183	164	123		Between Groups	1030.93	2	515.47	0.45
5		180	123	185		Within Groups	13868.80	12	1155.73	
6		167	162	165		Total	14899.73	14		
7										
8	AVERAGE()	170.8	151.2	156.4						
9	DEVSQ()	8090.8	1098.8	4679.2						
10										
11						Between	=DEVSQ(B8:D8)*5	1030.93		
12						Within	=SUM(B9:D9)	13868.80		
13						Total	DEVSQ(B2:D6)	14899.73		

Figure 4.5 provides the following data:

- The range B2:D6 contains a small data set.
- The range F3:J6 contains an ANOVA table output by the Data Analysis add-in's single-factor ANOVA tool, using the data in B2:D6 as a basis.
- The range B8:D8 contains the group means.
- The range B9:D9 contains the sum of the squared deviations in each group, using Excel's DEVSQ() function to calculate them.
- The range G11:G13 calculates the sums of squares in the ANOVA using the worksheet functions SUM() and DEVSQ().

> **NOTE** The DEVSQ() function finds the average of the values in its argument. It then takes the difference of each value from the average, squares the difference, and totals the squared differences.

Notice first that the values in cells G11:G13 are the same as those in the ANOVA table in G4:G6. The formulas used to calculate the values in G11:G13 are shown in F11:F13. In words:

- The Sum of Squares Between uses DEVSQ() to take the sum of the squared deviations of each group mean from the grand mean, and multiplies by the number of observations in each group.
- The Sum of Squares Within uses the instances of DEVSQ() in B9:D9 to get the sum of the squared deviations of each observation from the mean of its group; then, the results from DEVSQ() are totaled.
- The Sum of Squares Total uses DEVSQ() to return the sum of the squared deviations of each observation from the grand mean.

The concept to bear in mind is that a univariate ANOVA squares the deviation of a value from a mean. The means that are used to calculate the deviations differ, depending on the kind of sum of squares you're calculating, and there are other issues such as multiplying by the number of observations in each group. But the basis for all these figures is the notion of finding the deviations of a set of values from their mean, squaring them and summing the results.

Multivariate ANOVA uses the same sorts of patterns of calculation. But it's more general than univariate ANOVA in part because MANOVA does the following:

- It multiplies a deviation by itself and sums the deviations, just as ANOVA does: A sum of squares.
- It multiplies a deviation calculated on one variable by a deviation calculated on another variable, and sums the products: A sum of cross-products.

The result is a matrix that consists of sums of squares and sums of cross-products, or an *SSCP matrix*.

The next section shows how the pattern plays itself out in a MANOVA.

Using SSCP Instead of SS

When you carry out a univariate ANOVA, you take the ratios of one variance to another, and the route to the variances is by way of sums of squared deviations. For example, in a simple single-factor ANOVA, you divide the Sum of Squares Between by its degrees of freedom to get a Mean Square Between. And you divide the Sum of Squares Within by its degrees of freedom to get a Mean Square Within. Finally, divide the Mean Square Between by the Mean Square Within to get the F-ratio.

The various sums of squares are all built on the squared deviations of *the* dependent variable from means of *the* dependent variable (its group means and its grand mean). But in a multivariate ANOVA, there is no single dependent variable. Instead there is a *centroid*, a vector of the means of the dependent variables, from which the deviations of individual values are taken and either squared to reach a sum of squares, or multiplied by the individual's deviation on another dependent variable to reach a sum of cross-products.

Figure 4.6 begins to show how this is managed.

Don't worry about all the spadework shown in Figure 4.6 and subsequent figures. It's usually taken care of in code, such as the VBA subroutines that accompany this chapter's MANOVA.xls workbook. But to understand what's going on when you type **manova** into R, or otherwise call a multivariate ANOVA in some other application, it's often helpful to see the sausage being made in the context of a worksheet.

Figure 4.6
It's helpful to create a range of mean-corrected values as preparation for a MANOVA, as in the range E2:F16.

	A	B	C	D	E	F
		F2 ▾	fx	=C$22-C2		
1	Group	Dep Var 1	Dep Var 2		Mean-Corrected	
2	Group A	100	41		59.5	34.6
3	Group A	224	96		-64.5	-20.4
4	Group A	183	82		-23.5	-6.4
5	Group A	180	73		-20.5	2.6
6	Group A	167	70		-7.5	5.6
7	Group B	151	78		8.5	-2.4
8	Group B	156	69		3.5	6.6
9	Group B	164	88		-4.5	-12.4
10	Group B	123	72		36.5	3.6
11	Group B	162	71		-2.5	4.6
12	Group C	118	71		41.5	4.6
13	Group C	191	95		-31.5	-19.4
14	Group C	123	72		36.5	3.6
15	Group C	185	83		-25.5	-7.4
16	Group C	165	73		-5.5	2.6
17						
18		**Means**			**Means**	
19	Group A	170.80	72.40		-11.33	3.20
20	Group B	151.20	75.60		8.27	0.00
21	Group C	156.40	78.80		3.07	-3.20
22	Grand Means	159.47	75.60		0.00	0.00

> **NOTE**
> There are easier and quicker ways to reach, on a worksheet, the results this section and the next demonstrate. But the point here is not to obtain the required matrices in the smallest possible compass. The point is to get a clear idea of what's going on with the numbers.

4

Figure 4.6 shows data from three groups that are identified in A2:A16. Measures on two dependent variables are shown in B2:C16.

As you've seen, Excel has a useful worksheet function, DEVSQ(), which returns the sum of squared deviations of a set of values from their mean. But although that function is useful in a MANOVA, you also need to multiply deviations not only by themselves but by deviations from the mean of a different dependent variable. And Excel has no worksheet function that returns the sum of deviations from one mean as multiplied by deviations from another mean. (Yes, Excel does have the SUMPRODUCT() function and I get to it shortly.)

So it's necessary first to make the deviations explicit, and that's done in E2:E16 in Figure 4.6. The mean-centered values in Column E represent the deviations of the original values in Column B from their mean in cell B22. The original values for the first dependent variable in B2:B16 are each subtracted from their grand mean to produce the mean-corrected values in E2:E16. Similarly, the original values for the second dependent variable in C2:C16 are each subtracted from their grand mean in cell C22 to produce the mean-corrected values in F2:F16.

The means of each group, along with the grand mean, for each dependent variable appear in the range B19:C22. The group means of the mean-corrected values are shown in

E19:F21. The grand means of the mean-corrected values in E22:F22 are of course 0.0: The total of deviations from a mean always equal 0.0, and therefore so must their average. The grand means of the deviations are shown mainly as a check on the intermediate calculations.

Figure 4.7 shows the first steps in the MANOVA.

Figure 4.7
The Total SSCP is analogous to the Total Sum of Squares in a univariate ANOVA.

	H5 ▾	f_x {=MMULT(TRANSPOSE(E2:F16),E2:F16)}	
	G	H	I
1	Total SSCP		
2		14899.7	4715.8
3		4715.8	2401.6
4			
5		14899.7	4715.8
6		4715.8	2401.6
7			
8	=DEVSQ(B2:B16)		=SUMPRODUCT(E2:E16,F2:F16)
9	=SUMPRODUCT(E2:E16,F2:F16)		=DEVSQ(C2:C16)
10			
11	=MMULT(TRANSPOSE(E2:F16),E2:F16)	=MMULT(TRANSPOSE(E2:F16),E2:F16)
12	=MMULT(TRANSPOSE(E2:F16),E2:F16)	=MMULT(TRANSPOSE(E2:F16),E2:F16)

The two ranges H2:I3 and H5:I6 in Figure 4.7 are termed *matrices* in the jargon of multivariate analysis. The values are identical, but they are calculated in two different ways; the formulas for H2:I3 are shown in H8:I9 and for H5:I6 in H11:I12.

This matrix is called a *sum of squares and cross-products* matrix, or more frequently *SSCP*. The term *sum* applies both to the squares and to the cross-products. You can see most easily what's going on in the matrix from the formulas shown in H8:I9.

Notice first the formulas in the diagonal elements of the matrix, in cells H8 and I9. Once again DEVSQ() is used to calculate the sum of the squared deviations for a single variable: for the values in B2:B16 (refer to Figure 4.6) in H8, and for the values in C2:C16 in I9. The value in H2, calculated by the formula shown in H8, is identical to the sum of squared deviations shown in cells G6 and G13 of Figure 4.5. There's nothing mysterious about that: Both figures employ the same underlying data set, and the DEVSQ() function of course works the same way in both figures.

The value in cell I3 of Figure 4.7 is new, but that's only because the second dependent variable is new. It's calculated in the same way as the value in cell H2, but in cell I3 you point DEVSQ() at the second dependent variable in C2:C16.

The values in cells I2 and H3 of Figure 4.7 are analogous to the sums of squares in H2 and I3, but they are termed *sums of cross-products* rather than *sums of squares*. The need for the mean corrected values in E2:E16 and F2:F16 is now apparent: You want to multiply each person's deviation from the mean on one dependent variable by the corresponding deviation on another dependent variable, and then sum the results. The results of the multiplications are, again in the jargon of multivariate analysis, *cross-products*.

Although Excel has no worksheet function that calculates two sets of deviations, gets their products, and sums the results, it does have a SUMPRODUCT() function that gets the products of the members of two vectors and sums the results. That function is used to get the cross-products of the mean corrected values in E2:E16 and F2:F16. The deviations are already calculated in those two vectors (again, refer to Figure 4.6), and SUMPRODUCT() takes care of calculating the products of the two deviations belonging to each observation and then summing the products.

Although using DEVSQ() and SUMPRODUCT() makes it easier to see what's going on behind the scenes in the SSCP matrix, it's easier to get the result with a couple of Excel's matrix functions, pointed at the two vectors of deviations in E2:E16 and F2:F16. In Figure 4.7, the range H5:I6 contains the result, which is identical to the result in H2:I3. The formula used in H5:I6 appears in H11:I12.

You can tell from the formula that it has been array-entered in H5:I6 by looking at the Formula Box. There, the formula is surrounded by curly brackets, which indicate that Excel has interpreted it as an array formula. (The user doesn't enter the curly brackets. Excel takes care of that.) The steps to get the array formula in H5:I6 are similar to the steps for entering any array formula:

1. Select the range that the results of the array formula will occupy. In this case you would select H5:I6.

2. Type the formula but do not yet press Enter. Instead, hold down the Ctrl and Shift keys simultaneously and continue to do so as you press Enter. This keyboard sequence signals Excel that you want it to treat the formula you typed as an array formula. Excel displays the results in the selected range and surrounds the formula (in the Formula Box) by curly brackets.

> **NOTE** Array formulas have wide applicability in Excel in general and statistical analysis in particular. For example, you can't get as basic a function as LINEST() to work properly if you don't array-enter it. But it takes a fair amount of study and trial-and-error to get a good grounding in what array formulas can do for you—and what their traps are.

In the case of the array formula in H5:I6 of Figure 4.7, you're combining two of Excel's matrix functions in one array formula. You use the TRANSPOSE() function to turn the array E2:F16 90 degrees. (Notice that in this version of the SSCP matrix you're working with the two-column array E2:F16, not with two single-column vectors, E2:E16 and F2:F16, as you do in H2:I3).

Then you use the MMULT() function to perform what's termed *matrix multiplication* on the transposed and the original arrays of mean-centered values in E2:F16. The process of matrix multiplication is somewhat tedious: It involves multiplying two corresponding elements in two arrays, going through each column of one array and each row of the other.

The resulting products are then summed. You wind up with a matrix that has as many rows as the first array and as many columns as the second: In this case, you wind up with a 2×2 array.

> **NOTE**
> Matrix multiplication depends on getting the order of the matrices right. It's not a commutative process like ordinary algebraic multiplication. Although $x \times y = y \times x$, it's not true that MMULT(X,Y) necessarily equals MMULT(Y,X). So it's important to keep in mind that if you're calculating an SSCP matrix, you *postmultiply* the transpose of a matrix by the matrix itself: MMULT(TRANSPOSE(X),X).

When, as here, you point TRANSPOSE() and MMULT() at an array of mean-centered values, they do precisely what DEVSQ() does for a single variable and what SUMPRODUCT() does for two variables. They return an SSCP matrix.

But so far you've obtained only what's called the Total SSCP matrix, analogous to the Total Sum of Squares in a univariate ANOVA. It remains to divide, or *partition*, the Total SSCP matrix into the multivariate versions of a univariate ANOVA's Sum of Squares Between and its Sum of Squares Within. The next section describes how to do that. Relax: Most of the work has already been done.

Getting the Among and the Within SSCP Matrices

Figure 4.8 shows how simply you can calculate the Among SSCP matrix: the multivariate analog of the univariate ANOVA's Sum of Squares Between.

Figure 4.8
Two versions of the same SSCP matrix, using the same techniques as shown in Figure 4.7.

	D	E	F	G	H	I
18		**Means**			**Among SSCP**	
19		-11.3	3.2		1030.933333	-230.4
20		8.3	0.0		-230.4	102.4
21		3.1	-3.2			
22		0.0	0.0		1030.933333	-230.4
23					-230.4	102.4
24						
25					=DEVSQ(E19:E21)*5	=SUMPRODUCT(E19:E21,F19:F21)*5
26					=SUMPRODUCT(F19:F21,E19:E21)*5	=DEVSQ(F19:F21)*5
27						
28					=MMULT(TRANSPOSE(E19:F21),E19:F21)*5	=MMULT(TRANSPOSE(E19:F21),E19:F21)*5
29					=MMULT(TRANSPOSE(E19:F21),E19:F21)*5	=MMULT(TRANSPOSE(E19:F21),E19:F21)*5

The Among SSCP matrix is simple to calculate. All you need is the group means for each variable in mean-corrected form—again corrected by subtracting them from the grand mean. Those means appear in the range E19:F21 in Figure 4.8; they are identical to those shown in the same range in Figure 4.6.

The formulas that return the values in the ranges H19:I20 and H22:I23 appear as text in H25:I26 and in H28:I29. You can use either a combination of DEVSQ() and

SUMPRODUCT() as shown in H25:I26, or a combination of TRANSPOSE() and MMULT(), as shown in H28:I29. You simply point them at the group means of the mean-corrected dependent variables. As is the case with the univariate ANOVA, you need to multiply the results of the worksheet functions by the number of observations per group—in this example, that's 5.

Figure 4.9 shows how the final Within SSCP matrix is calculated.

Figure 4.9
The Within SSCP matrix uses mean-corrected values, but the means are group means rather than the grand mean.

	D	E	F	G	H		I
		E2 ▾		f_x =B$19-B2			
1		**Mean-Corrected**			**Within SSCP**		
2		70.8	31.4		13868.8		4946.2
3		-53.2	-23.6		4946.2		2299.2
4		-12.2	-9.6				
5		-9.2	-0.6		13868.8		4946.2
6		3.8	2.4		4946.2		2299.2
7		0.2	-2.4				
8		-4.8	6.6	=DEVSQ(E2:E16)		=SUMPRODUCT(E2:E16,F2:F16)	
9		-12.8	-12.4	=SUMPRODUCT(F2:F16,E2:E16)		=DEVSQ(F2:F16)	
10		28.2	3.6				
11		-10.8	4.6	=MMULT(TRANSPOSE(E2:F16),E2:F16)		=MMULT(TRANSPOSE(E2:F16),E2:F16)	
12		38.4	7.8	=MMULT(TRANSPOSE(E2:F16),E2:F16)		=MMULT(TRANSPOSE(E2:F16),E2:F16)	
13		-34.6	-16.2				
14		33.4	6.8				
15		-28.6	-4.2				
16		-8.6	5.8				

In Figure 4.9, the range E2:F16 is labeled "Mean-Corrected," just as in Figure 4.6. But the means that the values are corrected for are different. In Figure 4.6, *all* the values in B2:B16 are subtracted from the grand mean of the first dependent variable in B22 to produce the mean-corrected values in E2:E16. The same is true of the values in C2:C16. They are subtracted from their own grand mean in C22 to produce the mean-corrected values in F2:F16. The vectors in E2:E16 and F2:F16 are used to produce the Total SSCP matrix.

But in Figure 4.9, the mean-corrected values are corrected for each *group mean*, not for the *grand mean*. So, the mean-corrected values in E2:E6 are the result of subtracting the original values in B2:B6 from their group mean in cell B19. The mean-corrected values in E7:E11 are calculated by subtracting each value in B7:B11 from their group mean in cell B20. And so on, for the original values in B12:B16 with B21, C2:C6 with C19, C7:C11 with C20, and C12:C16 with C2.

After the values in E2:F16 have been found by subtracting the original values in B2:B16 and C2:C16 from their respective group means, the Within SSCP matrix is found by applying the same formulas as were used in Figure 4.7. That is, either of these two:

- DEVSQ() for the diagonal elements in the SSCP matrix, and SUMPRODUCT() for the off-diagonal elements. The results appear in the range H2:I3 in Figure 4.9, and the formulas themselves appear in the range H8:I9.

■ MMULT() and TRANSPOSE(), entered as a single array formula, to return all four elements of the Within SSCP matrix in H5:I6. The array formula is shown in H11:I12.

┌A SHORTCUT OR A TRAP?─

In a MANOVA with one factor, and similarly straightforward designs, you could calculate either the Among SSCP matrix or the Within SSCP matrix by simple subtraction. For example, calculate the Total SSCP matrix and the Among SSCP matrix by the methods outlined in this chapter. Then subtract each element in the Among SSCP from the corresponding element in the Total SSCP to get the Within SSCP.

As a matter of personal preference I don't care for that shortcut. It's how Microsoft got itself into trouble with the LINEST() worksheet function from Excel Version 3 through Excel 2002. The developers did not notice that if LINEST()'s third argument was used to force the constant to zero, the regression sum of squares would no longer equal the total sum of squares less the residual sum of squares. The result was to return nonsense such as negative values for the regression sum of squares, R^2 and the F-ratio.

In Excel 2003 Microsoft replaced the subtraction approach with one that calculates the residual sum of squares directly and independently, and that now returns correct results when the constant is forced to zero. (But please don't take this as a suggestion that forcing the constant to zero is a good idea. It usually isn't.)

4

Sums of Squares and SSCP Matrices

Recall that the simplest univariate ANOVA starts with the calculation of a total sum of squares: the sum of the squared deviations of each individual observation from the grand mean of the observations. The process then partitions the total sum of squares into two components: a sum of squares between and a sum of squares within. These two sums of squares are then converted to mean squares, or estimates of the variance in the population, via division by their degrees of freedom.

The result is that the mean square between is an estimate of the population variance derived solely from differences *between* the group means. The mean square within is an estimate of the population variance derived solely from deviations of individual observations *around* each group mean, and therefore without reference to differences between group means.

To the degree that the mean square between is larger than the mean square within, as expressed in the F-ratio, the inference that you're working with a noncentral F distribution is strengthened. Put another way, larger F-ratios provide greater support for the hypothesis that the sampled groups represent different populations with different means.

NOTE A *central* F distribution is one in which the mean square between and the mean square within estimate the same population parameter: its variance. It's the F distribution that you refer to in the back of statistics textbooks and in Excel's F.DIST() and F.INV() functions. When the samples that constitute the experimental groups come from different populations with different means, you're working with a *noncentral* F distribution, one that's stretched out to the right as compared with the central F distribution. Chapter 3 discusses noncentral F distributions in slightly greater detail.

The parallels to the multivariate ANOVA are straightforward. The basis for the Total SSCP matrix is an array of deviations of each observation from the grand mean of their dependent variable. The total sum of squares in the univariate ANOVA is the sum of the squared deviations of each observation from the (one and only) grand mean.

The basis for the Among SSCP matrix is an array of deviations of each group mean from the grand mean of each dependent variable. The same is true of the univariate ANOVA, with the proviso that there is only one dependent variable to worry about.

The basis for the Within SSCP matrix is an array of deviations of each observation from the mean of the observation's group, for each dependent variable. Again, the univariate ANOVA calculates the within (also known as *error*, and in regression analysis as *residual*) sum of squares by totaling the sum of the squared deviations of each observation from the mean of its own group.

In sum, the main conceptual difference between the calculations in a univariate and a multivariate ANOVA is that in an ANOVA you're working with three sums of squares: SS Total, SS Between, and SS Within (and with sums of squares for interactions in higher level ANOVA designs). You get to an F test by dividing sums of squares first by their degrees of freedom to obtain mean squares, and finally you divide one mean square by another to obtain an F-ratio.

In contrast, in a MANOVA you're not working with three individual sums of squares but three matrices that consist of sums of squares *and cross products*. In each case, the matrix is created by multiplying one dependent variable's deviation by itself (the squares) and also by another dependent variable's deviation (the cross products).

At this point the math involved in a MANOVA departs somewhat from that involved in an ANOVA. The next section gets into the specifics, which are not as abstruse and forbidding as you might have been led to believe.

Getting to a Multivariate F-Ratio

The route from the SSCP matrices to a multivariate F-ratio does not proceed through mean squares as it does from sums of squares in a univariate ANOVA. Instead, it involves a different ratio called *Wilks' lambda*. (The ratio is named for Samuel Wilks, the mathematician who developed it and explored its application in various areas of multivariate statistical analysis.)

Excel makes it easy to calculate Wilks' lambda. It is defined as the ratio of the determinant of the Within SSCP matrix to the determinant of the Total SSCP matrix. It's often symbolized as follows:

$$\frac{|W|}{|T|}$$

> **NOTE** In the literature, the name of the matrix is represented by its first letter: here, **W** for Within and **T** for Total. The vertical bars on either side of the letter denote the determinant of the matrix, so |**W**| means the determinant of the **W** matrix.

Because Excel has a worksheet function that calculates the determinant of a matrix, you simply form the ratio of the two determinants that are returned by Excel's function, MDETERM(). Figure 4.10 has an example based on the data set that this chapter has analyzed.

Figure 4.10
You can obtain Wilks' lambda in a single formula; the intermediate steps are shown here only for clarity.

G9	▾	*fx*	=E7/E11		
	A	B	C	D	E	F	G
1		Among SSCP					
2		1030.933	-230.4				
3		-230.4	102.4				
4							
5		Within SSCP					
6		13868.8	4946.2		Determinant		
7		4946.2	2299.2		7422250.52		
8							Lambda
9		Total SSCP					0.5480
10		14899.7	4715.8		Determinant		
11		4715.8	2401.6		13544429.93		

Figure 4.10 shows the determinants of the Within SSCP matrix and of the Total SSCP matrix in cells E7 and E11. Wilks' lambda is in cell G9 and is shown as the ratio of cell E7 to E11. Of course you can skip the display of the determinants in their own cells and simply enter something like this formula:

=MDETERM(B6:C7)/MDETERM(B10:C11)

> **NOTE** Excel has a variety of functions that pertain to matrix algebra, including MMULT(), MINVERSE(), TRANSPOSE(), and MDETERM(). They generally require that you array-enter them with Ctrl+Shift+Enter. MDETERM() is an exception and can be entered normally by simply pressing Enter.

What's a *determinant*? It's a good question, and it has no easy, straightforward answer. The meaning of a determinant depends on the sort of analysis you're conducting, and therefore the nature of the matrix whose determinant you want to use.

For just one example, suppose that you're running a principal components analysis (this type of analysis is discussed in Chapter 7, "Principal Components Analysis"). One of the results of the analysis is a matrix that contains the correlations between each of the underlying variables and the principal components that the analysis derives.

If you square the correlations between a given component and the original variables, and total the resulting R^2 values, you get the component's *eigenvalue*. And the continued product of the eigenvalues for all the components equals the determinant of the correlation matrix of the original set of variables.

> **NOTE** This all has to do with, among other issues, the fact that a correlation matrix that contains a linear dependency has a determinant of 0.0; such a matrix has no inverse. The determinant of 0.0 can come about only when one of the eigenvalues is 0.0, and that can happen only when two or more variables in the matrix have a correlation of 1.0—thus, a linear dependency exists. In that case all the available variability in the principal component will have been absorbed into prior R^2 values, subsequent R^2 values must therefore be 0.0, and the eigenvalue itself must be 0.0. That results in a determinant of 0.0.

But in the context we're examining in this chapter, you can also think of a determinant as an extension of the concept of variance in a univariate context to a multivariate context. Because the underlying SSCP matrices are measures of multivariate dispersion, their determinants are scalar (that is, single-number) expressions of the amount of dispersion in the underlying matrix.

And when you take the ratio of two determinants based on multivariate dispersion matrices, you get something analogous to a univariate ratio of two variances—that is, an F-ratio.

Wilks' Lambda and the F-Ratio

It turns out that Wilks' lambda, when you apply just a few transformations, is often distributed *exactly* as the F-ratio is distributed. That fact makes Wilks' lambda a powerful and useful method of determining the probability of observing differences among sample centroids as large as were obtained, when there is no difference among the population centroids. The logic of the situation is precisely analogous to the univariate case, where the probability of a given univariate F determines the probability of observed sample mean differences, assuming no mean differences in the population.

In many cases, Wilks' lambda (as transformed) is distributed exactly as the F-ratio, and so you can use Excel's F.DIST() functions to evaluate it. In other cases the distribution of lambda only approximates the distribution of the F-ratio, but it's a close approximation and so long as you're aware of the fact it's not a matter of great concern. The next section discusses the transformations and the situations in which a transformed lambda follows an F distribution.

Converting Wilks' Lambda to an F Value

Figure 4.11 shows what's involved in converting Wilks' lambda to an F value.

Figure 4.11
You supply the values in cells B1:B4, and the F value is automatically calculated.

	A12	▼	f_x	=IF(OR(Groups<4, DepVars<3),"Exact F","F Approximation")
	A		B	C
1	Groups		3	
2	Dependent Variables		2	
3	Total N		60	
4	Lambda		0.5480	
5				
6	Denominator check		8	=DepVars^2+(Groups-1)^2
7	S		2	=IF(B6=5,1,SQRT((DepVars^2*(Groups-1)^2-4)/(DepVars^2+(Groups-1)^2-5)))
8	DF Numerator		4	=DepVars*(Groups-1)
9	DF Denominator		112	=S*((TotalN-1)-(DepVars+(Groups-1)+1)/2)-(DepVars*(Groups-1)-2)/2
10				
11	Y		0.7403	=Lambda^(1/S)
12	Exact F		9.8243	=((1-Y)/Y)*(DFDenom/DFNum)

The material in Figure 4.11 is due to C.V. Rao, who developed this transformation in 1952. As shown, you need to supply the number of groups, the number of dependent variables, the total number of observations, and the value of Wilks' lambda itself. Given those four inputs, the formulas in the worksheet calculate the corresponding value of F.

You can then use the calculated F in conjunction with the degrees of freedom in cells B8 and B9 to obtain the probability of observing an F as large as the one you get in B12, given the degrees of freedom and assuming that the F-ratio in the population is 1.0. One way to do so in Excel 2010 is

=F.DIST.RT(B12,B8,B9)

There are several aspects of Figure 4.11 to take note of.

Avoiding a #DIV/0! Error

Notice the divisor in cell B7, spelled out in cell C7:

(DepVars^2+(Groups–1)^2–5)

There are a couple of cases in which that denominator can equal 0.0, and in that case the division in cell B7 would result in a division-by-zero error. In those cases, the value of S in B7 is deemed to be 1. The worksheet handles that situation by calculating this quantity:

DepVars^2+(Groups–1)^2

in B6. The formula in B7 checks the value in B6. If it is 5, so that the result of the divisor would be 0.0, the formula returns a 1. Otherwise, the full calculation is completed for S. (S is the standard terminology for this factor in the literature about transforming Wilks' lambda to an F value.)

Number of Groups

The number of groups depends on the hypothesis you're testing. If you're testing a single factor (whether the overall design uses one factor only or is a factorial design with two or more factors), then the number of groups is the number of levels that factor takes on. If you're testing an interaction between two factors, then the number of groups equals the number of cells created by the intersection of the two factors.

Named Cells

Eight of the cells in the worksheet shown in Figure 4.11 are named. The names are created by using the Define Name button in the Defined Names area of the Ribbon's Formulas tab; or, prior to Excel 2007, using Insert, Name, Define on the main Excel menu. The scope of the names has been limited to the worksheet on which they're defined.

The cells that have defined names are as follows:

- B1: Groups
- B2: DepVars
- B3: TotalN
- B4: Lambda
- B7: S
- B8: DFNum
- B9: DFDenom
- B11: Y

> **NOTE** The names of the cells in Column B are as shown in the previous list. For convenience, the meanings of those names are shown in the corresponding row of Column A; so, cell B2 is named "DepVars" and the meaning of that name, Dependent Variables, appears in cell A2.

It's hard enough to develop a feel for what each of the numbers is there for, when you're working with traditional but meaningless labels like "S" and "Y." It's even worse when the formulas use cell references instead of names. So I've named the important cells, in order that (for example) the formula for F is this:

=((1-Y)/Y)*(DFDenom/DFNum)

instead of this:

=((1-B11)/B11)*(B9/B8)

Exact F or Approximation

It's possible that you'll see, in other sources, formulas for Rao's transformation that are similar to but not precisely the same as given in Figure 4.11. There are four general cases in which the transformation is exactly distributed as an F-ratio:

- Two groups, any number of dependent variables
- Three groups, any number of dependent variables
- One dependent variable, any number of groups (thus a standard univariate ANOVA design)
- Two dependent variables, any number of groups

Various sources provide special formulas for those cases, partly because they're a little easier to calculate than the ones provided in Figure 4.11 if you're using paper and pencil or a hand calculator, and partly because under the conditions just given the transformation yields values that are exactly distributed as F.

However, with an application such as Excel, the tedium of (for example) taking the square root of lambda is no longer a real obstacle. The general formula provided in Figure 4.11 returns exactly the same results as the special-case formulas.

Furthermore, when the conditions for those cases are met, the label in cell A12 is "Exact F," and when they are not met the label appears as "F Approximation." This is managed by a simple IF() function in cell A12, which checks the number of groups and the number of dependent variables in cells B1 (Groups) and B2 (DepVars).

Calculations Included in the Code

The calculations described in this section, concerning the transformation of Wilks' lambda to an F value, are included in the MANOVA code found in MANOVA.xls (a workbook that is compatible with all versions of Excel from 97 through 2013 and which you can download from the publisher's website). This section is here primarily to describe how that code in particular, and how multivariate ANOVA generally, gets to an F value from Wilks' lambda.

Running a MANOVA in Excel

The downloads available for this book from quepublishing.com/title/9780789751683 include a workbook named MANOVA.xls. That workbook includes Visual Basic for Applications (VBA) code that performs a one-factor MANOVA. This section describes how to use it.

Laying Out the Data

There are a few requirements for the data inputs, as follows:

- You can include as many dependent variables as you want, but you must supply at least two.
- The data must be laid out as an Excel list (or as a table in Excel 2007 or later), with the values of the independent variable in one column and the associated values of the dependent variables in two or more *adjacent* columns.

■ The independent variable may consist of text or numeric values. The dependent variables must consist of numeric values.

■ The records need not be in independent variable order, although of course they can be, and that's normally the most convenient setup.

■ You can include a label for the independent variable, and for each dependent variable, in the first row of the list or table. In that case, use the MANOVA dialog box to warn Excel that the first row contains labels, not numeric observations.

Figure 4.12 shows an example of how the data might be laid out.

Figure 4.12
The independent variable is in Column A. Two dependent variables are in Columns B and C.

	A	B	C
1	Group	Dep Var 1	Dep Var 2
2	Group A	100	41
3	Group A	224	96
4	Group A	183	82
5	Group A	180	73
6	Group A	167	70
7	Group B	151	78
8	Group B	156	69
9	Group B	164	88
10	Group B	123	72
11	Group B	162	71
12	Group C	118	71
13	Group C	191	95
14	Group C	123	72
15	Group C	185	83
16	Group C	165	73

Running the MANOVA Code

To run the MANOVA code, begin by opening the MANOVA.xls workbook. When you do so, you might get a warning message from Excel that you are opening a workbook that contains "macros," or (depending on your version of Excel) some similar message. Whether you see such a message depends on the Excel security settings you have selected. You should continue to open the workbook if you trust it not to do damage. I trust it. But then I wrote it, and that's cogent for me but not for you.

Then open or switch back to a workbook that contains your data. What happens next depends on the version of Excel that you're running:

■ If you're using Excel 2007 or later, find the Add-Ins tab on the Ribbon. If you don't see it, click the File tab, click Customize Ribbon in the navigation bar, and fill the Add-ins checkbox. Back in worksheet view, click the Add-Ins tab and then click MANOVA.

■ If you're using Excel 2003 or earlier, you find MANOVA in the Data menu. Click it.

The dialog box shown in Figure 4.13 appears.

Figure 4.13
The independent variable
need not be adjacent to
the dependent variables,
but the dependents must
be adjacent.

You know what to do. Click in the Range with Independent Variable box and drag through the range where you stored its values. Click in the Range with Dependent Variables box and drag through that range. Select the Variable Labels in First Row check box or leave it cleared as necessary, and click OK.

The code runs and returns results in three general areas:

- Strictly descriptive statistics (means, standard deviations, counts, dispersion determinants, and SSCP matrices).

- A test of the equality of the dispersion—in fact, the equality of the variance-covariance matrix in the populations from which the groups were sampled. This test is analogous to the test of homogeneity of variance in a univariate ANOVA.

- F-tests that include a different univariate ANOVA for each dependent variable, followed by the multivariate F-test.

The results are output to a new worksheet in the workbook that contains your input data. The following sections depict and describe the results in greater detail.

Descriptive Statistics

Figure 4.14 shows the descriptive statistics area of the output.

The area of the worksheet that contains the descriptive statistics expands as the number of groups or the number of dependent variables increases. It always shows a matrix of the means and standard deviations for each dependent variable in each group. For each group, it also shows the counts and a dispersion determinant.

Figure 4.14

Notice that the cells in the Among and the Within SSCP matrices total to the corresponding cells in the Total SSCP matrix.

▲	A	B	C	D	E	F	G	H	I	J
1		Means			Std Devs			Counts		Dispersion
2		Dep Var 1	Dep Var 2		Dep Var 1	Dep Var 2				Determinant
3	Group A	170.800	72.400		44.974	20.256		5		15227.050
4	Group B	151.200	75.600		16.574	7.701		5		14300.550
5	Group C	156.400	78.800		34.202	10.257		5		39339.538
6	Full Sample	159.467	75.600		33.996	13.842		15		51543.406
7										
8	Total SSCP	14899.733	4715.800							
9		4715.800	2401.600							
10										
11										
12	Among SSCP	1030.933	-230.400							
13		-230.400	102.400							
14										
15										
16	Within SSCP	13868.800	4946.200							
17		4946.200	2299.200							

The dispersion determinant for each group is the determinant of the SSCP matrix for that group: in other words, a matrix with sums of squares in its main diagonal and sums of cross products off the main diagonal. These sums are based on the observations for a particular group only. The final determinant is of the SSCP matrix based on the observations in all the groups.

> **NOTE**
>
> The SSCP matrix is always a square matrix, just as a full correlation matrix is always square. The *main diagonal* is the set of cells in the matrix running from the leftmost, uppermost cell to the rightmost, lowermost cell in the matrix. (In a correlation matrix, the main diagonal is the one with 1.0 throughout.)

The determinants are used in the next section of the results, which tests the equality of the dispersion (or the variance-covariance) matrices.

The final three items in this section are the Total, the Among, and the Within SSCP matrices. They are used in the third section of the results to calculate Wilks' lambda (and therefore the multivariate F-ratio).

Equality of the Dispersion Matrices

The multivariate ANOVA makes an assumption about the variability of the dependent variables, and about their covariation, in the different groups. Like univariate ANOVA, MANOVA assumes that the variances are equal in the populations from which the samples were taken, and the covariances as well. Therefore, the assumption takes the position that any differences in the groups' SSCP matrices are due to sampling error. This section of the MANOVA output tests that assumption.

In univariate ANOVA, it has been shown that there's little reason to worry about the assumption of homogeneous variances if the group sizes are equal—that is, each group contains the same number of observations. Even when there are different numbers of observations in the different groups, there's no reason to worry when the group variances are equal, or nearly so. It's only when you have major discrepancies in the group sizes *and* in the group variances that the probability statements you make about the F-ratios become a matter for concern.

The same considerations apply in multivariate ANOVA. Many researchers ignore violations of the assumption on the same grounds as apply to the univariate situation: Probability statements are seriously affected only when group sizes are very unequal, and when the differences in the variance-covariance matrices are pronounced.

But the test is easily performed, and the MANOVA code supplied with the downloads for this book provides it. It appears in Figure 4.15.

Figure 4.15
You would probably conclude from this F-ratio that the within-group variance-covariance were equivalent.

▲	A	B	C	D	E	F
20		M	F	DF, numerator	DF, denominator	Prob. of F
21	Test of equality of dispersions	11.087	1.400	6	3588.923	0.211

The M value of 11.087 in Figure 4.15 is called *Box's M*, after G. E. P. Box, who developed it, building on earlier work by M. S. Bartlett. It is calculated as follows:

$$[(N-G) \times LN(|D_W|)] - \sum_{k=1}^{G} (n_k - 1)(LN(|D_k|))$$

where:

- N is the total number of observations.
- G is the total number of groups.
- LN indicates that a natural logarithm is taken.
- $|D_W|$ is the determinant of the matrix that results from dividing the Within SSCP matrix by the total degrees of freedom (that is, $N - G$).
- n_k is the number of observations in the kth group.
- $|D_k|$ is the determinant of the matrix that results from dividing the Within SSCP matrix for the kth group by the degrees of freedom for that group (that is, $n_k - 1$).

The value for M can be converted to an F value, which you can test against the F distribution with given degrees of freedom.

> **NOTE**
> The conversion of Box's M to an F value is complex and is not discussed here. However, you can find it demonstrated in a worksheet named *M to F* in the workbook for this chapter.

In the case of the data in Figure 4.15, you would continue to entertain the null hypothesis of no difference in the groups' variance-covariance matrices, and could proceed to the multivariate test of the differences between the group centroids (see the following section).

The degrees of freedom for the denominator shown in Figure 4.15 probably looks like a typographical error, given that there are only 15 observations in the complete design. But it's correct: The denominator of the F-test for the variance-covariance matrices uses degrees of freedom whose calculation involves division by small fractions. See the *M to F* worksheet in the accompanying workbook for the details.

The Univariate and Multivariate F-Tests

The third section of the MANOVA results contains the inferential tests on both a univariate and a multivariate basis (see Figure 4.16).

Figure 4.16
The MANOVA results include a univariate F-test for each dependent variable.

	A	B	C	D	E	F	G
23	Univariate F-ratios						
24	Variable	Source	Sum of Squares	DF	Mean Square	F-Ratio	Eta Square
25	Dep Var 1	Among	1030.933	2	515.467	0.446	0.069
26		Within	13868.800	12	1155.733		
27	Dep Var 2	Among	102.400	2	51.200	0.267	0.043
28		Within	2299.200	12	191.600		
29							
30	Multivariate tests						
31		Wilks Lambda	Eta square				
32		0.548	0.452				
33							
34	Multivariate F	DF, Numerator	DF, Denominator	Prob of F			
35	1.930	4	22	0.141			

The univariate ANOVAs return the results that you get if you run a standard single factor ANOVA on the data that you use in the MANOVA run, one dependent variable at a time. (More about this in the next section.)

The MANOVA reports Wilks' lambda, defined earlier in this chapter as the ratio of the determinant of the Within SSCP matrix to the determinant of the Total SSCP matrix:

$$\frac{|W|}{|T|}$$

Both of these determinants are generalized measures of variance. In fact, Wilks called lambda "the generalized variance," and the determinant of a dispersion matrix such as **W** or **T** is often thought of as the multivariate analog of the variance of a single variable.

In turn, lambda can be thought of in the same terms as an F-ratio, the ratio of two variances, with the following caveat. In ANOVA, the F-ratio is formed by dividing the variance estimate (usually termed the mean square) based on differences between group means, by the variance estimate based on differences between individual observations within groups. And so the larger the F-ratio, the greater the differences between group means.

But Wilks' lambda divides an estimate of the multivariate variability *within groups* by an estimate of the total multivariate variability. The Within variation and the Among variation together make up the Total variation. Therefore, the smaller the value of Wilks' lambda, the greater the differences between group centroids.

So F and lambda move in opposite directions. The farther apart the univariate group means, the larger the F. The farther apart the multivariate group centroids, the smaller the lambda.

But it's convenient to be able to test an F value, and therefore it's usual to convert lambda to an F value and test it against a central F distribution with a given number of degrees of freedom for the numerator and the denominator. That conversion was discussed in an earlier section, "Converting Wilks' Lambda to an F Value." The MANOVA code does it on your behalf, and displays the F value, the degrees of freedom, and the probability that it was sampled from a central F distribution. See the range A35:D35 in Figure 4.16.

One further statistic reported in the MANOVA results is eta-squared. This statistic generalizes R^2, the proportion of variance in a dependent variable that's shared with the predictor variables in a multiple regression, to an analysis of variance context.

In the univariate case, eta-squared is this ratio:

$SS_B / (SS_B + SS_W)$

or more simply with just one factor:

SS_B / SS_{TOT}

In the multivariate case, eta-squared is 1 – lambda. Because Wilks' lambda is the ratio of generalized within variance to generalized total variance, 1 minus that ratio is generalized between (or among, if you prefer) variance to generalized total variance.

> **NOTE** Some statistical software applications calculate eta-squared by first raising lambda to the power (1/s), where *s* is the smaller of the degrees of freedom for the factor being tested and the number of dependent variables. The MANOVA routine included in the workbook for this chapter does not adopt this approach.

You can think of eta-squared as a handy descriptive statistic that gives you a sense of the proportion of variance in an outcome measure or measures that can be accounted for by independent or predictor variables.

After the Multivariate Test

Statisticians disagree about the nature of the proper procedure following a significant multivariate F-test. The two procedures most often followed are to pay attention to the univariate tests or to follow up with a discriminant function analysis.

Some attend to the univariate tests on the argument that a significant multivariate result affords protection against errors due to correlations between the dependent variables.

Others contend that the univariate F-tests ignore the fact that the multivariate test is sensitive not only to differences in the centroids but to different linear combinations of the individual dependent variables. That fact leads to the use of discriminant function analysis, the topic of Chapters 5 and 6 of this book.

Discriminant function analysis, *very* briefly, enables you to determine how continuous variables (treated as dependent variables in MANOVA) combine to best discriminate between nominal variables (which constitute the grouping factor or factors in MANOVA). This sort of analysis provides weights that, when applied to the continuous variables, result in functions that are uncorrelated, and that maximize the differences among the nominal groups. However, it's not always possible to interpret the meaning of these functions in the context of the research being conducted.

Among those who move directly from a significant multivariate result to the univariate tests, the approach generally involves dividing the alpha level used for the multivariate test by the number of groups involved for the factor in question.

For example, suppose that you have adopted an alpha level of .05 for your multivariate test, and that it has returned a multivariate F that is significant at, say, the .04 level. You proceed to the univariate tests, of which there are three: You have three dependent variables. One course at this point is to divide the original multivariate alpha of .05 by three and adopt an alpha of (0.5 / 3) or 0.16 for your univariate tests. This is sometimes referred to (not entirely appropriately) as the Bonferroni approach.

You can use multiple comparison procedures (for example, planned orthogonal contrasts or Newman-Keuls) with a factor or interaction if the univariate test is significant at the chosen alpha level.

You can instead or in addition run a discriminant function analysis after a significant MANOVA result to determine the linear combination (or combinations) of the dependent variables that best discriminates among the groups used as MANOVA's independent variables. You can then turn around and use those combinations as dependent variables in univariate ANOVAs: Because the combinations will not be correlated there's no reason to deploy MANOVA.

And it's time now to move on to discriminant function analysis.

Discriminant Function Analysis: The Basics

5

A traditional analysis of variance, or *ANOVA*, helps you decide whether different groups have different average values on some continuous variable. The groups are usually defined in terms of some category. For example:

- Which political party gives a higher favorability rating to a particular legislative proposal? The party is the category, and the rating is the continuous variable.

- Do people who eat meat have a different mean cholesterol level than vegetarians? Type of diet is the category, and cholesterol level is the continuous variable.

- Do smokers miss more workdays due to illness than nonsmokers? Smoking behavior is the category, and days missed is the continuous variable.

In each of these cases—and depending on how the data was gathered—you're asking whether belonging to a particular category has an effect on a numeric measure such as political rating, cholesterol level, or frequency of illness. Here's another way of posing that question: Do the outcome measures define different populations that have different average values? Or is there really just one population, and the different averages you got in the study just due to sampling error?

As discussed in this and the next chapter, discriminant function analysis (sometimes termed discriminant analysis, multiple discriminant analysis, or MDA) turns that logic around. Like the MANOVA examples in Chapter 4, "Multivariate Analysis of Variance (MANOVA)," discriminant analysis typically uses two or more numeric variables. But instead of asking whether the groups differ according to the averages on the numeric variables, discriminant analysis asks questions such as these:

■ Can you distinguish Republicans from Democrats on the basis of voters' attitudes toward a proposal and their ages?

■ Is it possible to classify someone's eating preferences according to cholesterol level and body weight?

■ Can you predict whether a person is a smoker or a nonsmoker from the number of sickdays they take and their performance on a treadmill?

Before you can undertake a discriminant function analysis, though, you need to arrange to treat a nominal, categorical variable such as Make of Automobile as a numeric variable. The software you use to run the analysis usually takes care of this for you, but it's helpful to understand something about what's going on with that coding process. The next section discusses the issues involved and shows how it's done.

Treating a Category as a Number

If you've used ANOVA to help investigate questions such as these, you might well have come across what's called the *regression approach* to the analysis. In contrast to the regression approach, the traditional approach accumulates sums of squared deviations from mean values, converts those sums of squares to estimates of variance, and then compares those estimates by means of an *F-ratio*.

The regression approach and the traditional approach return identical results in cases where both approaches can be used. (The reason for the identical results is that each approach is just a different way of expressing something called the *general linear model*. My book *Statistical Analysis: Microsoft Excel 2010* spends a couple of chapters discussing both the traditional and the regression approach.) The regression approach enables you to complete a credible analysis in situations that are much more difficult for the traditional approach—for example, the analysis of multiple factors in which different cells have different numbers of observations.

Very briefly, to use the regression approach to the analysis of variance, you convert your categorical labels to numeric values by means of one coding scheme or another. If your categorical variable (often termed a *factor*) has just two levels, you might assign a 0 to one level and a 1 to the other. If there are three categories, you might use -1, 0, and 1 as numeric codes to represent the categories.

It's a little more complicated than that, and if you have more than two categories, you need to create more than one set of codes. But the basic idea is that you convert nominal categories such as Ford, Toyota, and GM to numeric values such as -1, 0, and 1.

After that conversion has taken place, you're in a position to use regression analysis to analyze your data. Consider a standard multiple regression analysis in which you might predict cholesterol levels from subjects' type of diet—coded so that it's a numeric variable (0 and 1) rather than nominal categories (carnivore and vegan). Figure 5.1 shows how the traditional and the regression approaches can be equivalent.

Figure 5.1

The same data set analyzed by ANOVA and by regression. This figure abbreviates the output of the ANOVA and the regression tools.

	A	B	C	D	E	F	G	H	I	J	K	L	M	N
1	Cholesterol levels for:													
2		Carnivore	Vegan					Group	Cholesterol		SUMMARY OUTPUT			
3		55	48					1	55		Regression Statistics			
4		50	45					1	50		Multiple R		0.6991	
5		54	45					1	54		R²		0.4888	
6		58	49					1	58		Adjusted R²		0.4249	
7		49	51					1	49					
8	ANOVA							0	48		ANOVA			
9	Source of Variation	SS	df	MS	F			0	45		Prop. of Variance	df	"MS"	F
10	Between Groups	78.4	1	78.4	7.65			0	45		Regression	0.4888	1	0.489 7.65
11	Within Groups	82	8	10.25				0	49		Residual	0.5112	8	0.064
12	Total	160.4	9					0	51		Total	1.0000	9	

In Figure 5.1, the data is laid out in two ways. First, in the range A3:B7, it's laid out for analysis by the Data Analysis add-in's ANOVA: Single Factor tool. In the traditional analysis, you estimate the variance of the scores using the group means (the mean square between, in cell D10) and the variance of the scores using the individual observations within each group (the mean square within, in cell D11). The mean squares are the sums of squares in column B divided by the associated degrees of freedom in column C. The ratio of the two variance estimates in column D is the F-ratio in cell E10, in this case 7.65.

The second data layout appears in the range G3:H12. Notice that the category names in cells A2 and B2 have been replaced by 1s and 0s in G3:G12. Laid out for regression analysis and with the numeric values 1 and 0 instead of the category labels "Carnivore" and "Vegan," it's possible to evaluate the correlation between group membership and cholesterol. The regression tool's output does that in cell K4: The correlation is 0.6991—check it yourself if you like using the CORREL() worksheet function.

The square of the correlation, 0.4888, expresses the proportion of the Cholesterol variance that's associated with variability in the Group variable. That's the same value as the R² shown in cell K10. The remaining proportion of variance, 0.5112, is usually termed the *residual* variation, in cell K11.

Using the regression approach, you bypass the sums of squares and instead work with the proportion of the total sum of squares due to the regression (0.4888 or 48.88%) and the residual proportion that's left over (0.5112 or 51.12%). Divide each proportion by the associated degrees of freedom to get a "mean square." The ratio of those "mean squares," 0.489 / 0.064, is 7.65 in cell N10, precisely the same F-ratio as is returned by the traditional ANOVA in cell E10.

The foregoing is just a simple demonstration of the fact that by coding information about group membership as a numeric variable, you can get the same results from regression analysis as you do from traditional analysis of variance.

5

And you might extend the benefits of the analysis by adding a variable. As long as you're going to the expense of getting cholesterol measures on 10 people, and asking them about their dietary habits, you might as well record each person's sex. Then you could use a two-factor ANOVA (possibly the Data Analysis add-in's ANOVA: Two-Factor with Replication tool) to test simultaneously the relationships of diet and sex to cholesterol levels.

Further, if you coded the Sex factor as you did the Diet factor, with 1s and 0s, you could analyze the data using regression. You'd have the added benefit that if you had a different number of observations in each design cell (for example, 10 vegetarian males but 15 vegetarian females), you'd be able to put together a credible analysis of the data. It's not necessarily true that the traditional approach would yield credible results in this situation (often termed an *unbalanced design*).

The Rationale for Discriminant Analysis

I've inflicted this material on you to set the stage for turning the whole analysis on its head. What if you knew subjects' ratings of a legislative proposal, as well as their ages and party preferences? Why not use rating and age to forecast the political preference of registered voters who have not declared a party affiliation? You've already coded the categorical variable so that it's numeric. You could use rating and age as predictors to help you decide whether a given subject is more likely to vote Republican or Democrat.

Multiple Regression and Discriminant Analysis

And that's what discriminant function analysis does (anyway, one of the things). It enables you to classify subjects according to nominal categories. Instead of using categorical variables as independent or predictor variables—with continuous variables as the dependent or predicted variables—you use continuous variables as the predictors and numerically-coded categories as the predicted variables.

The analysis provides you with a *function*, much like a regression equation, that helps you *discriminate* between the levels of the category.

Ronald Fisher developed discriminant function analysis in the 1930s, and one of the first applications of discriminant analysis was in the field of botany. It's often called the *Iris Study*, and its purpose was to determine whether it's possible to correctly classify irises into one of three species from knowledge of size measurements. The available variables were the sepal length, sepal width, petal length, and petal width. Of 150 cases, 147 were correctly classified as *Iris setosa*, *Iris virginica*, or *Iris versicolor*.

I bring it up in part because it's a frequently cited application, and also because it's an example of using discriminant analysis to distinguish among not just two but three groups, using not just two but four numeric predictor variables. There's no particular limit to the number of predictors, or the number of groups to classify into, but as a practical matter you seldom see more than four or five predictors and four or five groups.

Discriminant analysis has many parallels with what might be a more familiar approach, multiple regression, and those parallels are easiest to understand in the context of a discriminant analysis that uses just two groups, such as Republican and Democrat or buys and doesn't buy. This chapter discusses the parallels between the two types of analysis in that two-category context. Chapter 6, "Discriminant Function Analysis: Further Issues," extends the discussion to three groups and more.

Adjusting Your Viewpoint

It's twilight. You're outside, trying to referee a rugby game and you can barely tell one team from the other. The players are all covered with mud. You know that there are two teams on the field, and each team's players are standing close to one another, getting ready for the scrum. Worse for you as an observant referee, from where you're standing one of the teams is behind the other.

What with the sun going down, all the mud, the way the players are positioned, and with one team standing behind the other, you can't tell whether to start the scrum or not. You're supposed to wait until the two teams have separated and are standing apart. The players might be separated into the two sides, but from where you're standing it all looks like one muddy, mobile mess (see Figure 5.2).

Figure 5.2
You can barely tell one player from another. It's hopeless to tell one team from another.

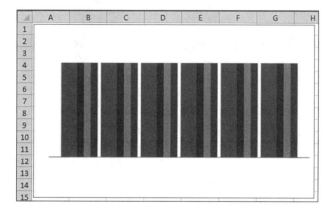

If you were taller than the players you could look down from a different perspective. Then things might resolve themselves as you look on from a greater height (as in Figure 5.3). But if you were that much taller you'd be playing instead of refereeing.

But when you move off to one side, your angle changes. Now you can see at least that the teams are separated, even if the individual players are not yet positioned for the scrum (see Figure 5.4).

5

Figure 5.3
Peering down at the players you have a better idea of how they're arrayed.

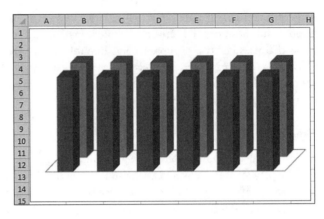

Figure 5.4
By changing the angle from which you're viewing the players you can tell one team from another.

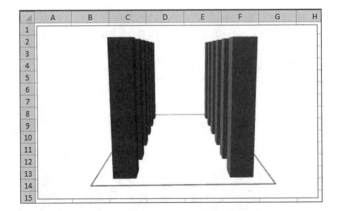

In a literal sense, what you might do to get a better view of two teams—or categories—is what discriminant analysis does to give you a better view of how individual data points can be resolved into two or more categories. The mathematics of discriminant analysis helps to resolve an undifferentiated mass of data points such as irises or rugby players or undeclared voters into two or more distinct categories. Two things happen:

- A new axis, besides the original vertical and horizontal axes, is established at an angle from the original axes, much as you established a new position to view the rugby players from, at an oblique angle to the sideline.

- The new axis has two properties: When you view the data points from the perspective of the new axis, the distances between the categories are maximized and the distances between the category members are minimized. For example, compare what you see in Figure 5.2 with what you see in Figure 5.4.

Discriminant Analysis and Multiple Regression

If the topic of discriminant analysis crossed your desk in college or grad school, someone very likely pointed out that when the predicted variable takes on two values only, discriminant analysis and multiple regression amount to the same thing.

And that's true in part. With just two values for the predicted variable—buys or doesn't, Independent or Libertarian, survives or doesn't—there are several parallels between discriminant analysis and regression analysis. There are also some important differences. Because both the parallels and the differences can help to illuminate the nature of both types of analysis, I'm going to dip into them in this section. Chapter 6 examines them more formally and in greater detail.

Regression, Discriminant Analysis, and Canonical Correlation

Why are the parallels limited to analyses with just two values for the predicted variable? Actually, they're not. The predicted, categorical variable could have three, four, or more values. But the resemblance that discriminant analysis bears to multiple regression is much more clear with two values in the predicted variable.

Furthermore, when the predicted variable is actually a nominal variable—also termed a *categorical* variable—ordinary regression analysis limits you to two categories. Here's how it works out:

The various approaches to inferential statistical analysis that you studied in school are all special cases of what's termed *canonical correlation*. The various types of correlation and regression analysis seek to quantify the relationships between two sets of data. Those two data sets are sometimes termed predictor variables and predicted variables, or independent variables and dependent variables, depending on the type of inference that you want to draw.

At the simplest level, each data set might consist of one continuous variable, such as height and weight. The Pearson correlation coefficient quantifies the relationship between the two continuous variables and, depending on how you got your sample and how large it is, might return a value as small as 0.2 or as large as 0.9.

At roughly the same level of complexity, a t-test quantifies the strength and reliability of the relationship between a nominal variable with two values and a continuous variable. You might use a t-test to address whether two categories, males and females, have reliably different average salaries for the same job descriptions. Changing one data set from a continuous variable (as in Pearson correlation analysis) to a nominal variable (as in a t-test) has profound consequences for how you analyze the data and interpret your conclusions.

Taking things a step further, you use ANOVA to assess whether different groups and combinations of groups have different averages on a continuous variable. On average, do male MDs have different salaries than female MDs? Do oncologists have different salaries than obstetricians? What about male oncologists versus female obstetricians? The ANOVA is designed to tell you whether any combination of groups differs on the continuous variable from any other combination of groups. If it looks as though differences exist, you often follow up with t-tests to make specific comparisons, but you use ANOVA to help you decide whether further comparisons are warranted.

ANOVA takes you beyond the two-group-only limitation of the t-test. The analysis of covariance, or ANCOVA, adds one or more continuous predictor variables into the mix of one or more categorical variables. But ANCOVA still deals with one continuous predicted variable only.

Similarly, multiple regression deals with a single predicted variable and multiple predictor variables. The predicted variable is typically a continuous one: salary or cholesterol level or miles per gallon. The predictor variables also are often continuous: years of education or body weight or age of automobile. But the use of coding techniques can turn a categorical variable into a numeric one (for example, 1 to represent Ford, 0 to represent GM, and -1 to represent all other makes). More on this issue shortly.

With MANOVA you begin to deal with what's termed *multivariate analysis*. Of course, as simple a technique as Pearson correlation analysis is multivariate: Even there you're examining two variables instead of only one. But statistical jargon reserves the term *multivariate* to analyses in which there exist at least two dependent or predicted variables. And MANOVA, or *multivariate analysis of variance*, takes you into analyses with one data set consisting of multiple, continuous, predicted variables, and (on the other side of the equals sign) another data set consisting of one or more nominal variables that you think of as independents or predictors.

Discriminant analysis turns MANOVA around. Instead of asking whether the centroids of dependent or predicted variables differ by group, as in MANOVA, discriminant function analysis asks whether it's possible to distinguish one group from another by examining two or more continuous variables. Can you use discriminant analysis to distinguish, for example, Democrats from Republicans if you know their annual income and years of education? And can you classify people whose party affiliation is unknown by applying the results of that discriminant analysis?

By examining structure coefficients (a topic I discuss in Chapter 6), it's possible to go beyond the omnibus findings available in MANOVA. Recall from Chapter 4 that a significant multivariate finding, even supported by significant univariate F-tests, does not show you how the continuous variables work to result in a reliable outcome. Structure coefficients can do so, although it's good to keep in mind that drawbacks to their use exist, and that they tend to be less useful in discriminant analysis than they are in, for example, principal components analysis.

Again, MANOVA and discriminant analysis both reserve one of the two data sets for continuous variables, and the other data set for variables that represent categories or groups. One difference between the two types of analysis is which data set you want to regard as the predictors and which you want to regard as the predicted.

Canonical correlation is the most general of these analyses. Both data sets can consist of multiple variables. Not just one of each as with Pearson correlation or t-tests; not just one predicted variable and multiple predictors as with multiple regression and ANOVA; not just multiple predicted variables and multiple categories that have been converted to numeric values by means of coding. Canonical correlation allows for the combination of multiple continuous variables, as well as numerically coded nominal variables, in both data sets.

As such, it's both plausible and useful to view all the other types of analysis as special cases of canonical correlation. Viewed from that perspective it's possible to see the parallels between multiple discriminant analysis and canonical correlation when the predicted, nominal variable takes on more than two values.

Coding and Multiple Regression

When you use a coding technique to represent a nominal variable with numeric values, it's typical to use 1s, 0s, and sometimes -1s. Figure 5.5 reviews how this is done with what's called *dummy coding*, which employs 1s and 0s only.

Figure 5.5
The purpose of coding is to distinguish one category from another using numbers instead of text labels.

	A	B
1	Brand	Coded Brand
2	Ford	1
3	Ford	1
4	Ford	1
5	Ford	1
6	Ford	1
7	GM	0
8	GM	0
9	GM	0
10	GM	0
11	GM	0

The idea behind coding is to present the data to a statistical analysis with values that it can deal with. For example, using multiple regression, it's possible to calculate a correlation coefficient between a variable such as price and another variable whose values consist of 1s and 0s. It's not possible to calculate a correlation between a variable of dollar amounts and a variable whose values are "Ford" and "GM." To calculate the correlation, you first must code "Ford" and "GM" as, say, 1 and 0.

When you get to three or more categories, things get slightly more complicated (see Figure 5.6).

With three categories (here they are Ford, GM, and Toyota) you need two coded vectors to tell one category from another. Only Ford has a 1 in vector A, only GM has a 1 in vector B, and only Toyota has a 0 in both vectors. In general, you need as many vectors as you have groups, minus 1. (It's not coincidence that the number of vectors equals the number of degrees of freedom.)

Figure 5.6

When you get beyond two categories you need additional coded variables, or vectors.

	A	B	C
		Coded Brand	Coded Brand
1	Brand	Vector A	Vector B
2	Ford	1	0
3	Ford	1	0
4	Ford	1	0
5	Ford	1	0
6	Ford	1	0
7	GM	0	1
8	GM	0	1
9	GM	0	1
10	GM	0	1
11	GM	0	1
12	Toyota	0	0
13	Toyota	0	0
14	Toyota	0	0
15	Toyota	0	0
16	Toyota	0	0

> **NOTE**
>
> There are other methods of coding, including effect coding and planned orthogonal contrasts, which have special properties. For example, effect coding in multiple regression causes the value of the regression coefficient to equal the deviation of the mean for a given group from the grand mean—that's the *effect* of being in that group. Planned orthogonal coding forces the predictor variables to be uncorrelated with one another, and you must have specified in advance the comparisons you want to make. But each of these types returns the same overall results for the regression equation: the values of R^2, the standard error of estimate, the F-ratio and the degrees of freedom.

Why restrict yourself to 1s and 0s? (Or in the case of effect coding, 1s, 0s, and -1s?) You could, after all, assign 1 to Ford, 2 to GM, 3 to Toyota, 4 to Nissan, and so on. Then you would need one vector only.

One reason is that so doing is the same as pretending that a nominal variable is a continuous one, or at least an ordinal one (an ordinal variable's values are rankings, such as 1st, 2nd, 3rd, and so on). To assign numeric codes to a series of categories is to act as though the categories existed in some intrinsic order: that there is more "car-ness" in a Ford than in a GM, more in a GM than in a Toyota, and so on. Furthermore, it would imply that there is an average brand, determined by getting the average of the numeric codes and then looking up the brand name that's closest to the average of the codes. The implication is obviously ridiculous.

Furthermore, multiple regression depends on quantifying the correlations between the predictor variables. That's perfectly feasible when you have two vectors consisting of 1s, 0s and -1s. It's impossible when you have Vector 1 only, consisting of 1s, 0s and 2s; where is Vector 2, which you need in order to establish a correlation with Vector 1?

The *only* purpose served by a coding system is to enable the analysis to distinguish one category from another, using numbers instead of words. In that case another name for Vector A in Figure 5.6 might be "Is a Ford," and for Vector B "Is a GM." The combined effect of the information in both vectors enables both you and the computer to decide which record "Is a Toyota."

Now it's possible to see the reason that multiple regression resembles discriminant analysis when there are two groups only. With more than two groups you need more than one vector to capture the information about group membership. In discriminant analysis, these coded vectors constitute the predicted variables, and ordinary multiple regression *allows for one predicted variable only*. And with just one coded vector as the predicted variable you're restricted to two groups.

> **NOTE** There are, of course, other related reasons. To evaluate more than one dependent variable you need to examine SSCP matrices, not simply the sum of the squares of a single variable. Ordinary multiple regression makes no provision for that sort of analysis. Nevertheless, all these reasons stem from the fact that you need more than one vector—or predicted variable—to represent membership in more than two groups.

With the rationale for that limitation out of the way, let's take a closer look at how discriminant function analysis resembles multiple regression.

The Discriminant Function and the Regression Equation

Both discriminant function analysis and multiple regression return coefficients (as well as constants) that you use to multiply actual values. (These coefficients are often termed *weights*, but I'll use *coefficients* in this book.) The results of those multiplications are totaled and then added to the constant, and the result is a predicted score. For example, your regression analysis of two continuous predictor variables and a predicted variable with two values might return this equation:

$$\hat{Y} = 0.47X_1 + 2.12X_2 + 3.5$$

where:

- $\hat{Y}$ is the predicted value.
- X_1 is the first predictor variable.
- 0.47 is the regression coefficient for X_1.
- X_2 is the second predictor variable.
- 2.12 is the regression coefficient for X_2.
- 3.5 is the constant or *intercept*—the point at which the regression line intercepts the vertical axis.

You get the same sort of result from discriminant analysis—coefficients and a constant—but the actual values of the coefficients and the constant are almost certain to be different from those returned by regression analysis. That's because the two types of analysis are intended to do different things:

■ Regression analysis returns coefficients that, used in conjunction with the sample's values, maximize the *correlation* between the predicted values and the observed values on the predicted variable. The correlation is quantified by the projection of the individual data points onto two orthogonal axes (that is, axes that are at right angles to one another). One axis represents the predicted variable and the other axis represents the predicted values: the results of the regression equation as applied to each record.

■ Discriminant analysis returns coefficients that, used in conjunction with the sample's values, maximize the *distance* between the centroids of each group. The projections are made onto an axis that is typically at other than a 90 degree angle from the two original, orthogonal axes.

> **NOTE**
> Recall that a *centroid* is a vector of (typically) the means of each variable for the members of a particular group.

These objectives are not at all incompatible but they are different and so, therefore, are the coefficients. Nevertheless, the values of the regression coefficients and those of the discriminant coefficients are tightly coupled. I demonstrate that coupling next.

From Discriminant Weights to Regression Coefficients

Figure 5.7 shows a small data set that can be analyzed using both regression and discriminant analysis. It includes two continuous predictor variables and a predicted variable that takes on just two values (and therefore it's compatible with ordinary multiple regression).

Figure 5.7
The range E2:G6 contains the results of Excel's LINEST() worksheet function.

⏴	A	B	C	D	E	F	G
1	Group	X1		X2				
2	1	6		2		-0.110858	0.28246	-0.61617
3	1	5		4		0.048084	0.089396	0.490718
4	1	6		3		0.629309	0.363854	#N/A
5	1	8		4		5.941827	7	#N/A
6	1	7		4		1.573273	0.926727	#N/A
7	0	3		3				
8	0	6		8		Ratio of coefficients:		-2.54795
9	0	6		9				
10	0	5		5				
11	0	4		0				

In Figure 5.7, notice the two values in cells E2 and F2. They are the regression coefficients to be applied to the predictor variables in columns B and C.

NOTE Remember that LINEST() returns the coefficients in the wrong order. In this example, you use the coefficient in E2 with the values in Column C, and the coefficient in F2 with the values in Column B.

Figure 5.8 shows partial results of running the MANOVA code from Chapter 4 on the data in Figure 5.7.

Figure 5.8
You'll need the Total and the Within SSCP matrices to complete a discriminant analysis.

	A	B	C
1		Means	
2		X1	X2
3	0	4.800	5.000
4	1	6.400	3.400
5	Full Sample	5.600	4.200
6			
7	Total SSCP	18.400	10.800
8		10.800	63.600
9			
10			
11	Among SSCP	6.400	-6.400
12		-6.400	6.400
13			
14			
15	Within SSCP	12.000	17.200
16		17.200	57.200

Figure 5.9 shows partial results from a discriminant function procedure written in Visual Basic for Applications (VBA) and available from the publisher's download site in the file named Discriminant.xls. Later sections of this chapter and the next discuss that procedure in some detail.

Figure 5.9
The values in cells C11 and D11 are the discriminant coefficients.

	A	B	C	D
6	Chi-square tests			
7	Roots Removed	Canonical R	R Squared	Eigenvalue C
8	0	0.7933	0.6293	1.6977
9				
10	Row coefficient vectors			
11	Discriminant Function	1	1.0462	-0.4106
12				
13			Ratio of coefficients:	
14			-2.54795	

The discriminant coefficients are used in much the same fashion as the regression coefficients (but they are returned in the correct order). So you would multiply the coefficient in C11 by the values of the first predictor variable, and the coefficient in D11 by the values of the second predictor variable.

But what's really interesting is the relationship between the two coefficients. If you form a ratio of the first discriminant coefficient to the second, you get the same result as you do by forming the ratio of the regression coefficients. Compare cell C14 in Figure 5.9 with cell G8 in Figure 5.7.

Figure 5.10 compares the results of applying the discriminant function with the results of applying the regression equation.

Figure 5.10
Predicted values from regression and from discriminant analysis.

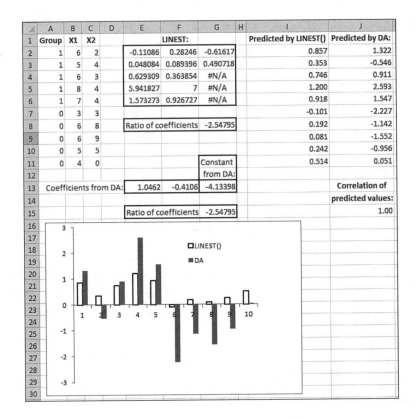

	A	B	C	D	E	F	G	H	I	J
1	Group	X1	X2			LINEST:			Predicted by LINEST()	Predicted by DA:
2	1	6	2		-0.11086	0.28246	-0.61617		0.857	1.322
3	1	5	4		0.048084	0.089396	0.490718		0.353	-0.546
4	1	6	3		0.629309	0.363854	#N/A		0.746	0.911
5	1	8	4		5.941827	7	#N/A		1.200	2.593
6	1	7	4		1.573273	0.926727	#N/A		0.918	1.547
7	0	3	3						-0.101	-2.227
8	0	6	8		Ratio of coefficients		-2.54795		0.192	-1.142
9	0	6	9						0.081	-1.552
10	0	5	5						0.242	-0.956
11	0	4	0				Constant		0.514	0.051
12							from DA:			
13	Coefficients from DA:				1.0462	-0.4106	-4.13398			Correlation of
14										predicted values:
15					Ratio of coefficients		-2.54795			1.00

There's a lot to notice in Figure 5.10. To start with the coefficients, notice that the regression coefficients are in cells F2 (for variable X1) and E2 (for variable X2). The ratio of the first coefficient to the second coefficient appears in cell G8 and is about -2.548.

The coefficients from the discriminant analysis appear in cells E13 (for variable X1) and F13 (for variable X2). Their ratio is given in cell G15, and it is identical to the ratio for the regression coefficients. Therefore, the coefficients returned by multiple regression and those returned by discriminant analysis, although different, are identically proportional. The first coefficient in both cases is -2.548 larger than the second coefficient.

In turn, the results of multiplying the coefficients times the original variables to obtain predicted results will differ: The regression coefficients are different from the discriminant coefficients. But because the coefficients of each kind are proportional to one another in exactly the same degree, the predicted results will covary exactly.

That effect is demonstrated by the ranges I2:I11 and J2:J11 in Figure 5.10. The values in Column I are the result of applying the LINEST() equation to the original X1 and X2 variables. The values in Column J are the result of using the discriminant coefficients and constant (the latter is calculated in cell G13 and is the result of applying the coefficients to the variable means and multiplying by -1).

The correlation between the two sets of predicted values appears in cell J15 and is precisely 1.0: a perfect correlation.

Now have a look at the column chart in Figure 5.10. It shows the pairs of predicted values, with the regression predictions showing up as empty columns and the discriminant predictions as filled columns. Notice that the variability between the groups is greater for the discriminant predictions: The first five are farther above zero than their paired regression predictions, and the second five are farther below zero than the associated regression predictions.

This effect is consistent with the intent of discriminant analysis, to separate the groups as much as possible. The discriminant function creates a new axis in what's called *discriminant space* at an angle from the usual horizontal and vertical axes, and projects the observed data points onto that new axis. The angle of the axis is computed so as to separate the groups as much as possible, and when the original data points are projected onto that new axis the separation between the groups—that is, the discrimination—is achieved.

Eigenstructures from Regression and Discriminant Analysis

The term *eigenstructure* generally means the combination of *eigenvalues* and *eigenvectors*. You often have several eigenvalues to deal with, and each eigenvalue is associated with another set of values, its eigenvector.

Eigenvalues and the members of their eigenvectors have different meanings depending on the situations in which they're used and interpreted. In principal components analysis, for example, you can interpret an eigenvalue as the sum of the squared loadings of each original variable on the derived component.

But in discriminant function analysis, an eigenvalue is a way of expressing the ratio of the Among SSCP to the Within SSCP. There is a different eigenvalue for each discriminant function that your analysis derives.

> **NOTE** The number of discriminant functions that you get from your analysis depends on the number of groups in the predicted variable and on the number of predictor variables you're using. If you have more variables than groups (or the same number of each), then the maximum number of discriminant functions is the number of groups, minus 1. But if you have more groups than variables, you could derive as many discriminant functions as you have variables. You want to stop, of course, when the functions become meaningless in either a substantive or a statistical sense.

The associated eigenvectors in discriminant analysis are the coefficients that you apply to the observed variables in the discriminant equation. There are different ways of *scaling* the values in the eigenvector. These different scales depend on whether you want the coefficients in the raw score form or standardized, and whether you are working with the Total SSCP matrix or the Within SSCP matrix. I cover these issues in greater detail in Chapter 6.

This chapter uses the two-group case with two predictor variables as an example of the relationship between multiple regression and discriminant analysis. The number of groups minus 1 is 1, and therefore only one discriminant function is available.

It turns out that in the two-group case the regression coefficients constitute the eigenvector. Figure 5.11 shows how the eigenvalue can be calculated from either the regression analysis or the discriminant analysis.

Figure 5.11
The eigenvalue is easy to retrieve from the LINEST() results.

	A	B	C	D	E	F	G	H	I	J	K	L
L12						f_x	{=MMULT(F9:G9,MMULT(I9:J10,L9:L10))}				
1	Group	X1		X2								
2	1	6		2					Among SSCP			
3	1	5		4		1.0462	-0.4106		6.400	-6.400		1.0462
4	1	6		3					-6.400	6.400		-0.4106
5	1	8		4								
6	1	7		4		{=MMULT(F3:G3,MMULT(I3:J4,L3:L4))}						13.5813
7	0	3		3								
8	0	6		8					Within SSCP			
9	0	6		9		1.0462	-0.4106		12.000	17.200		1.0462
10	0	5		5					17.200	57.200		-0.4106
11	0	4		0								
12						{=MMULT(F9:G9,MMULT(I9:J10,L9:L10))}						8
13	-0.11086	0.282460137	-0.61617									
14	0.048084	0.089395912	0.490718									
15	0.629309	0.363853858	#N/A							=L6/L12		1.6977
16	5.941827	7	#N/A									
17	1.573273	0.926727411	#N/A									
18												
19		Ratio of SS:	1.6977									

As I noted earlier in this section, in discriminant analysis the eigenvalues can be thought of as a ratio of the SSCP Among to the SSCP Within. This is consistent with the purpose of discriminant analysis, to maximize the distance between groups in the context of minimized variability of individual observations within groups.

This chapter has already pointed out several times that with just one predicted vector it's possible to emulate a discriminant analysis using multiple regression. In that case there are no cross products among the predicted variables, just a sum of squares for the (single) predicted vector. The regression analysis partitions the total sum of squares into a component due to the regression and a residual component.

So, as shown in Figure 5.11, you can determine the eigenvalue for the (sole) discriminant function by taking the ratio of the sum of squares regression to the sum of squares residual. This is done in cell C19 to return the value 1.6977. The sum of squares regression is therefore more than half again the sum of squares residual, and the differences between the group means are a good bit larger than the differences between individual observations within groups.

You might want to refer to Figure 5.9, which shows the eigenvalue for the discriminant function in cell D8. The value shown there is 1.6977 and is calculated by the VBA code in the downloadable workbook named Discriminant.xls.

For the two-group situation as managed by discriminant analysis, you can also calculate the eigenvalue directly on the worksheet. The process is also shown in Figure 5.11. Three sets of values are needed:

- The SSCP Among matrix, in the range I3:J4
- The SSCP Within matrix, in the range I9:J10
- The discriminant coefficients, in the range F3:G3

The discriminant coefficients appear four times, in a row in F3:G3 and F9:G9, and in a column in L3:L4 and L9:L10.

With that data in hand, it's easy to calculate the eigenvalue. Cell L6 contains an array formula that's displayed immediately to its left. The array formula uses the MMULT() worksheet function twice, once to postmultiply the Among SSCP matrix by the transpose of the coefficients, and then to premultiply that matrix multiplication by the coefficients. The result is a scalar (in the jargon of matrix algebra, a single number) that expresses the amount of variability in the Among SSCP matrix.

Similarly, cell L12 makes the same calculation as cell L6, except that the Within SSCP matrix is used instead of the Among SSCP matrix. The result expresses the variability in the Within SSCP matrix.

Finally, cell L6 is divided by cell L12 in cell L15. The result is 1.6977, the eigenvalue for the discriminant function, identical in value to the ratio of the sum of squares regression to the sum of squares residual in the regression analysis—and, of course, identical to the eigenvalue shown in Figure 5.9.

5

Structure Coefficients Can Mislead

I've mentioned structure coefficients a couple of times in this chapter, and Chapter 6 discusses them in greater detail. But because structure coefficients are frequently valuable sources of information, I want to show you here how they can also mislead you.

Structure coefficients turn up in multiple regression, principal components analysis, and discriminant function analysis, as well as in other techniques. A structure coefficient is the correlation between a predictor variable and a predicted variable. So, if you're using age and height to predict weight in a multiple regression, two structure coefficients are available: the correlation of age with predicted weight and the correlation of height with predicted weight.

The square of a structure coefficient is the proportion of variance that the predictor variable shares with the predicted variable. As such, you can think of it as a measure of the importance of a given predictor to the predicted values. In the jargon of principal components analysis, a structure coefficient indicates the degree to which a predictor variable loads on a predicted variable. As such, structure coefficients can be particularly valuable in discriminant analysis where the focus is often on how the predictor variables combine to distinguish different groups.

But the numeric context in which you calculate a structure coefficient is critical to interpreting it properly. Figure 5.12 illustrates a situation that you would easily recognize because it's such an extreme example. But it shows the mechanics of how it's possible to go wrong.

Figure 5.12
Even a large structure coefficient is meaningless when the overall R^2 is small.

	A	B	C	D	E	F	G	H	I
	Predicted variable	Predictor variables			Predicted values		LINEST()		
1									
2	34	81	80		59.4		0.05	0.02	53.71
3	47	58	19		55.9		0.21	0.27	14.71
4	62	50	74		58.4		0.00	25.76	#N/A
5	99	87	74		59.2		0.04	17.00	#N/A
6	90	73	68		58.6		55.70	11282.30	#N/A
7	39	31	95		59.0				
8	30	82	33		57.2				
9	47	44	6		55.0		Structure coefficients		
10	50	44	38		56.5		0.62	0.96	
11	67	71	27		56.6				
12	50	56	22		56.0				
13	62	33	18		55.3				
14	36	57	69		58.3				
15	7	37	17		55.4				
16	81	18	29		55.5				
17	40	21	13		54.8				
18	73	34	80		58.3				
19	99	64	27		56.5				
20	80	1	13		54.4				
21	47	65	92		59.6				

Figure 5.12 shows a variable to be predicted in Column A and two predictor variables in Columns B and C. A multiple regression analysis in the form of LINEST() is in G2:I6 and the resulting predicted values are in the range E2:E21. Two structure coefficients, one for each predictor variable, are shown in G10:H10.

Those structure coefficients are quite strong. Their squares indicate that 38% and 92% of the variance in the predicted values is shared with the two predictors. Unfortunately that's meaningless.

The LINEST() formula also shows that the R^2 for the overall regression is 0.00. In other words, there is no relationship between the actual values for the predicted variable and the predicted values themselves. Therefore the squares of the structure coefficients indicate that the predictor variables share 38% and 92% of a random outcome.

Admittedly this is an extreme example, ginned up to demonstrate a point. I assume that the first thing you do when you run a multiple regression is to check the R^2, or the largest eigenvalue in a principal components analysis, or the Wilks' Lambda in a discriminant analysis or MANOVA. If those figures do not appear as though you would obtain similar results from another sample, taken similarly, you would very likely move on to another problem, leaving the question of structure coefficients behind with the rest of the statistics.

Wrapping It Up

The purpose of this chapter has been to call on your existing knowledge of multiple regression analysis to begin an exploration of discriminant function analysis. The parallels, both conceptual and computational, between regression and discriminant analysis appear throughout, from the structure of the regression and the discriminant equations, to the values of the coefficients (more precisely, to their ratios), to the eigenvalues that express the degree of variability among the group centroids to the degree of variability within the groups.

5

Discriminant Function Analysis: Further Issues

Chapter 5, "Discriminant Function Analysis: The Basics," provides a relatively brief look at the purposes of discriminant analysis and its relationships to multiple regression analysis—at least in the two-group case. Those relationships go well beyond the simple two-group case, although it's more difficult to demonstrate them with three groups or more.

This chapter takes the discussion further. It provides examples of discriminant analysis with more than just two groups and more than just two continuous variables. You'll see how to use freeware code, which you can download for this book to move beyond the MANOVAs discussed in Chapter 4, "Multivariate Analysis of Variance (MANOVA)." (Recall that MANOVA itself does not tell you how its continuous variables combine to result in a significant outcome; for that you need discriminant analysis.) And you'll see graphic examples of how discriminant analysis can use the continuous variables that you supply to classify new cases according to *a priori* categories.

Let's start by walking through the Excel workbook.

Using the Discriminant Workbook

You can download several Excel workbooks from the publisher's website, www.quepublishing.com/title/9780789751683. Among them is one named Discriminant.xls, found among the files for Chapter 6 of this book.

The workbook contains Visual Basic for Applications (VBA) code. The code performs a discriminant function analysis, given the results from a preliminary MANOVA.

Opening the Discriminant Workbook

When you open the workbook, Excel might warn you that it contains code that could harm your computer. Whether you see such a warning depends on how you have set the security options for your copy of Excel. Obviously it's up to you how to proceed, if at all. I can only say that as I supplied the workbook to the publisher it contained nothing harmful, and as the publisher offers it to you the workbook is entirely benign.

After the workbook is open, you should see an Add-Ins tab on the Ribbon. That tab might have already been there if you have other Excel add-ins open, and if so you see a new item in the Add-Ins tab called Discrim. If you have opened the Discriminant.xls file and still don't see an Add-Ins tab on the Ribbon, click the Ribbon's File tab, click Options in the navigation bar, and then click Customize Ribbon on the Excel Options navigation bar. Make sure that the Add-Ins box is checked in the Main Tabs list box.

If that checkbox is filled, if you have opened the Discriminant.xls workbook, and if you still can't locate an Add-Ins tab on the Ribbon or a Discrim item in that tab, there's a problem that I'm unable to solve for you here.

You also need to open another workbook, either before or after you open Discriminant.xls, but in any case before you start to run the VBA code in the Discriminant workbook. That other workbook must contain three ranges:

- A Total Sum of Squares and Cross Products (SSCP) matrix.
- A Within SSCP matrix.
- A matrix with group and total sample means; groups must occupy rows and continuous variables must occupy columns.

The output produced by the MANOVA workbook, discussed in Chapter 4, provides just the sort of layout that you need, although of course any source that writes the SSCP and group means matrices (again, groups in rows and variables in columns) will do fine.

Figure 6.1 shows an example of what's needed. It employs the layout provided by the MANOVA code discussed in Chapter 4.

It can be helpful if the matrix of group means (and the grand means) has variable labels immediately above it and group names immediately to its left. Figure 6.1 shows the variable labels in the range B2:E2 and the group names in the range A3:A5.

You'll read a good bit more in this chapter about the data set that's summarized in Figure 6.1, but for now a brief overview will support a discussion of the matrices. The data set dates back to the 1930s, when a botanist collected measurements on three different species of irises: I. setosa, I. versicolor and I. virginica. The botanist collected data on 50 irises from each species: its petal length, its petal width, its sepal length, and its sepal width. The data set was turned over to Sir Ronald Fisher, who used the data in his development of discriminant function analysis procedures.

Figure 6.1
These data layouts are needed for the discriminant analysis, regardless of their source.

	A	B	C	D	E
1			Means		
2		Sepal length	Sepal width	Petal length	Petal width
3	I. setosa	5.006	3.428	1.462	0.246
4	I. versicolor	5.936	2.770	4.260	1.326
5	I. virginica	6.588	2.974	5.552	2.026
6	Full Sample	5.843	3.057	3.758	1.199
7					
8	Total SSCP	102.168	-6.323	189.873	76.924
9		-6.323	28.307	-49.119	-18.124
10		189.873	-49.119	464.325	193.046
11		76.924	-18.124	193.046	86.570
12					
13					
14	Among SSCP	63.212	-19.953	165.248	71.279
15		-19.953	11.345	-57.240	-22.933
16		165.248	-57.240	437.103	186.774
17		71.279	-22.933	186.774	80.413
18					
19					
20	Within SSCP	38.956	13.630	24.625	5.645
21		13.630	16.962	8.121	4.808
22		24.625	8.121	27.223	6.272
23		5.645	4.808	6.272	6.157

That explains something of the meaning of the data in the range B3:E6 of Figure 6.1. Columns B through E contain the means of the four continuous variables, petal and sepal length and width. Rows 3 through 5 contain the means of the three species, and Row 6 contains the grand means.

Using the Discriminant Dialog Box

With a worksheet such as the one shown in Figure 6.1 active, click the Discrim item in the Add-Ins tab. The dialog box shown in Figure 6.2 appears.

The dialog box shown in Figure 6.2 asks the user to supply the number of predictor variables. In the context of discriminant analysis, that means the number of continuous variables you want to use to discriminate between the categorical groups. In the context of the data shown in Figures 6.1 and 6.2, that means four predictor variables: petal length and width and sepal length and width.

Notice that this is the reverse of the roles played by the variables in the MANOVA that precedes the discriminant analysis. There, group membership is treated as the predictor variable—more typically termed the independent variable—and the continuous variables are treated as the predicted or dependent variables. Discriminant analysis turns things around and treats the continuous variables as predictors and the group membership as the predicted variable.

The dialog box also asks you for the number of groups: the number of distinct categories that you want to discriminate among. In Figure 6.2, that number is 3—the number of species whose means are represented in the range B3:E6.

6

Figure 6.2
If you supply either group names or variable labels in the group means range, you must supply both the names and the labels.

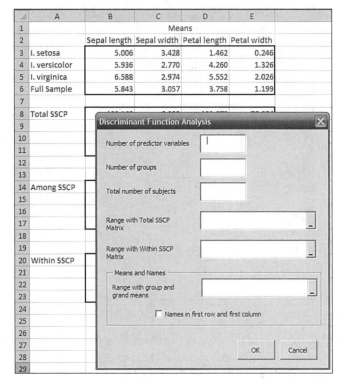

(Yes, I could pick up the number of variables from the width of the means matrix and the number of groups from its height. I explain shortly why I chose not to do so.)

The SSCP and means matrices provide no information about the number of cases represented in the data, so the dialog box asks you for that figure. It's used in the inferential tests that the code provides. In the case of the Iris data set, the figure is 150: There are 50 cases in each of three groups. This is not meant to imply that your groups must each have the same number of observations. They don't.

The dialog box also asks the user for the worksheet addresses of the ranges that contain the Total and the Within SSCP matrices. You can click in the two associated range edit boxes and drag through the appropriate cells on the worksheet (B8:E11 and B20:E23, respectively, in Figure 6.1). You might find it quicker to simply type the addresses into the edit boxes, but that's a little more error prone.

The third matrix, which contains the group means and grand mean on each variable, is just a little trickier. The MANOVA analysis discussed in Chapter 4 picks up and outputs group names and variable labels if you supply them with your input data. If not, the MANOVA code supplies default labels and names.

Notice in Figure 6.2 that you can choose to tell the Discriminant code to pick up variable labels and group names from worksheets such as the one shown in Figure 6.1. Fill the checkbox if you want to use both the labels and names that are on the worksheet; otherwise, leave it unchecked.

With the data as laid out in Figures 6.1 and 6.2, you could

- Fill the dialog box's checkbox and select A2:E6 as the range for the group and grand means. Notice that doing so picks up the group names in Column A and the variable labels in Row 2.

- Clear the checkbox and select B3:E6 as the range for group and grand means. So doing keeps the code's hands off the group names and variable labels, and the output uses default values.

> **TIP**
>
> I urge you to select your own variable labels and group names when you run Chapter 4's MANOVA routine. Then MANOVA will supply them in its output, and you can reuse them if and when you run the discriminant code. That will make it easier to compare the two sets of results.

Why does the dialog box first ask you for the number of variables and number of groups when that information is available from the size of the matrix of means? Because I didn't want to take the time to code the IF-THEN-ELSEIF or SELECT CASE structures needed to get the counts right depending on the interaction of the range address for the matrix and whether the checkbox is filled or cleared.

When you have finished providing the information requested by the dialog box, click OK to continue the analysis or Cancel to bail out. Excel responds by creating two new worksheets in the workbook where the SSCP and group means matrices are located.

One new worksheet, named Discriminant Results, contains inferential tests such as an F-ratio derived from Wilks' lambda and the necessary degrees of freedom, information about how the raw variables correlate with the discriminant functions (structure coefficients) and chi-square tests of the roots. (I discuss the meaning of these statistics in later sections of this chapter.)

The other new worksheet is named Eigenstructure and Coefficients. It contains information about the structure of the discriminant functions (the eigenvalues and eigenvectors) as well as the discriminant coefficients. The coefficients come in four flavors: raw and standardized (much like b weights and beta weights in multiple regression), and based on the Within SSCP and the Total SSCP matrices. Again, I discuss the meanings of and differences between these types of coefficients as this chapter continues.

You can get the Discrim item out of the Ribbon's Add-Ins tab simply by closing the Discriminant.xls workbook. If you still have a workbook open with a VBA project that Excel regards as an add-in, the Add-Ins tab remains on the Ribbon. Otherwise the Add-Ins tab goes away when you close Discriminant.xls. The tab reappears when you once again open Discriminant.xls.

Why Run a Discriminant Analysis on Irises?

There's something a little artificial about running a discriminant analysis on a data set full of petal widths, sepal lengths, and species names that only a botanist could love. It's not the flowers that are artificial. I'm hardly a botanist, but I bet a good one could tell representatives of the three species in question apart just by glancing at them.

But Fisher's main purpose for the iris data set, 80 years ago, was as a test bed to demonstrate how his discriminant functions could accurately and reliably distinguish between categorical groups (here, iris species) on the basis of continuous variables (here, petal and sepal lengths and widths).

Evaluating the Original Measures

Making those distinctions couldn't be done on the basis of any straightforward combination of the continuous variables. For example, Figure 6.3 shows how the sepal length and the sepal width covary among the three iris species.

Figure 6.3
Sepal lengths and widths do not do a good job of distinguishing among these species of iris.

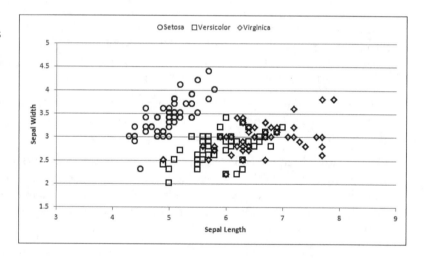

Notice that Figure 6.3 shows that the three iris species are thoroughly mingled on the chart. The distributions of the markers that identify members of the three species overlap considerably, on both the horizontal sepal length axis and the vertical sepal width axis. The setosa do tend to have shorter sepals and the virginica longer sepals. Nevertheless, if you had only sepal size measurements from one of the 150 irises, grabbed at random, you could not with any real confidence state that it's a setosa, versicolor, or virginica.

You can do a little better using petal width and sepal length. You can see in Figure 6.4 that the petal widths of setosa irises are—in this sample, at least—consistently smaller than in virginica and versicolor. With knowledge of the petal width alone you could tell a setosa from either of the other two species. But you could not confidently distinguish a virginica from a versicolor.

Figure 6.4
Petal width helps to separate setosa from virginica and versicolor.

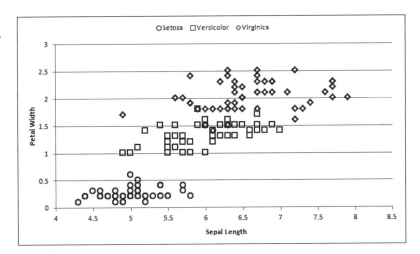

You could create four other bivariate charts from the six measures available. I don't do so here because it would be a waste of space. The results are similar to those you see in Figures 6.3 and 6.4: Some discrimination exists, but not enough across all three species to hang your hat on.

> **NOTE**
>
> The workbook for this chapter contains all the measurements: For 150 irises, you'll find petal and sepal length and width along with the species. So if you really want to, you can chart all six pairs of variables.

Discriminant Analysis and Investment

I'll make the assumption, quite possibly unwarranted, that you're more interested in commercial applications for discriminant analysis than in botanical applications. So let's generalize this discussion from plants to borrowers. Suppose that you have a set of 150 people who have borrowed money from your financial institution in the past. On that sample of 150 borrowers you have available continuous measures such as credit rating, annual income, age, and net worth. You also know whether the loans were repaid on a timely basis, repaid late, or not repaid.

You chart the data on those 150 borrowers, looking for a clue regarding whether you could make reliable decisions about *future* borrowers on the basis of age and credit rating, or annual income and net worth, or some other pair of continuous variables. If your results resembled those shown in Figures 6.3 and 6.4, you could be forgiven if instead you resorted to reading tea leaves. (Of course, that's apparently what was done from 2004 through 2007, and it turned out badly.)

I've done precisely that for a client who was in the business of purchasing debt. (Well, there were roughly 500 borrowers rather than the 150 irises involved in Fisher's seminal work.) And I started work with the data set by getting the bivariate correlations between the predictor variables and plotting them using scattercharts. Nothing suggested any good line of univariate analysis, but the distributions indicated that the variables would meet the assumptions needed for MANOVA and discriminant analysis. Because those approaches tend to have greater statistical power than logistic regression when the assumptions are met, I started looking further with MANOVA. (There have been plenty of occasions when the data have told me that assumptions for MANOVA were violated so seriously that logistic regression was the only sensible approach to classifying the records for subsequent decision making.)

The initial MANOVA run returned a significant multivariate F-ratio and four significant univariate F-ratios. As noted in earlier chapters on MANOVA and discriminant analysis, we avoid making conclusions on the basis of univariate F-ratios, even when the multivariate F-ratio is thought to be significant. Instead, the next step is discriminant analysis.

The discriminant analysis returned one significant discriminant function. I plotted the 500 records, Function 1 against Function 2, and got acceptable classification. There was some overlap on Function 1 and considerable overlap on Function 2, but Function 1 correctly classified 470 of the 500 cases. Plenty close enough for the client's purposes.

I can't show you that data, but the iris data set has no non-disclosure agreement attached to it, so let's return to botany for a while. Figure 6.5 shows what happens with the iris data set when it is run through a discriminant analysis.

Figure 6.5
The first discriminant function separates setosa from the other two species and leaves only a small region of overlap between versicolor and virginica.

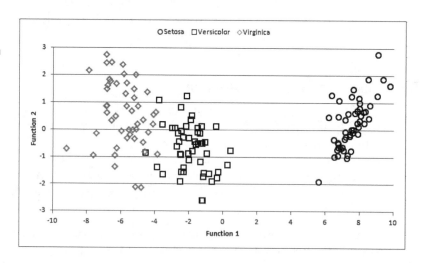

Figure 6.5 charts a variable—more precisely, a discriminant function—called Function 1 against another discriminant function called Function 2. Function 1 does a good job of distinguishing between all three species. Function 2 does a poor job, and I have left it in the chart partly to give it a vertical dimension (so you can distinguish the data points) and partly to suggest that there are data sets where *both* of two functions are useful.

The discriminant functions charted in Figure 6.5 are new variables, created by discriminant function analysis. These new variables are based in the original measurements (sepal length and width, petal length and width). They are analogous to the predicted values that you obtain from a multiple regression analysis. Of course, in multiple regression, there is only one set of predicted values, whereas discriminant analysis frequently returns two, three or more discriminant functions. Furthermore, the values predicted by multiple regression are calculated so as to maximize their correlation with a linear combination of the predictors. In contrast, the values calculated by discriminant analysis, when projected onto their axes, best separate the groups they belong to—axes that are rotated much as the rugby referee in Chapter 5 rotated his point of view to best separate the teams.

Benchmarking with R

It can be a good idea to benchmark the results of a discriminant analysis using a different application. This section shows you how to set up a discriminant analysis using the freeware statistical application R.

This section also briefly describes how to obtain R if you don't have it already. You can then benchmark the results that Excel provides, as shown in the previous section, against R's results for the same data set.

I show you R's results, and how to get them, in this section, so that you can run the analysis in a different environment. Or, if you prefer, you can make the comparison without obtaining R; this section shows you R's results on the iris data set discussed in the previous section and analyzed, using Excel, in the next section.

Downloading R

You can obtain the R software from this website: http://cran.r-project.org/.

The site gives you free access to R's base system and its associated statistical routines. It also provides instructions for installing R on your local machine.

The base R system does not include the software needed for discriminant analysis. That software, as well as software that performs other analyses such as logistic regression, is available in the form of what R terms *contributed packages*: libraries of routines that R can use, much like an Excel add-in, to extend its analysis capabilities.

One such package is called MASS, named after *Modern Applied Statistics with S* (Springer, 2002, ISBN 0-387-95457-0). The S programming language is a precursor to R. Although MASS is typically installed with the R base system, you must make reference to it in your R commands to get access to the discriminant analysis routine. I show you how to do that shortly.

6

Arranging the Data File

I find it's convenient to use Excel to create a data file that I will want to analyze using R. Most often I use Excel to run the analysis, and there are times when I want to benchmark the results using R, and occasionally with yet another application. In that sort of case it's handy to be able to export the data from Excel to a text file, usually a Comma Separated Values (CSV) file, for import into R.

A CSV file (so known because Excel provides the letters csv as the filename extension) is a file that consists solely of text values, including numbers. It has none of the structures that a native Excel file has, such as multiple worksheets, charts and pivot tables. It does maintain the row-by-column structure of an Excel worksheet, separating rows by means of carriage returns and columns by means of commas. That makes the csv arrangement useful as a general method of moving data between applications.

In most cases you will want to structure a worksheet as an Excel list or table, with different variables occupying different columns, different records occupying different rows, and a header row that names each variable on the worksheet. Have that worksheet active when you're ready to create the CSV file: The active sheet is the only worksheet that will be saved in the CSV format. (If the active sheet is a chart sheet, as distinct from a worksheet with an embedded chart, Excel will not allow you to save it as a CSV file.)

Give a little thought to the variable labels you put into the first header row. R is case-sensitive when it comes to variable labels, so if you import a variable named "Species" into R, you can't subsequently refer to that variable as "species".

Embedded blanks are fine, but bear in mind that R inserts periods in their place. The same is true of special characters such as % and ^. So either "sepal length" or "sepal%length" would become "sepal.length". If both "sepallength" and "sepal.length" look awkward to you, consider using "SepalLength". Whatever you use as the column header is what R uses as the variable's name.

After you have the data layout the way you want it, and the variables with the labels you want in the header row, click the Ribbon's File tab and choose Save As from the navigation bar. In the Save As Type drop-down box near the bottom of the Save As dialog box, choose CSV (Comma delimited) (*.csv) and then click the Save button.

> **TIP**
>
> I suggest that before you choose a file type in the Save As Type drop-down box, you use the Folders pane in the Save As dialog box to navigate to a location whose path is easily typed. Bear in mind that you have to type that path when you direct R's attention to the CSV file. If you have to type a lengthy string that includes a Users folder, the username, perhaps a Documents or Desktop folder, and who knows what other hurdles are sitting in the obstacle course, all the while remembering to type forward slashes instead of backslashes—if all of that's true then you're apt to make a mistake somewhere. This is the reason that I have so many CSV files in my C: root.

When you click Save, Excel displays a warning that CSV files may contain one worksheet only. If you have all the data you want to import into R on the active worksheet, you're fine, and you should click OK. Otherwise, click Cancel and make whatever changes to the structure of the workbook are necessary before saving it.

Your file may contain features that are not compatible with a CSV file. Don't worry about it. If the active worksheet contains nothing but data values, the resulting CSV file will contain them, too, and that's all you want it to have. The source file you're saving from retains the special Excel features and remains open.

> **CAUTION**
>
> Although the source workbook remains open along with Excel features and multiple worksheets, it has been renamed with the .csv extension. To avoid losing the features and worksheets, along with any changes you have made since the last time you saved it as a native Excel file, you should usually save it once again, this time as an xls, xlsx, xlsm, or some other native Excel file type.

Running the Analysis

After you have saved the data in a text file, the next step is to have R read the data. Begin by starting R (normally from a taskbar or desktop icon that the R installation routine takes care of for you). After a few introductory messages and disclaimers, you get R's prompt, a greater-than symbol:

```
>
```

Enter the following commands. I show what you are expected to type in **boldface**. R's responses appear in `this typeface`.

Bring the data in the .csv file into R and place it into a data frame. Here, I have named the data frame *irisdata*. Notice that the separators between folder names are forward slashes rather than the backslashes you ordinarily see in Windows addresses. (You can use two consecutive backslashes rather than a single forward slash if you prefer.)

```
>irisdata <- read.csv("C:/Users/C^2/Desktop/Iris.csv")
```

R has now created a data frame named *irisdata*. It contains all the variables' names and values on all the records that you included in the .csv file. Next, attach the data frame:

```
>attach(irisdata)
```

The effect of the *attach* command here is to add the data frame *irisdata* to R's search path. With the data frame in the search path it's possible to refer, for example, to *species* without qualifying the variable name by the data frame (*irisdata$species*). The small increment in convenience might be lost due to confusion if you have, say, two data frames attached and both have a variable named *species*. To remove a data frame from the search path use the *detach* command.

6

It's a good idea to take a look at a summary of the data that R has put into the data frame. This can help you recover early if a problem has occurred in saving or acquiring the data:

```
>summary(irisdata)
 Sepal.length    Sepal.width     Petal.length    Petal.width
 Min.   :4.300   Min.   :2.000   Min.   :1.000   Min.   :0.100
 1st Qu.:5.100   1st Qu.:2.800   1st Qu.:1.600   1st Qu.:0.300
 Median :5.800   Median :3.000   Median :4.350   Median :1.300
 Mean   :5.843   Mean   :3.057   Mean   :3.758   Mean   :1.199
 3rd Qu.:6.400   3rd Qu.:3.300   3rd Qu.:5.100   3rd Qu.:1.800
 Max.   :7.900   Max.   :4.400   Max.   :6.900   Max.   :2.500
        Species
 Setosa    :50
 Versicolor:50
 Virginica :50
```

R responds by showing a count of each category in a text variable (here, *Species*) and descriptive statistics for each numeric variable: minimum, first quartile, median, mean, third quartile and maximum. If any of those values look wrong to you, you should probably have a look at the .csv file again, probably in Excel's graphical user interface.

If it all looks right to you, load the library that contains R's discriminant analysis software:

```
>library(MASS)
```

After the software is loaded, execute the *lda* (linear discriminant analysis) routine using the *irisdata* data frame. Specify the variables that you want to use. Because the .csv file in this example is set up with the four continuous variables in its first four columns, you can refer to them using R's *c(1:4)* syntax. Place the results in a new variable named IRIS.

```
>IRIS = lda(irisdata[, c(1:4)], Species)
```

Finally, display the contents of the new IRIS variable. (Note that R abbreviates the names of the continuous variables. For example, *Sepal.Length* is shown as *SL*.)

```
>IRIS
Call:
lda(irisdata[, c(1:4)], Species)

Prior probabilities of groups:
    Setosa Versicolor  Virginica
 0.3333333  0.3333333  0.3333333

Group means:
             SL    SW    PL    PW
Setosa     5.006 3.428 1.462 0.246
Versicolor 5.936 2.770 4.260 1.326
Virginica  6.588 2.974 5.552 2.026

Coefficients of linear discriminants:
         LD1         LD2
SL  0.8293776 -0.02410215
SW  1.5344731 -2.16452123
PL -2.2012117  0.93192121
PW -2.8104603 -2.83918785

Proportion of trace:
   LD1    LD2
0.9912 0.0088
```

If you want to see each record's value on each discriminant function, use the *predict* command:

```
>predict(IRIS)$x
   [1,]   7.5724707   0.805464137
   [2,]   6.5605516   1.015163624
    .
 [149,]  -6.7967163  -0.863090395
 [150,]  -5.2204877  -1.468195094
```

(I have omitted the 3rd through the 148th records.) R displays a different row for each record and as many columns as there are discriminant functions (in this case, that's 2: the number of groups minus 1).

There are a couple of things you should know about the individual discriminant function values as provided by the *lda* package in R.

Coefficients and Constants

To duplicate R's discriminant function scores, returned as in the previous section by means of the *predict* command, you need to multiply each record's values on the original continuous variables by the corresponding coefficient. R provides the coefficients (labeled Coefficients of Linear Discriminants in the previous section). These are the raw score coefficients returned using the Within SSCP matrix. The four types of discriminant coefficients are discussed shortly, in the section titled "Eigenstructures and Coefficients."

However, R does not provide the constants associated with the raw score coefficients for each discriminant function. They are easy to calculate. You simply multiply the grand mean of each original continuous variable by the discriminant function's coefficient for that variable. Total the results and multiply by -1. Figure 6.6 shows an example.

Figure 6.6
Calculating the constant for the second discriminant function using the grand means of each continuous variable and the function's coefficients.

	A	B	C	D	E	F	G
G6			f_x	=-1*SUM(B6:E6)			
1		Sepal length	Sepal width	Petal length	Petal width		
2	Coefficients, Function 2	0.0241	2.1645	-0.9319	2.8392		
3							
4	Grand Means	5.843	3.057	3.758	1.199		
5							=-1*SUM(B6:E6)
6	Products	0.1408	6.6177	-3.5022	3.4051		-6.6615

It's fairly easy to calculate the constants, so you can handle it in a minute or two directly on a worksheet. (The Discriminant.xls code that you can download with other files for this chapter calculates and displays the discriminant function constants along with the coefficients.)

In sum: Be aware that the *lda* package in R displays the raw score coefficients but not the constants. You need both to calculate the discriminant function scores for each record. If you're willing to accept R's results, this isn't a big deal. Because there are so many different ways to calculate the discriminant scores, though, I much prefer to know what's going on. I also appreciate knowing why I don't get the results I expect if I leave out the constants.

Understanding the Coefficient Signs

Different applications that perform multivariate analyses such as discriminant, principal components, and factor analysis from time to time report different loadings (the term used in factor analysis for "structure coefficients") and factor or discriminant score coefficients, even when the data to be analyzed is identical. The differences are not in the absolute values of the loadings and other coefficients, but in their *signs*.

The signs are arbitrary, although they might cause you to interpret the meaning of a factor differently according to whether a loading is positive or negative. For example, suppose you were investigating a measure of a person's intelligence among a variety of other variables such as income and education, in an effort to classify unaffiliated voters according to tendency to vote as a social liberal or as a social conservative.

Your numeric analysis might reveal a factor that appears to identify that tendency. When you run the numbers through one statistical application, you find that the "intelligence" variable exhibits a strong loading such as .92 on the factor. When you do the same analysis with another application (or even in another instance of the same application), you find that its loading is -.92. The two applications return the same loading but one is positive and one is negative.

They're probably both right. The strength of the loading is the same in both cases. It's simply that one set of results suggests that you interpret the factor as being influenced by the subject's intelligence, whereas the other set of results suggests that the factor is defined in part by an absence of fatuity.

Because the sign is arbitrary, some applications such as SYSTAT (1986) count the number of negative loadings for a given component (or, in the context of discriminant analysis, for a given discriminant function). If the number of negative loadings exceeds the number of positive loadings, the direction of the component is reversed. The effect is to change positive loadings to negative and vice versa. If you see discriminant function coefficients from one application that differ only in their signs from the coefficients reported by another application, the difference is probably due to switching arbitrarily negative signs to arbitrarily positive ones. The *lda* package in R appears to use this approach.

The Results of the Discrim Add-In

With the R results in hand to use as a benchmark, as discussed in the previous section, it's time to look at the results of using the Discrim add-in supplied with this book's downloadable Excel files.

NOTE The file named Discriminant.xls, which contains the Discrim code, is not formally an add-in. Excel saves true add-ins with the extension .xla (through Excel 2003) or .xlam (Excel 2007 and later). But to make the code compatible with versions of Excel both through 2003 as well as subsequent to 2003, I decided to save it in .xls format. The result is that versions of Excel that have the Ribbon toss the command that starts the code into the Add-Ins tab—even though the file's not a true add-in. In consequence I refer to the file, and the code inside it, as an add-in even though it's an .xls file.

The Discriminant Results

The Discrim add-in creates two new worksheets in the workbook that is active when you start Discrim. One is named Discriminant Results, and I describe its contents in this section. The other is named Eigenstructure and Coefficients, and it's described in the next section.

The Discriminant Results worksheet brings together various descriptive and inferential analyses that help you evaluate the usefulness of the analysis as applied to your data set. Figure 6.7 shows the upper portion of the Discriminant Results worksheet.

Figure 6.7
The overall usefulness of the discriminant analysis is summarized in this portion of the results.

	A	B	C	D	E	F	G	H
1	Wilks Lambda:	0.0234	Eta-Square:	0.9766				
2								
3	F-ratio for Overall Discrimination:	199.1453						
4	NDF1	8	NDF2	288				
5								
6	Chi-square tests							
7	Roots Removed	Canonical R	R Squared	Eigenvalue	Chi Square	N.D.F	Lambda	Percent Trace $W^{-1}A$
8	0	0.9848	0.9699	32.1919	546.1153	8	0.0234	99.1213
9	1	0.4712	0.2220	0.2854	36.5297	3	0.7780	0.8787
10								
11	Structure Coefficients							
12	Variable	Function 1	Function 2					
13	Sepal length	-0.7919	0.2176					
14	Sepal width	0.5308	0.7580					
15	Petal length	-0.9850	0.0460					
16	Petal width	-0.9728	0.2229					
17								
18	Communalities							
19		Function 1						
20	Sepal length	0.6655						
21	Sepal width	0.8449						
22	Petal length	0.9593						
23	Petal width	0.9828						

6

Figure 6.7 begins by reporting the multivariate significance of the discriminant analysis. In the case of the iris data set, it reports a Wilks' lambda of .0234 in cell B1 and the corresponding eta-square value in cell D1. Clearly, both are highly significant values.

> **NOTE**
>
> Eta-square is also termed the *correlation ratio*. In multivariate and discriminant analysis, it is equal to 1 minus Wilks' lambda. In univariate ANOVA, eta-square equals the Sum of Squares (Between) divided by the Sum of Squares (Total). In a multivariate context, therefore, eta-square is the determinant of the SSCP Among divided by the determinant of the SSCP Total. Similarly, as other chapters in this book have noted, Wilks' lambda is the determinant of the SSCP Within divided by the determinant of the SSCP Total.

The transformation of Wilks' lambda to the F-ratio appears in cell B3, with the degrees of freedom for the F-test in cells B4 and D4. With such a large F-ratio and so many degrees of freedom for the denominator there is little point in testing the F-ratio, but if you wanted to do so you could, using this formula:

=F.DIST.RT(B3,B4,D4)

which in this case does not return a value that Excel can distinguish from zero.

> **NOTE**
>
> You can find the procedure to transform Wilks' lambda to a multivariate F-ratio (as well as the correct degrees of freedom) in Figure 4.11. Chi-square approximations also exist but they are less accurate, particularly with small values for the degrees of freedom.

Tests of the discriminant functions follow in rows 8 and 9. Bartlett's approximation is used to return a chi-square value for each discriminant function, and the degrees of freedom are supplied so that you can compare each chi-square to a reference chi-square distribution. As already indicated, the first discriminant function is highly significant, and there is little attributable variance left over for the second function.

The canonical correlations (and their squares) also appear in the range B8:C9. These values represent the correlation between a linear function of the predictor variables, and a linear function of the coded dummy variables that represent group memberships. In the iris example, of course, the group memberships are the species of which each iris is a member. Again, after the first discriminant function has been accounted for, the canonical correlation drops from .98 to .47.

With the eigenvalues in hand (from either the Eigenstructure and Coefficients or the Discriminant Results worksheet) it's easy to calculate the canonical correlations. For a given discriminant function, the canonical correlation is the square root of an eigenvalue divided by the eigenvalue plus 1. So, in Figure 6.7, the following formula returns the first canonical correlation:

=SQRT(D8/(1+D8))

Interpreting the Structure Coefficients

You can interpret the structure coefficients in the range B13:C16 of Figure 6.7 in much the same way that you interpret loadings in a principal components or factor analysis. Or, in a multiple regression, you might assess the importance of a given predictor variable by calculating its correlation with the values that are predicted by the regression equation. An original predictor variable's correlation with a principal component, or with the predicted values from a multiple regression, or with scores on a discriminant function, is often taken as an indicator of the importance of a given predictor.

These correlations are typically termed *structure coefficients*. You could of course calculate them yourself by getting the discriminant function scores of each record (discussed later in this chapter) and correlating them with the original predictors. But with many records that can be awkward, and the Discrim results include the structure coefficients on the Discriminant Results worksheet.

It is for this reason—the examination of structure coefficients—that many analysts follow up a significant MANOVA with a discriminant function analysis. A MANOVA does not tell you which variables are responsible for a significant multivariate F-ratio or Wilks' lambda. The pattern of the structure coefficients can provide you with that information.

Quantifying the structure coefficients is the main point of discriminant analysis. It's every bit as important as quantifying the loadings (just a different term for structure coefficients) in a principal components or factor analysis. By examining which predictor variables have strong structure coefficients on a given discriminant function, you can infer what it is that the discriminant function measures, just as examining the loadings on a principal component (normally, following rotation) enables you to infer what the component measures. And that's the rationale for discriminant analysis: a MANOVA will tell you if groups differ significantly on a continuous variable, but it doesn't tell you which variable or variables. For that you rely on the pattern of the structure coefficients.

In the case of the analysis of the irises, the first discriminant function appears to be defined by the sepal length, the petal length, and the petal width, where the structure coefficients are fairly high. The second discriminant function is principally defined by the sepal width. But as earlier analyses have indicated, the second discriminant function is of virtually no importance to distinguishing the species in discriminant space. Therefore, an analyst might not bother with the sepal width measure in subsequent research that involves distinguishing these species from one another.

The Discriminant Results worksheet also reports the communality of each predictor. (The term *communality* might be more familiar in the context of factor analysis.) The communality of a variable is the sum of the squares of the variable's structure coefficients. The higher the communality, the more the variable contributes to the discrimination. As the structure coefficients indicate, the contribution of the sepal width variable is less effective than that of the other predictors.

6

> **NOTE**
> Communalities in discriminant analysis are useful only when the number of groups minus 1 is less than the number of predictor variables. Otherwise, the communalities will all equal 1.0.

Eigenstructures and Coefficients

The second new worksheet provided by Discriminant.xls is named Eigenstructures and Coefficients. In the context of discriminant analysis, the term *eigenstructure* means the eigenvalues and eigenvectors associated with the discriminant functions and the predictor variables. The coefficients referred to in the name of the worksheet are used to calculate scores on each discriminant function, both for individual record profiles and for group centroids.

Figure 6.8 shows an example of this worksheet for the iris data set.

Figure 6.8
Each discriminant function has a different eigenvalue, and each discriminant function has a different eigenvector of predictor variables.

	A	B	C	D	E	F	G	H	I	J	K	L
1	Eigenvalues		Eigenvectors									
2	32.1919		0.2087	0.0065	0.3463	0.5012						
3	0.2854		0.3862	0.5866	0.1959	-0.4423						
4	0.0000		-0.5540	-0.2526	0.2695	-0.4874						
5	0.0000		-0.7074	0.7695	-0.8770	0.5617						
6												
7	Raw Coefficients based on Total SSCP							Standardized Coefficients based on Total SSCP				
8			Sepal length	Sepal width	Petal length	Petal width	Constant		Sepal length	Sepal width	Petal length	Petal width
9	Function 1		0.1449	0.2681	-0.3847	-0.4911	0.3679		0.1200	0.1169	-0.6790	-0.3744
10	Function 2		0.0214	1.9221	-0.8276	2.5212	-5.9154		0.0177	0.8378	-1.4609	1.9218
11												
12	Raw coefficients based on Within SSCP							Standardized coefficients based on Within SSCP				
13			Sepal length	Sepal width	Petal length	Petal width	Constant		Sepal length	Sepal width	Petal length	Petal width
14	Function 1		0.8294	1.5345	-2.2012	-2.8105	2.1051		0.4270	0.5212	-0.9473	-0.5752
15	Function 2		0.0241	2.1645	-0.9319	2.8392	-6.6615		0.0124	0.7353	-0.4010	0.5810
16												
17	Pooled within groups covariance matrix											
18	0.2650	0.0927	0.1675	0.0384								
19	0.0927	0.1154	0.0552	0.0327								
20	0.1675	0.0552	0.1852	0.0427								
21	0.0384	0.0327	0.0427	0.0419								
22												
23	Inverse of pooled within groups covariance matrix											
24	10.8435	-5.3772	-8.9919	3.4174								
25	-5.3772	14.2339	2.6698	-8.9063								
26	-8.9919	2.6698	14.7892	-8.9064								
27	3.4174	-8.9063	-8.9064	36.7724								

The eigenvalues are measures of the amount of variability in the variables that represent the different groups that can be accounted for by each discriminant function. As Chapter 5 notes, each eigenvalue is an expression of the ratio of the Among SSCP matrix to the Within SSCP matrix, for a given discriminant function.

Figure 6.8 shows in cell A2 that the eigenvalue for the first discriminant function is quite large: that the combined variance and covariance among the groups is over 32 times greater than the combined variance and covariance within the groups. In a univariate context such as a simple ANOVA, this situation is analogous to a large mean square between groups divided by a small mean square within groups, leading to a large F-ratio.

The eigenvectors are actually cosines of angles between the axes that are defined for the predictor variables within each discriminant function. You could use them to construct graphs that show where each record's profile falls on those axes.

A more prosaic use for the eigenvectors is to construct the vectors of coefficients that are used to produce the records' scores on each discriminant function. The Discriminant.xls file provides the coefficients for you, and in Figure 6.8 they appear in the range A7:K15. Discriminant function analysis provides for four different types of coefficients (discussed in the next section), and the Discriminant.xls file reports each type of coefficient.

The standard way to calculate discriminant scores for a record is to use that record's raw measured values and combine them with the coefficients labeled *Raw coefficients based on Within SSCP* in the range B14:E15 in Figure 6.8. When that combination has been accomplished, you add the constants in F14:F15. Figure 6.9 repeats the coefficients and constants, along with the actual sepal and petal measurements for the first and last two records.

Figure 6.9
You can use Excel's MMULT() function to calculate the discriminant scores, or perform the multiplications and additions explicitly.

	H14			f_x	=$C$4*C7+$D$4*D7+$E$4*E7+$F$4*F7+$G$4			
	A	B	C	D	E	F	G	H
1		Raw coefficients based on Within SSCP						
2			Sepal length	Sepal width	Petal length	Petal width	Constant	
3		Function 1	0.8294	1.5345	-2.2012	-2.8105	2.1051	
4		Function 2	0.0241	2.1645	-0.9319	2.8392	-6.6615	
5								
6	Record Number	Species	Sepal length	Sepal width	Petal length	Petal width		
7		1 Setosa	4.3	3	1.1	0.1		
8		2 Setosa	4.4	2.9	1.4	0.2		
9								
10		149 Virginica	7.7	3	6.1	2.3		
11		150 Virginica	7.9	3.8	6.4	2		
12								
13		Record Number	Function 1	Function 2		Record Number	Function 1	Function 2
14		1	7.5725	-0.8055		1	7.5725	-0.8055
15		2	6.5606	-1.0152		2	6.5606	-1.0152
16								
17		149	-6.7967	0.8631		149	-6.7967	0.8631
18		150	-5.2205	1.4682		150	-5.2205	1.4682

Figure 6.9 repeats the coefficients and constants from Figure 6.8, in the range C3:G4. Only four of the 150 irises appear in Figure 6.9, in rows 7 and 8, and rows 10 and 11. (The entire data set is in the worksheet named Fig 6.11 in the workbook that you can download for this

chapter.) I include four records in Figure 6.9 to demonstrate how to calculate the discriminant scores. You can compare the results with those reported by R and shown earlier in this chapter in the section "Running the Analysis."

Figure 6.9 shows two ways to calculate the discriminant scores, one in the range C14:D18 and one in the range G14:H18. The range C14:D18 uses a somewhat quicker method. Cell C14, for example, contains this array formula for the first iris's value on the first discriminant function:

> =MMULT(C7:F7,TRANSPOSE($C$3:$F$3))+$G$3

In words, this array formula tells Excel to multiply together the individual pairs of cells in C7:F7 and C3:F3 (for example, C7 times C3, then D7 and D3, and so on) and then sum the results of the multiplications; this is what the MMULT() function does. Finally, add the value of the constant in cell G3. The coefficients in C3:F3 and the constant in G3 are identified using absolute references so that the formula can be copied and pasted without changing their addresses.

The array formula for the first iris's value on the second discriminant function is in cell D14:

> =MMULT(C7:F7,TRANSPOSE($C$4:$F$4))+$G$4

Notice that the original measures in C7:F7 are the same as the ones used for the first discriminant function score in cell C14. The coefficients and the constant are different: The coefficients are found in C4:F4 and the constant in G4. Again, the addresses of the coefficients and constant are provided as absolute references.

With those two array formulas established in C14 and D14, you can copy and paste them down into the next 149 rows to get the two discriminant scores on each of 150 irises, distributed across three species. Notice that the discriminant scores for the first two and last two irises are the same as reported earlier in this chapter by R's lda package.

Still in Figure 6.9, another method of calculating the discriminant scores appears in the range G14:H18. It's a little more tedious to enter, but it does show explicitly how the multiplications and additions are carried out, rather than hiding them inside the MMULT() and TRANSPOSE() functions. Cell G14 contains this formula (which need not be array-entered) for the first discriminant function:

> =$C$3*C7+$D$3*D7+$E$3*E7+$F$3*F7+$G$3

Again, the original measurements in C7:F7 are multiplied by the corresponding coefficients in C3:F3 and the results are summed. Then the constant in G3 is added.

The formula for the second discriminant function, in H14, is

> =$C$4*C7+$D$4*D7+$E$4*E7+$F$4*F7+$G$4

The only difference from the first of the previous two formulas is that the coefficients and constant for the second discriminant function, in Row 4, are used.

After these two formulas have been set up, you can copy them down the worksheet to calculate the discriminant function scores for all 150 irises.

If you prefer, you could also use Excel's SUMPRODUCT() function instead of either matrix multiplication or explicit multiplication. For example:

=SUMPRODUCT($C$3:$F$3,C7:F7)+$G$3

and:

=SUMPRODUCT($C$4:$F$4,C7:F7)+$G$4

The discriminant scores can be charted to determine visually how and where the separation between the species occurs. Figure 6.5 shows such an analysis, using a scatter chart to display the relationship between the discriminant functions.

> **TIP**
> It's best to start by charting the first 50 Setosa irises. Then activate the chart, click the Design tab in the Chart Tools group, and click the Select Data button. In the Select Data Source dialog box, click the Add button to add the Versicolor records. This adds a new data series with different markers, so that you can distinguish the Setosa irises from the Versicolor irises. Finally, repeat the process for the Virginica irises to replicate the chart in Figure 6.5.

Other Uses for the Coefficients

Different analysts (and different writers on the subject of discriminant function analysis) prefer to use different sets of discriminant coefficients. These preferences are usually due to the fact that they want to emphasize different aspects of the discriminant analysis.

For example, a writer or an analyst who wants to emphasize the calculation of the discriminant scores (discussed in this chapter in the previous section) might focus the discussion on the coefficients and constants based on the Within SSCP matrix—just as was done in the previous section.

There are four sets of coefficients and two sets of constants that you can derive for a given discriminant analysis. So-called *raw* coefficients and constants are used with the raw measures, sometimes as corrected for group or grand means. *Standardized* coefficients can be used with standardized measures, usually standardized to zero mean and unit variance (such as z-scores). Because the values have a zero mean, standardized coefficients are not accompanied by a constant.

Both raw and standardized coefficients can be based on either a Total SSCP or a Within SSCP matrix.

The Eigenstructure and Coefficients worksheet produced by the Discrim add-in provides all four sets. Should you want to use one set rather than another, each is available. Suppose, for example, that you do not have access to the original data on a case-by-case basis but want to calculate the structure coefficients. One way of doing so is to find the correlation (perhaps using Excel's CORREL function) between the calculated scores for a discriminant function and the original measures. But you can't do that if you don't have access to each original observation.

Figure 6.10 shows how you can get around that difficulty by using the Total SSCP matrix and the standardized coefficients based on it.

Figure 6.10
Compare the calculated structure coefficients with those shown in Figure 6.7.

	J15			f_x	{=MMULT(B15:E18,G15:H18)}					
	A	B	C	D	E	F	G	H	I	J	K
1	Total SSCP	102.1683	-6.3227	189.8730	76.9243						
2		-6.3227	28.3069	-49.1188	-18.1243						
3		189.8730	-49.1188	464.3254	193.0458						
4		76.9243	-18.1243	193.0458	86.5699						
5							Variances				
6	C_t	0.6857	-0.0424	1.2743	0.5163		0.6857				
7		-0.0424	0.1900	-0.3297	-0.1216		0.1900				
8		1.2743	-0.3297	3.1163	1.2956		3.1163				
9		0.5163	-0.1216	1.2956	0.5810		0.5810				
10											
11	Variances	0.6857	0.1900	3.1163	0.5810						
12											
13							Standardized Coefficients			Structure	
14							Based on Total SSCP			Coefficients	
15	R Matrix	1.0000	-0.1176	0.8718	0.8179		0.1200	0.0177		-0.7919	0.2176
16		-0.1176	1.0000	-0.4284	-0.3661		0.1169	0.8378		0.5308	0.7580
17		0.8718	-0.4284	1.0000	0.9629		-0.6790	-1.4609		-0.9850	0.0460
18		0.8179	-0.3661	0.9629	1.0000		-0.3744	1.9218		-0.9728	0.2229

Begin with the Total SSCP matrix in the range B1:E4. This matrix is taken from the MANOVA results shown in Figure 6.1. You can convert that matrix to a variance-covariance matrix (symbolized as C_t, where the "t" subscript stands for Total) in B6:E9 by dividing by the Total degrees of freedom. Because there are 150 irises in the data set, the Total degrees of freedom (or N − 1) is 149. Each cell in B6:E9 is a cell in B1:E4 divided by 149, so the formula in cell B6 is

   =B1/149

You can convert a variance-covariance matrix to a correlation (or R) matrix by dividing each cell by the product of the standard deviations of the variables that it comprises. The standard deviations are available from the variances of the variables involved in the specific correlation being calculated. Those variances are shown in Figure 6.10 in two ranges: B11:E11 and G6:G9. Pick them up from the main diagonal of the C_t matrix in the range B6:E9. For example, the value in cells C11 and G7 is the same as the value in cell C7.

Placing the variances in those ranges enables you to populate the R matrix by entering just one formula and then autofilling to the right and down. The formula in the upper-left corner of the R matrix, in cell B15, is

=B6/SQRT(B$11*$G6)

The formula divides the variance in cell B6 by the square root of the product of the variances in B11 and G6. Because all three variances refer to the same variable, the result is 1.0; a variable's correlation with itself is, trivially, 1.0.

The use of the dollar signs in the references to the variances in column B and in Row 6 means that you can copy the formula to the right, through column E, and down, through row 9, to finish populating the R matrix. For example, the formula in cell E17 turns out to be

=E8/SQRT(E$11*$G8)

so the covariance between Petal Length and Petal Width is divided by the square root of the product of the proper variances.

An R matrix is, of course, a set of standardized values, unaffected by either the means or the variances of the variables that it includes. Therefore it's appropriate to use it in conjunction with standardized coefficients, and they have been brought into Figure 6.10 (in the range G15:H18) from the range H9:K10 of Figure 6.8. The latter figure reproduces the Eigen-structure and Coefficients worksheet produced by the Discrim add-in. In Figure 6.10 the matrix of standardized coefficients based on the Total SSCP has been transposed from Figure 6.8, using Excel's TRANSPOSE() function.

Finally, the structure coefficients are calculated by this array formula, entered in J15:K18 of Figure 6.10:

=MMULT(B15:E18,G15:H18)

Notice that the values the array formula returns are exactly equal to those returned by the Discrim add-in, in B13:C16 of Figure 6.7.

One final word about structure coefficients: It's important to evaluate them in light of more general results. In the case of the iris data set, you've already seen that both descriptive statistics (the eta-square in cell D1 of Figure 6.7) and inferential statistics (the F-ratio in cell B3 of the same figure) support the notion that the discriminant function analysis is successful in distinguishing the three species from one another.

In that case, and in similar situations, it's appropriate to look carefully at the structure coefficients to determine which original variables contribute most strongly to the discrimination. (Recall that one principal reason to do a discriminant analysis at all is to determine which continuous variables are responsible for a significant MANOVA result.)

6

But you can get apparently strong structure coefficients even if the overall discrimination is borderline. (Or if it is clearly weak—although in that case you might wonder why you were doing a discriminant analysis at all; it's tantamount to running multiple comparison tests following a nonsignificant ANOVA result.)

It's entirely possible to calculate strong correlations between the original predictor variables and the discriminant scores even if the discriminant scores fail to distinguish between groups. Bear that in mind if you find yourself examining a discriminant analysis that's been run as a follow-up to a marginal MANOVA result.

Classifying the Cases

I may as well tell you right now that even after you've gotten significant results from a MANOVA, and after you've run a discriminant analysis with significant outcomes, what remains—the classification step—is still a mess.

Plenty of books and articles discuss classification based on discriminant analysis, but I have yet to see one that clearly explains how it's done in a situation involving more than two groups and more than two predictor variables. (No, I haven't read all those books, and, yes, there might well be some that describe the process clearly and completely.) In this section I use the iris data set and the results of the discriminant analysis to show how the sausage gets made.

Four basic steps are needed to move from the raw measures (the petal and sepal lengths and widths) and the known groups (the species) to a measure of the distance of each record from the centroid of each group. The basic steps are as follows:

1. Represent each observation as the deviation of its value on each of four predictors from the predictor's grand mean.

2. Find the average mean corrected value for each predictor in each species. These constitute the group centroids—in this example, of course, the group centroids are the species centroids.

3. We now have individual records' values corrected for the grand mean of each variable. We also have species' centroids, corrected for the grand means. Next, find the individual values of each record as a deviation from *each species*' centroid, including that of its own species. This is in preparation to determine which species' centroid a given iris is closest to.

4. Convert the four deviations for each iris to a single Mahalanobis' D^2 value. The result is, for each iris, three values for D^2, one for each species. Assign each iris to the species with the smallest value of D^2 for that iris.

I detail these four basic steps in the remainder of this section.

Distance from the Centroids

One good method of classifying individual cases according to the categories you started with goes by the fearsome name *Mahalanobis' D^2*. It's named for the statistician who developed the method in 1927, when he was working on ways to make classifications according to anthropological measurements. It is a way of determining the distance of any given measurement in your data set from each value in the data set's centroids. Each case has a distance from each centroid, and the smallest distance indicates which centroid—therefore, which category—the case belongs to. Here's why D^2 is so useful:

Imagine that you're working with three predictor variables and, say, two groups. The three variables define a three-dimensional space that's occupied by the groups. The individual cases you're working with create a swarm of points in that space, and an individual's measures on the three variables place him relatively close to or far from a group's centroid. Each individual is classified (rightly or wrongly, of course) into the group where the centroid is closest to his measured scores.

It's a little more complicated than that. One problem is that the measures may use different scales. That difficulty is usually managed by converting the scores to the multivariate analog of the univariate standard score or *z-score*.

Another problem is that the swarms of individual data points might not be spheres. It would be handy if they were spherical, because then any two individuals who are the same distance from the centroids would have the same probability of belonging to that swarm.

But if a swarm is elongated, an ellipse instead of a sphere, John might be close to the edge of the swarm if he's located on the ellipse's short axis. And Mary, with the same distance measure, might be equally close to the centroids and well away from the swarm's edge if she's located on the ellipse's long axis. In that case, John (close to the edge defined by the short axis) has a lower probability of belonging to the swarm than does Mary (far from the edge defined by the long axis), even though both are equally close to the swarm's centroids.

In addition to standardizing the scales of the measures, Mahalanobis' D^2 takes account of the direction of an individual's scores from a swarm's centroid. Distances and directions in a swarm are the foundation of probability statements. It's easier to visualize with the distribution of a single predictor variable, where in a normal curve the probability of a given value depends on its distance from the mean, regardless of its direction from the mean. A z-score of 1.96 has the same probability of occurrence as a z-score of -1.96. In a multivariate swarm, the probability of a given observation depends on its distance *and* direction from the centroid. You get those measures by dividing an observation by the swarm's variance-covariance matrix—or, in terms of matrix algebra, you multiply it by the inverse of the variance-covariance matrix.

You'll see this occur in the context of the Excel worksheet in the following sections of this chapter. Then you'll see how to use the resulting values of D^2 to classify the individual observations.

6

Correcting for the Means

Figure 6.11 shows some of the original, raw data from Fisher's 1936 discriminant analysis of irises. The data set includes the sepal length and width, the petal length and width, and a botanist's assignment of each iris to one of three species: setosa, versicolor, and virginica. The full data set is available in the workbook for this chapter, which you can download from the publisher's website, quepublishing.com/title/9780789751683. The data set is also available from a number of sources online; if you want to obtain it that way, search the Web using the terms *fisher, iris, data, set.*

Figure 6.11
The full data set includes 50 observations of each species.

⬚	A	B	C	D	E	F	G	H	I	J	K
		Sepal	Sepal	Petal	Petal			Average of	Average of	Average of	Average of
1	Species	length	width	length	width		Row Labels ▾	Sepal length	Sepal width	Petal length	Petal width
2	Setosa	4.3	3	1.1	0.1		Setosa	5.006	3.428	1.462	0.246
3	Setosa	4.4	2.9	1.4	0.2		Versicolor	5.936	2.770	4.260	1.326
4	Setosa	4.4	3	1.3	0.2		Virginica	6.588	2.974	5.552	2.026
5	Setosa	4.4	3.2	1.3	0.2		Grand Total	5.843	3.057	3.758	1.199
6	Setosa	4.5	2.3	1.3	0.3						
7	Setosa	4.6	3.1	1.5	0.2						
8	Setosa	4.6	3.4	1.4	0.3						
9	Setosa	4.6	3.6	1	0.2						

Figure 6.11 also shows a pivot table with the average value of each of the four predictor variables for each species. The pivot table also shows the grand mean of each variable across species. This pivot table is useful for the next step in the analysis, which is to convert each observation to a deviation from a mean value. Figure 6.12 shows the start of that process.

Figure 6.12
Each value is expressed as a deviation from a different mean, and each observation as a deviation from a different centroid.

A3	▾	f_x	='Fig 6.11'!B2-'Fig 6.11'!H$5

⬚	A	B	C	D	E	F	G
1		Deviations from Grand Means					
2	Sepal Length	Sepal Width	Petal Length	Petal Width			
3	-1.543	-0.057	-2.658	-1.099			
4	-1.443	-0.157	-2.358	-0.999			
5	-1.443	-0.057	-2.458	-0.999			
6	-1.443	0.143	-2.458	-0.999			
7	-1.343	-0.757	-2.458	-0.899			
8	-1.243	0.043	-2.258	-0.999			

Figure 6.12 begins to demonstrate the reason that you seldom see a display of the full process of discriminant analysis. It's not conceptually complex, but for any really interesting problem it takes up an awful lot of space. So the calculations detailed in this chapter usually take place in the memory arrays established and managed by coding languages such as C# or VBA. In normal situations it's fine to keep the intermediate calculations out of the way, but learning about the specifics of an analysis is not a normal situation.

Therefore, you see in Figure 6.12 the mean-corrected values of each of the 600 original measures (four predictor variables measured on 150 irises). In each case the mean of the predictor variable is subtracted from the original value to yield a deviation, or *mean-corrected value*.

As you can see in Figure 6.12, the formula in cell A3 is

='Fig 6.11'!B2-'Fig 6.11'!H$5

If you refer to Figure 6.11, you see that the formula subtracts the grand mean for sepal length (in the pivot table) from the first iris's value for sepal length.

> **TIP**
>
> In the previous formula, notice the dollar sign before the 5 in the mixed reference H$5. That dollar sign anchors the reference to row 5. With that dollar sign in place, you can drag the formula three columns to the right, ending up with this formula in cell D3:
>
> ='Fig 6.11'!E2-'Fig 6.11'!K$5
>
> Now the range A3:D3 can be copied and pasted, or autofilled using the fill handle, down through the next 149 rows. The references to cells that contain the grand means, H$5:K$5, remain unchanged, so that (for example) cell A152 contains this formula:
>
> ='Fig 6.11'!B151-'Fig 6.11'!H$5

The deviations from the grand means in Figure 6.12 have but two purposes:

- To create the species centroids shown in Figure 6.13
- To provide deviations from the species centroids shown in Figure 6.14

In Figure 6.13, cell B4 contains this formula:

=AVERAGE('Fig 6.12'!A3:A52)

Figure 6.13
Each species' centroid includes the four means of the mean-corrected values shown in Figure 6.12.

	B4		f_x =AVERAGE('Fig 6.12'!A3:A52)		
	A	B	C	D	E
1	Centroids of Mean Corrected Values				
2					
3		Sepal Length	Sepal Width	Petal Length	Petal Width
4	Setosa	-0.837	0.371	-2.296	-0.953
5	Versicolor	0.093	-0.287	0.502	0.127
6	Virginica	0.745	-0.083	1.794	0.827

It is the average of the mean-corrected sepal length of the first 50 irises, all of which belong to the setosa species. In other words, the average sepal length of setosa irises is 0.837 *below* the mean sepal length of all 150 irises. Similarly, the average sepal length of versicolor irises is 0.093 *above* the mean sepal length of all 150 irises.

Other cells in the range B4:E6 in Figure 6.13 calculate the means of the mean-corrected (or *deviation*) values of the other three predictor variables for each species. So the range B4:E4 shows the average deviation of 50 setosa irises, on four variables, from each variable's grand mean across 150 irises.

Similarly, the range B5:E5 shows the average deviation of 50 versicolor irises, on four variables, from each variable's grand mean across 150 irises. The range B5:E5 contains the centroid of the versicolor irises.

> **NOTE**
>
> There are quicker and more elegant ways to get the mean deviations shown in Figure 6.13, typically making use of the =SUM(IF structure in array formulas. If you're comfortable with those techniques in Excel worksheets, by all means use them. Although those formulas are more elegant, some readers find that the array formulas tend to obscure the purpose of the calculations.

At this point, we have each individual observation expressed as a deviation from the four grand means of all 150 irises (refer to Figure 6.12). We also have the centroid of each species (that is, the vector of the four mean values of each species) expressed as a deviation from the grand mean (refer to Figure 6.13).

The next step, shown in Figure 6.14, is to get the deviation of each individual value (mean-corrected for the grand mean as shown in Figure 6.12) from each species mean (also mean-corrected for the grand mean as shown in Figure 6.13).

Figure 6.14

Deviations of each iris's profile from the centroid of each species.

A3				f_x	='Fig 6.12'!A3-'Fig 6.13'!B$4						
	A	B	C	D	E	F	G	H	I	J	K	L
1		Deviations from Setosa Centroid				Deviations from Versicolor Centroid				Deviations from Virginica Centroid		
2	Sepal Length	Sepal Width	Petal Length	Petal Width	Sepal Length	Sepal Width	Petal Length	Petal Width	Sepal Length	Sepal Width	Petal Length	Petal Width
3	-0.706	-0.428	-0.362	-0.146	-1.636	0.23	-3.16	-1.226	-2.288	0.026	-4.452	-1.926
4	-0.606	-0.528	-0.062	-0.046	-1.536	0.13	-2.86	-1.126	-2.188	-0.074	-4.152	-1.826
5	-0.606	-0.428	-0.162	-0.046	-1.536	0.23	-2.96	-1.126	-2.188	0.026	-4.252	-1.826
6	-0.606	-0.228	-0.162	-0.046	-1.536	0.43	-2.96	-1.126	-2.188	0.226	-4.252	-1.826
7	-0.506	-1.128	-0.162	0.054	-1.436	-0.47	-2.96	-1.026	-2.088	-0.674	-4.252	-1.726
8	-0.406	-0.328	0.038	-0.046	-1.336	0.33	-2.76	-1.126	-1.988	0.126	-4.052	-1.826
9	-0.406	-0.028	-0.062	0.054	-1.336	0.63	-2.86	-1.026	-1.988	0.426	-4.152	-1.726
10	-0.406	0.172	-0.462	-0.046	-1.336	0.83	-3.26	-1.126	-1.988	0.626	-4.552	-1.826
11	-0.406	-0.228	-0.062	-0.046	-1.336	0.43	-2.86	-1.126	-1.988	0.226	-4.152	-1.826

> **NOTE**
>
> The same result comes about by subtracting the mean of a given variable for a given species from the value of that variable for a given iris from each species, but that approach can get even more unwieldy.

One of the effects of this step, and therefore of the steps that lead up to it, is to remove the effect of the grand mean of each variable from each measurement. For example, petal lengths tend to be greater than petal widths. By expressing each measure as a deviation first from the grand mean and then from its species mean, we remove the effect of the (largely irrelevant) fact that a petal length tends to be quantitatively larger than a petal width, just by virtue of the fact that it's a length rather than a width.

Figure 6.14 shows the deviation of the four measures taken on each iris from the mean *of a particular species*. For example, cell A3 in Figure 6.14 shows the deviation of that iris's raw sepal length from the mean sepal length of all setosa irises in the sample. As you get farther down the worksheet into the versicolor and virginica irises, you see that the cells display the difference of a versicolor iris's sepal length from the mean setosa sepal length.

The same is true for the sepal width, petal length, and petal width measures in columns B, C, and D in Figure 6.14. In each case, the deviation of an iris's measure is taken from the mean of that measure for all setosa irises.

> **NOTE** You might find that some authors who write on the topic of discriminant analysis use the term *profile* to denote the set of measures on the predictor variables for a given case. That makes it easier to distinguish the *profile* measures for a specific record (for example, person or iris) from the *centroid* measures for a particular category (for example, political affiliation or species).

It's these deviations that form the basis for the D^2 measures. The smaller the deviation from a species' mean on a given measure, the greater the likelihood that an iris belongs to that species.

Figure 6.14 repeats the calculations in columns A through D in columns E through H and in columns I through L. Columns E through H deviate each iris's measures from the mean values for the versicolor species, and Columns I through L deviate the measures from the mean values for the virginica species.

Adjusting for the Variance-Covariance Matrix

The final step in classifying cases using Mahalanobis' D^2 is to adjust the cases' profiles for the predictor variables' variances and covariances with other predictors. Figure 6.15 shows how this is done.

Each of the 150 irises is assigned three D^2 values in Figure 6.15. Each D^2 value expresses the iris profile's Mahalanobis distance from a different species centroid. For example, the iris in Row 10 of Figure 6.15 is about 2.4 units from the setosa centroid, but about 90 and about 181 units from the versicolor and virginica centroids. Because it is much closer to the setosa centroid, D^2 classification would assign the iris to that group.

Figure 6.15

The covariance matrix is provided by the Discrim add-in.

B10	▾	fx	{=MMULT('Fig 6.14'!A3:D3,MMULT($B$3:$E$6,TRANSPOSE('Fig 6.14'!A3:D3)))}				
	A	B	C	D	E	F	G	H	I

▲	A	B	C	D	E	F	G	H	I
1		Inverse of pooled within groups covariance matrix							
2		Sepal length	Sepal width	Petal length	Petal width				
3	Sepal length	10.8435	-5.3772	-8.9919	3.4174				
4	Sepal width	-5.3772	14.2339	2.6698	-8.9063				
5	Petal length	-8.9919	2.6698	14.7892	-8.9064				
6	Petal width	3.4174	-8.9063	-8.9064	36.7724				
7									
8			D^2						
9		Setosa	Versicolor	Virginica			Group per D^2	Actual species
10		2.366	89.642	181.417			1	Setosa
11		3.850	71.641	155.927			1	Setosa
12		2.578	78.000	164.475			1	Setosa
13		2.005	84.033	171.863			1	Setosa
14		15.800	64.904	144.357			1	Setosa

Here's how you arrive at the D^2 values. The formula that returns the 2.366 value in cell B10 is

=MMULT('Fig 6.14'!A3:D3,MMULT($B$3:$E$6,TRANSPOSE('Fig 6.14'!A3:D3)))

The formula must be array-entered, using Ctrl+Shift+Enter instead of simply Enter. Note the curly brackets around the formula in Figure 6.15's Formula box, which indicate that Excel has interpreted it as an array formula.

In contrast, the array formula that returns 89.642 in cell C10 is

=MMULT('Fig 6.14'!E3:H3,MMULT($B$3:$E$6,TRANSPOSE('Fig 6.14'!E3:H3)))

The difference between the formulas in B10 and C10 is entirely due to the deviation profile for that iris found in Figure 6.14. In the second instance of the formula, the deviation profile in the range E3:H3 is used. That is the deviations of the iris's measurements from versicolor's centroid, whereas in the first instance of the formula the deviations are from setosa's centroid.

Each of the two previous formulas involves a matrix and a vector. The vector is used twice: once oriented as a row (A3:D3) and once as a column (TRANSPOSE(A3:D3)). The range A3:D3, found in Figure 6.14, consists of the deviations of an iris's raw profile from the setosa species centroid. It is the multivariate version of a value minus a mean, as in the numerator of a z-score.

The matrix in the previous formula is used once. It is the *inverse* of the pooled within-groups variance-covariance matrix, and it is provided in the results of running the Discrim add-in (it is found on the worksheet named *Eigenstructures and Coefficients*). In Figure 6.15 it is located in the range B3:E6.

The formula for D^2 premultiplies the iris's deviation profile in A3:D3 by the inverse of the variance-covariance matrix and therefore divides the profile by the variance-covariance matrix. (Recall that matrix algebra does not have a "matrix division" procedure in the sense that it has a matrix multiplication procedure. Instead of matrix division, matrix algebra takes the inverse of a matrix and then postmultiplies the result by another matrix.)

Finally, the formula once again uses the iris's deviation profile to premultiply the result of "dividing" the deviations by the variance-covariance matrix.

So, making allowances for the complications induced by the conventions of matrix algebra, the formula for D^2 comprises the square of some deviation scores (those scores are used as both a pre- and a postmultiplier) and divides by a variance-covariance matrix. The variance is, of course, the square of the standard deviation. The covariance is closely analogous to the variance, as you likely know. The variance of a given variable is precisely equivalent to the variable's covariance with itself.

What we have, therefore, in D^2 is a multivariate version of a chi-square value, the square of a z-score:

$$(X - \bar{X})^2 / s^2$$

And some analysts treat the generalized distance measure as a chi-square, interpreting the probability associated with its value as a chi-square variate as the proportion of cases as close to, or closer to, a group's centroid than does the individual record with that particular D^2.

By "dividing" by the variance-covariance matrix, D^2 removes the effect of different variances and covariances for different variables, much as a univariate z-score removes the effect of the size of the standard deviation from the difference between an observed value and the mean of the group that the observation belongs to.

Assigning a Classification

For a given case, the smallest value of D^2 indicates which group the case should be classified into. So, in Figure 6.15, all the visible cases in rows 10 through 24 have as their smallest D^2 the value in column B. Because that is the D^2 calculated using the setosa centroid, we classify those irises into that group.

Although you can't see it in Figure 6.15, the values for row 60 are, in order, 66.849, 5.598, and 37.608. So the smallest D^2 of 5.598 is the second of the three and corresponds to the deviations from the versicolor centroid and the case is assigned to that group.

Excel provides an easy way to classify all the cases. In Figure 6.15, notice the value 1 in cell G10. Its formula is

=MATCH(MIN(B10:D10),B10:D10,0)

Working from the inside out, this fragment

MIN(B10:D10)

returns the smallest value in the range B10:D10, which is 2.366.

The MATCH function finds a value inside a range of values and returns its position within that range. So, simplifying the original formula, we have

=MATCH(2.366,B10:D10,0)

That formula tells Excel to find 2.366 in the range B10:D10 and return its position in the range. Because it's the first value in the range, Excel returns the value 1. (The final argument to the MATCH function, which in this case is 0, instructs MATCH that an exact match is required and that the values in the range are not necessarily in a sorted order.)

Copying the formula in cell G10 through cell G159 results, for each iris, in a classification as 1, 2, or 3, which correspond to setosa, versicolor, or virginica due to the way the profiles in Figure 6.14 are set up: Setosa in columns A through D, versicolor in columns E through H, and virginica in columns I through L.

Creating the Classification Table

Classification procedures usually involve creating a table that shows how actual classifications line up with predicted classifications. (Various scientific fields and many different analysts refer to this sort of table by a variety of names, including *contingency table* and *confusion table*.)

Still in Figure 6.15, I supplied the original species identifications for each iris in column H. Now the range G10:H159 is used as the source data for the pivot table shown in Figure 6.16.

Figure 6.16
The predicted classifications are almost perfectly accurate.

	A	B	C	D	E
1					
2	Count of Actual species				
3		1	2	3	Grand Total
4	Setosa	50			50
5	Versicolor		48	2	50
6	Virginica		1	49	50
7	Grand Total	50	49	51	150

According to the table in Figure 6.16, 147 of the 150 irises (98%) have been correctly classified by the combination of discriminant analysis and D^2. This outcome is not surprising, given the separation of the three groups shown previously in Figure 6.5. There, the first discriminant function separates setosa clearly from the other two species, whereas there is no such clear separation between versicolor and virginica. Although some overlap exists between versicolor and virginica on the first function, it's narrow, and the two species remain well separated on the horizontal axis.

That outcome is echoed by the table in Figure 6.16, which shows that D^2 has mis-assigned two versicolors as virginica and one virginica as versicolor.

Training Samples: The Classification Is Known Beforehand

If you do much work or reading in the area of discriminant analysis you're likely to encounter the terms *training* and *test* samples (alternatively, the terms *supervised* and *unsupervised* are sometimes used). These terms have to do with whether you allow discriminant analysis to corroborate the existing classifications for a given data set (as with the iris data set), or you use classification figures from one data set on a second data set that has no known classification information. In effect, the use of both a training and a test sample is an exercise in cross-validation of the sort discussed in Chapter 2, "Logistic Regression."

One problem with methods based on the General Linear Model (and those methods include everything from t-tests to canonical correlation) is that they are apt to overestimate their own accuracy.

This phenomenon might be most familiar in the context of multiple regression analysis, where most statistical packages include something called the *adjusted R²*. The math that underlies multiple regression treats the bivariate correlations between the variables (and therefore the measurements they depend on) as though they were free of error. That perfection never comes about in practice.

Suppose that you apply the regression coefficients that you obtain from a multiple regression analysis to a different set of data than you used to calculate the coefficients. Then, calculate the correlation between the predicted and actual Y values in the second data set—in effect, that's a multiple R. The second multiple R is generally smaller than the multiple R reported by your original analysis. The errors that lead to an inflated multiple R in the first data set are different from the errors that exist in the second data set, and therefore the regression coefficients can't take advantage of them in the second set. They're not there.

A popular and apt term for this sort of thing is *capitalization on chance*. (Another is *shrinkage*.) The adjusted multiple R reported by many regression applications is an attempt to account for shrinkage by adjusting the multiple R down, according to the relationship between the number of predictor variables and the sample size. An adjusted multiple R can help in your interpretation of the results, but it's not as strong a check as is cross-validation. Of course, it costs nothing to calculate an adjusted R, whereas it can be terribly expensive to get your hands on another sample, especially of people, to validate your results with.

Group probabilities are determined in different ways by different packages. Some use what's termed *equal priors* and assume that cases are equally distributed across groups in the population from which your sample was taken. Other packages default to *proportional priors*, which assume that the probabilities of group membership in the population are identical to

6

the distribution of cases in your sample. (The Discrim add-in for this chapter assumes proportional priors.)

And most packages enable you to specify custom probabilities when you know or suspect that the priors are not equal in the population and that your sample does not reflect the population memberships.

Now suppose that you withhold a randomly selected subset of your cases from the analysis—you omit, say, half or two-thirds of your cases. Treat the remaining cases as a training sample, run a discriminant analysis on them, and record the coefficients and constants that result. Apply these discriminant functions to your withheld data and determine the degree to which the results agree with the *a priori* classifications. You can also use the differences from centroids, in combination with the inverse of the pooled within groups covariance matrix as shown previously in Figure 6.15, to calculate Mahalanobis' D^2 measures on the withheld data. Then check whether the resulting group assignments agree with the *a priori* classifications.

This second analysis is clearly a version of the cross-validation discussed in Chapter 2.

And if you have the resources to conduct a discriminant analysis on both a training sample and a test set, using a respectable number of records in each case, it's definitely worth doing. If you find substantial disagreement in the two analyses, you'll want to back off the results from the training sample. But if you find substantial agreement as to classifications in the two analyses, you can feel much more comfortable with your original findings.

6

Principal Components Analysis

7

This book's chapters on MANOVA and discriminant function analysis discuss how you can apply intermediate statistical techniques—specifically, multivariate analysis—to decision making. In particular, MANOVA provides you with tools that can help with decisions regarding which of two or more categories a person or a flower or a treatment belongs to: Someone who will buy versus someone who won't; one species of iris versus another; a longer life versus a shorter one. Discriminant function analysis can help you fine-tune the preliminary results of a MANOVA, clarifying how the predictor variables work alone and in combination to distinguish those categories from one another.

The final two chapters of this book—Chapter 8, "Cluster Analysis: The Basics," and Chapter 9, "Cluster Analysis: Further Issues"—discuss a technique whose purpose is similar to MANOVA and discriminant analysis, but with a major twist. In discriminant analysis, you know at the outset which category a particular record belongs to (leaving aside the issue of misidentification, which is really just an extreme sort of measurement error). With cluster analysis, you don't know beforehand which category—or *cluster*—a record belongs to, or how many clusters there are, if any.

> **NOTE**
>
> Or, perhaps more often, you know which cluster each record belongs to, but you withhold that information from the analysis. In that way you can subsequently apply the results to a sample whose cluster membership you *don't* know.

You hope that the measures you have for continuous variables will cause the records to sort themselves into meaningful groupings.

This chapter discusses concepts and methods that are used in MANOVA and discriminant analysis, as well as some interesting possibilities for cluster analysis. That's why I decided to place this chapter between discriminant analysis and cluster analysis. I expect it to solidify some of the concepts and techniques discussed in previous chapters and also to lay the groundwork for cluster analysis. (In fact, it's been shown that principal components analysis [PCA] can itself define clusters, as you see in the final sections of this chapter.)

Establishing a Conceptual Framework for Principal Components Analysis

The idea of a principal component often seems mysterious and abstruse to people encountering the notion for the first time. That's especially true when principal components are tweaked a little and given names such as "latent traits" and "rotated factors."

At root, a principal component is a combination of scores on the variables the component comprises, as an SAT (Scholastic Assessment Test) score is a combination of 1s (correct) and 0s (incorrect) on the individual items the test comprises.

Let's begin by drawing some parallels between PCA and analysis techniques that you might find more familiar.

Principal Components and Tests

Suppose that your young cousin gets a score of 1500 on the two-section version of the SAT. That's a fine score. It puts your cousin in the top 1% of those who take the test, and your cousin's educational and professional prospects are quite bright.

But what is an SAT score? It's an arbitrary measurement. It's the total of the correct scores for dozens of questions regarding quantitative topics and critical reasoning. The questions change from year to year and are under frequent attack for cultural bias (and whether an officially correct answer is actually correct—even whether a verifiably correct answer *is* among the available options).

You can't take a scale of SAT scores and chop it up into equally spaced segments, like a ruler is chopped up into equally spaced inches. The 5-point difference between a score of 500 and 505, in the middle of the possible range of scores on the Quantitative section, might represent a difference of one correct answer. But answering one more question correctly might also represent the 25-point difference between a score of 700 and 725. It's a matter of standard deviations, and 34% of the test takers have scores between 500 and 600, whereas only 2% have scores between 700 and 800.

Furthermore, you can't take a scale of SAT Quantitative scores and turn them at a 90-degree angle to a scale of SAT Reasoning scores to create a sixteenth century cross-staff (a device which could measure the height of a building from a distance of a hundred feet). There's no absolute frame of reference to help us orient Quantitative with Reasoning scales, the way a right triangle's opposite and adjacent sides are automatically oriented.

Many people and groups have attacked the SAT over the years, often with good reason. That's probably inevitable, given the stakes. It has been a culturally biased instrument. It doesn't do a good job of predicting college grade point averages—the result of *restriction of range*, a phenomenon that comes about when not everyone who takes the SAT goes on to college.

But an SAT score has conceptual meaning. You can't close your eyes and visualize a score of 700 the way you can visualize the length of 12 inches, but you know what it means. It is built on the sum of many smaller scores, some of which have absolute meanings and some of which don't. Each of those smaller scores—or test items—has a measurable relationship with the total SAT score: One of the foundations of test design and analysis is the correlation between the 0-or-1 score on a given item and the total test score.

All of this makes the SAT much like a principal component. A principal component is a weighted combination of several measures that you can get your hands on. You build up an SAT score by getting scores on many individual test items. Just because an SAT score is an arbitrary construct doesn't imply that it has no intrinsic meaning. It does. You may find that meaning biased, or wrong, or invidious, but it has meaning.

PCA enables you to combine individual measures in quantitatively meaningful ways to construct a *principal component*. The SAT simply adds up the number of questions answered correctly and then applies some conversions to get a two-scale total that ranges from 400 to 1600. PCA looks further into the relationships between the individual measures to suggest exactly how much weight a given variable should have in determining a person's (or a thing's) score on the principal component.

PCA's Ground Rules

PCA also has some special rules that it applies to constructing the components. For example, it insists that as much variability as possible be assigned to the first component the analysis locates. The second component can lay claim only to some portion of whatever variance remains after the first component has been established. The third component has available to it only the variance that hasn't been attributed to the first two components, and so on. Yes, PCA can identify as many components as there are original variables, but it's normal for only the first few to have any useful meaning.

This approach has the effect of making the principal components you identify uncorrelated with one another. Recall that the statistic R^2, which can range from 0 to 1, expresses the percentage of variability that two variables share with one another.

Suppose you have access to, say, 50 variables that you use to measure different behaviors across a company's customers. You run a principal components analysis on those variables and customers. All the variability in those variables that *can* be assigned to the first principal component *is* assigned to that component. The analysis continues by extracting any variability that can be assigned to the second principal component from the remaining variability in the data set.

7

The second component cannot share any variability with the first component. Any variability that can be assigned to the first component is no longer available for attribution to the second component. Therefore the two components cannot share any variance, and their R^2 must be 0.0. Because R^2 is the square of the correlation coefficient, the two components must be uncorrelated. This aspect of PCA turns out to be valuable in situations where uncorrelated variables, such as principal components, help to remove ambiguity that correlated variables tend to obscure.

Correlation and Oblique Factor Rotation

Some analyses that can follow a principal components analysis, such as oblique factor rotation, rotate the components (which are then termed *factors*) so they are no longer at right angles to one another and therefore reintroduce the correlations. This isn't really perverse—there are usually good reasons for it.

For example, one important difference between PCA and factor analysis is that PCA's main intent is data reduction—the replacement of, say, 20 measured variables by perhaps 3 principal components without significant loss of information. Doing so makes subsequent analysis of the data more straightforward. It's almost always more effective to work with 3 inferred components than with 20 measured variables.

But factor analysis takes the position that there may well be underlying (or *latent*) traits that cannot be measured directly and are expressed only through the measurement of variables that you can measure directly. The well-known g-factor in psychometrics is a latent trait that's thought to underlie performance in verbal, quantitative, and other apparently unrelated tasks such as pattern recognition.

The idea is to measure those factors indirectly by quantifying the relationship between the factor that can't be measured and variables that can. It's helpful, of course, to reduce without major loss of information the relatively large number of measured variables to a relatively small number of inferred factors. But although that's an important purpose of PCA, factor analysis has a different goal: the verification that an underlying factor such as the g-factor exists, and the identification of what the factor represents.

The verification of a factor's existence, as well as its meaning, is managed by examining the correlations between the measured variables and the inferred factors. (In the context of PCA and factor analysis, these correlations are termed *loadings*.)

A subsequent section of this chapter, Rotating Factors to a Meaningful Solution, discusses how a procedure called *factor rotation* adjusts and clarifies the loadings so that it's easier to tell what a factor represents. But the rotation method discussed in that section is Varimax rotation, which forces the axes (which are a visual representation of the factors) to remain at 90 degrees from one another—that is, uncorrelated and orthogonal.

Many analysts regard orthogonal rotation such as Varimax as convenient for the purpose of interpretation but unrealistic for the purpose of representing reality. There's usually no special reason to expect two underlying traits, factors that cannot be directly measured, to be uncorrelated. It's probably more realistic to assume that they are correlated.

Oblique rotation methods such as *oblimin* permit the factors to rotate to a solution in which the factors are correlated. The angles between the axes are not forced to equal 90 degrees but are allowed to be oblique. Of course, 90 degree angles between axes are permitted, and if two factors are actually uncorrelated in nature, the oblique rotation is expected to result in an angle that's close to 90 degrees.

This book has no more to say about oblique rotation because it introduces complexities well beyond the book's scope. I have included this section so that when you run across the term "oblique rotation" you'll be familiar enough with it to understand something of the term's implications.

Using the Principal Components Add-In

Enough informal theory for the moment. Let's put some meat on the bones and have a look at a very spare analysis. Figure 7.1 shows measurements on three variables for ten records.

Figure 7.1
Such a small data set is seldom useful for anything other than an example of PCA.

◢	A	B	C	D	E
1	Record Number		Weight	Age	Height
2	1		6	32	27
3	2		5	25	0
4	3		29	5	21
5	4		10	32	26
6	5		1	47	8
7	6		41	20	22
8	7		42	11	5
9	8		18	45	15
10	9		11	11	34
11	10		30	16	36

The numbers shown in Figure 7.1 were created by entering the following formula in the range C2:E11.

=TRUNC(RAND()*50)

I selected C2:E11, typed the formula, and finished with Ctrl+Enter, which is Excel's keyboard sequence to enter multiple formulas in multiple cells. (This is different from the entry of an array formula, which enters *one* formula in multiple cells, each of which usually returns a different result.) Then, with C2:E11 selected, I used the keyboard sequence Ctrl+C to copy the cells, and Alt+E+S+V to paste the results of the formulas as values only. The previous action prevents Excel from recalculating the RAND() functions every time a change is made to the worksheet.

A workbook named Factor.xls is available for download from the publisher's website, quepublishing.com/title/9780789751683. When you open it (and after you have dealt with possible warnings from Excel that it came from the Web and has potentially harmful content in the form of Visual Basic for Applications [VBA] code), the Ribbon's Add-Ins tab gets a new item, Principal Components.

7

Activate the worksheet shown in Figure 7.1 (or one that's similar, with several variables and more records; or, one that contains a correlation matrix) and then click the Principal Components item in the Ribbon's Add-Ins tab. The dialog box shown in Figure 7.2 displays.

Figure 7.2
Use meaningful variable names whenever possible and fill the Variable Labels in First Row check box.

For the data shown in Figure 7.1 you would take these steps after the dialog box shown in Figure 7.2 has opened:

1. Click in the Input Range edit box and drag through the worksheet range C1:E11.
2. Click the Variable Labels in First Row check box.
3. Click in the Record IDs edit box and drag through the range A2:A11. With record IDs such as names, the scores on each component are associated in the results with the records' IDs.
4. Select the Raw Data option button. If you're using a correlation matrix instead of raw data, click its option button. The Number of Observations box becomes enabled, and you should enter the number of records that were used to create the correlation matrix.
5. Click OK.

> **NOTE**
> I discuss the use of the dialog box's Rotation tab later in this chapter. *Don't* run the Principal Components add-in until you've read the section Rotating Factors to a Meaningful Solution.

When you click OK, Excel runs a PCA using the code supplied with the Factor.xls workbook.

Figure 7.3 shows some of the PCA results for the data in Figure 7.1.

Figure 7.3
The variable labels supplied in Figure 7.1 are used to label the results in Figure 7.3.

◢	A	B	C	D
1	R Matrix			
2		Weight	Age	Height
3	Weight	1	-0.60266	0.07880
4	Age	-0.60266	1	-0.27612
5	Height	0.07880	-0.27612	1
6				
7	R Inverse			
8		Weight	Age	Height
9	Weight	1.59113	1.00058	0.15091
10	Age	1.00058	1.71176	0.39381
11	Height	0.15091	0.39381	1.09685
12				
13	Determinant of R matrix = 0.58057			
14				
15	For sphericity test, Chi-square = 3.897, and df = 3			
16	P(Chi-square) = 0.273			

The Correlation Matrix

Whether you supply a correlation matrix or raw observations as your input data, the results always start with the correlation matrix (or *R matrix*) of your variables (in the range B3:D5 in Figure 7.3) and its inverse (in B9:D11). There can be good reasons to base the principal components analysis on a covariance matrix rather than a correlation matrix. However, I find that using a correlation matrix makes it easier to interpret the eigenvalues. Regardless of whether you use a covariance or a correlation matrix to start an analysis, the eigenvalues sum to the *trace* of the matrix.

> **NOTE** The trace is the sum of the elements in the main diagonal of the matrix.

When you're using a correlation matrix, the trace is simply the number of variables in the matrix, because each element in the main diagonal equals 1.0. That makes it easy to see how much of the original variance is associated with each root.

> **NOTE** *Root,* or *characteristic root,* is simply another term for eigenvalue.

The Inverse of the R Matrix

The inverse of the R matrix, often symbolized as R^{-1}, is useful for a variety of reasons. For example, it makes it easy to get the R^2 (also termed a *squared multiple correlation,* or SMC) between each original variable and the remaining variables in the matrix.

7

Apart from the reasons that the inverse of an R matrix is useful, it helps to know what it is. The inverse of a matrix (which need not be an R matrix) is the multivariate version of a simple inverse or reciprocal. Only square matrices have inverses: a 3 row by 3 column matrix has an inverse; a 3 row by 4 column matrix does not. The inverse of a matrix has the same dimensions as the original matrix.

Although it takes a square matrix to have an inverse, it's not sufficient. Many square matrices do not have an inverse. A number called a *determinant* is associated with each square matrix, and it's a function of the specific numbers in the matrix. If a matrix has a determinant of specifically zero, the matrix cannot be inverted. A matrix with a determinant of zero typically has a linear dependency somewhere in it: for example, two variables whose correlation is 1.0, or two variables which, combined, bear a correlation of 1.0 with a third variable. An R matrix with a determinant of zero, which contains a linear dependency, and which therefore cannot be inverted, is useless for PCA. (A raw data matrix that results in an R matrix that can't be inverted is also useless for PCA.)

Relatively recent developments in the algorithms for the extraction of principal components have enabled the identification of the source of linear dependency in a matrix via *QR decomposition*. The resulting code removes from the matrix the source of the dependence. Since Excel 2003, the LINEST() function has employed QR decomposition.

CAUTION

Most mainstream statistical applications such as SAS and SPSS accompany their results with a warning that QR decomposition has removed one or more variables from the analysis—when that is true, of course. LINEST() does not do so. Instead, it sets both the coefficient and the standard error for one of the variables that creates the dependency to zero. I suggest that you try to make it a habit to glance at each predictor variable's coefficient and standard error, in the first two rows of the LINEST() results. If they are both zero for a given predictor variable, LINEST() has almost certainly removed that variable from the equation. So doing changes the degrees of freedom, and you'll therefore want to exercise special care in interpreting the inferential statistics in the third through fifth rows of the LINEST() results.

If you postmultiply a square matrix by its inverse (or if you postmultiply the inverse of a matrix by the original matrix), the result is an *identity matrix*. An identity matrix is a special case of a *diagonal matrix*. In a diagonal matrix, all cells that are not on the main diagonal each have a value of zero (the main diagonal consists of cells [1,1], [2,2], [3,3] and so on). An identity matrix is a diagonal matrix that has 1s in each cell of the main diagonal and, of course, 0s in all other cells.

Excel has an MINVERSE() function that returns the inverse of a square matrix, and an MDETERM() function that returns the determinant of a square matrix. These worksheet functions are welcome because for a data set with more than two variables, calculating a matrix inverse or a determinant is enormously tedious and error prone.

Continuing with the example data in Figure 7.1, suppose you want to find the R^2 between Weight as a predicted variable in a multiple regression analysis, and Age and Height as the predictors. In Excel, you need to use the LINEST() worksheet function, which returns R^2 in the third row, first column of its results. If you want to do the same for Age as a predicted variable and Height as a predicted variable, you need to deploy LINEST() twice more.

Why would you want to get those R^2 or SMC values? They are often used in factor analysis. An R matrix is a typical source of information for a factor analysis, which is interested in the variance shared by the variables in the R matrix, but not in variance that is specific or unique to particular variables. A variable's correlation with itself is 1.0, and so is its R^2: A variable shares 100% of its variance with itself. But some of that variance is unique to the variable and is not shared with any of the other variables in the R matrix.

Therefore, to put a ceiling on the proportion of variance in a particular variable that is to be considered by the factor analysis, the SMCs are used to replace the 1.0 values in the R matrix. Using a variable's SMC with the other variables in the analysis removes that variable's unique variance from the process—variance that would be included if values of 1.0 were used in the main diagonal of the R matrix.

If you have run a principal components analysis in preparation for a factor analysis, you can get the SMCs much more easily than by repeatedly entering LINEST() once for each variable. Figure 7.4 shows how to get them from the inverse of the R matrix.

Figure 7.4
LINEST()'s x-values, or predictors, must occupy contiguous columns, so you must provide different layouts of the precedent cells for different instances of LINEST().

	A	B	C	D	E	F	G	H	I	J	K
1	Weight	Age	Height		Age	Weight	Height		Height	Weight	Age
2	6	32	27		32	6	27		27	6	32
3	5	25	0		25	5	0		0	5	25
4	29	5	21		5	29	21		21	29	5
5	10	32	26		32	10	26		26	10	32
6	1	47	8		47	1	8		8	1	47
7	41	20	22		20	41	22		22	41	20
8	42	11	5		11	42	5		5	42	11
9	18	45	15		45	18	15		15	18	45
10	11	11	34		11	11	34		34	11	11
11	30	16	36		16	30	36		36	30	16
12											
13	-0.118	-0.660	37.701		-0.273	-0.557	40.443		-0.303	-0.110	28.914
14	0.388	0.327	13.128		0.344	0.276	9.108		0.381	0.363	15.213
15	0.372	13.627	#N/A		0.416	12.514	#N/A		0.088	13.173	#N/A
16	2.069	7	#N/A		2.491	7	#N/A		0.339	7	#N/A
17	768.328	1299.772	#N/A		780.217	1096.183	#N/A		117.649	1214.751	#N/A
18											
19	R Inverse				1-(1/R-inverse)						
20		Weight	Age	Height		Weight	Age	Height			
21	Weight	1.591	1.001	0.151	Weight	0.372					
22	Age	1.001	1.712	0.394	Age		0.416				
23	Height	0.151	0.394	1.097	Height			0.088			

7

Figure 7.4 shows three different R^2 values of interest as calculated by LINEST(), in cells A15, E15, and I15. Cell A15 is the result of regressing Weight on Age and Height; E15 is the R^2 for Age on Weight and Height; and I15 is the R^2 for Height on Weight and Age.

The range B21:D23 repeats the inverse of the R matrix that appears in Figure 7.3, cells B9:D11. The range G21:I23—more specifically, its main diagonal—contains these formulas:

    =1-(1/B21)

    =1-(1/C22)

    =1-(1/D23)

Note that G21:I23 returns the same values as are reported by LINEST() in A15, E15, and I15: the SMCs of each variable with the remaining variables in the original R matrix. This makes it easy to replace the 1.0 values in the R matrix, in preparation for a factor analysis.

> **N O T E**   The inverse of the R matrix has other uses. For example, its values are used when you want to get factor coefficients after the principal components, or the factors, have been rotated by Varimax or some other method of rotation.

The Sphericity Test

The sphericity test shown in rows 15 and 16 of Figure 7.3 checks the likelihood that the correlation matrix in the population from which the observations are sampled is actually an identity matrix, with values of 1.0 in the main diagonal and values of 0.0 elsewhere. If that is the case, the variables in the population have (trivially) correlations of 1.0 with themselves and 0.0 with all other variables in the matrix. Then the variables are already uncorrelated and independent of one another in the population, and there is no point to conducting a principal component analysis to locate combinations of variables that *are* uncorrelated.

For the example analyzed in Figure 7.3, the chi-square value is fairly small given the number of degrees of freedom. As shown in cell A16, you would expect to get a chi-square value at least this large 27% of the time that the correlation matrix in the population is the identity matrix. (Of course with a much larger sample than the 10 cases used here you might easily get a much larger value of chi-square: one that is significant at, say, the 0.01 level, or whatever alpha level is appropriate for the decision you're making.) Normally you would not proceed after these sphericity test results. They offer no compelling reason to reject the hypothesis that the correlation matrix is an identity matrix when it's based on a full population. But this is an example so we'll press on.

The sphericity test, developed by Maurice Bartlett in 1950, is a multivariate test for independence. The reason for the term *sphericity* is that in, say, three dimensions, a swarm of data points measured on three normally distributed variables would tend to resemble a sphere if the variables were uncorrelated. The resemblance would become more pronounced as you add more records to the data set. Similarly, in two dimensions, if you use a scatterplot to chart two uncorrelated variables, you tend to get a circle. (That circle elongates to an ellipse and then to a straight line if you change the correlation between the variables from 0.0 to 0.5 to 1.0.)

The conventional wisdom is that if you have a large number of records in your sample, you can skip the sphericity test and not worry too much about it. With a small sample, it's a good idea to pay attention to its results. In such a case it's all too easy to obtain moderately strong correlations that are due to sampling error from a population in which the correlations are effectively 0.0.

The sphericity test depends on the determinant of the correlation matrix as a measure of the generalized variance, and the principal components output reports the determinant (see Figure 7.3, cell A13).

Counting Eigenvalues, Calculating Coefficients and Understanding Communalities

Figure 7.5 shows more of the results on the Principal Components worksheet created by the Factor.xls workbook that accompanies this chapter.

Figure 7.5

This information completes the Principal Components worksheet. Additional information pertaining to Varimax rotations appears on separate worksheets.

	A	B	C	D	E	F
18	**Eigenvalues**					
19		Factor 1	Factor 2	Factor 3		
20		1.69525	0.94069	0.36406		
21						
22	**Eigenvectors**					
23		Factor 1	Factor 2	Factor 3		
24	Weight	0.63665	-0.40884	-0.65386		
25	Age	-0.68923	0.07864	-0.72026		
26	Height	0.34589	0.90921	-0.23172		
27						
28	**Factor Score Coefficients**					
29		Factor 1	Factor 2	Factor 3		
30	Weight	0.48897	-0.42153	-1.08367		
31	Age	-0.52936	0.08108	-1.19372		
32	Height	0.26565	0.93744	-0.38404		
33						
34	**Factor Structure**					
35		Factor 1	Factor 2	Factor 3		
36	Weight	0.82893	-0.39653	-0.39452		
37	Age	-0.89740	0.07627	-0.43459		
38	Height	0.45035	0.88184	-0.13981		
39						
40	**Squared Loadings**	Factor 1	Factor 2	Factor 3	h^2, 2 Factors	SMCs
41	Weight	68.7%	15.7%	15.6%	84.4%	0.37151
42	Age	80.5%	0.6%	18.9%	81.1%	0.41581
43	Height	20.3%	77.8%	2.0%	98.0%	0.08830
44						
45	**Factor Scores**					
46		Factor 1	Factor 2	Factor 3		
47		-0.57101	1.05205	0.08707		
48		0.95588	1.15283	1.67073		

The set of data that appears in Figure 7.5 helps you decide whether a principal component is worth retaining, and if so what the component means. The eigenvalues, shown in the range B20:D20 of Figure 7.5, are particularly important to your decisions regarding how many components you will regard as meaningful. The factor structure (perhaps more familiarly known as *loadings*) in the range B36:D38 can help you determine what a given component measures—and thus what its meaning is.

How Many Components?

The question of the number of components to retain can be a thorny one, and theorists have advanced various methods both objective and subjective to help get to an answer. Henry Kaiser, the developer of the Varimax method of factor rotation, proposed (and argued effectively) that although the decision should be guided by your understanding of the nature of the data set, you should retain only components that have eigenvalues of 1.0 or greater. Many purely statistical applications provide that decision rule as the default method of deciding how many components to retain.

> **NOTE**
>
> It's normal for the first component extracted to have the largest eigenvalue, the second component the next largest eigenvalue, and so on. This pattern has suggested another one of the decision rules, called the *scree test*. If you plot the eigenvalues on a line chart the result resembles the pattern of scree, or rocky debris, that collects at the bottom of a cliff due to erosion. The idea is that there's a perceptible elbow that you can see as the slope of the eigenvalues changes from more vertical to more horizontal, and that elbow tells you where to stop considering components. This is at root a subjective test, and I'm uncomfortable recommending it to you. Many would feel perfectly comfortable recommending the scree test, justifiably so.

The eigenvalues for this particular data set appear in Figure 7.5. Only one, the first, is greater than 1.0: The data suggest that these variables represent just one principal component.

Kaiser cited several reasons for his recommendation that only principal components with eigenvalues of at least 1.0 be retained. One largely intuitive reason that appeals to me is that a principal component is a measure of *common* variance—that is, variance to which more than one measured variable contributes. As such, a retained component ought to account for at least as much variance as any single variable. When the basis for the extraction of the components is a correlation rather than a covariance matrix, a single variable's contributed variance is 1.0, and therefore a retained component's eigenvalue ought to be at least 1.0.

But it often happens that the first component extracted has a much larger eigenvalue than subsequent components. Further, those subsequent components wind up with smaller eigenvalues than you might expect them to have, given your knowledge of the nature and strength of the relationships between the variables. Whatever considerations you decide to adopt as criteria for dropping components from subsequent analysis, your attention begins to shift from the eigenvalues to the eigenvectors. More precisely, your attention shifts to the structure of the components—the loadings—whose values are calculated from the eigenvectors.

7

It's at this point that you begin to move past PCA and into *factor analysis*. One common procedure in factor analysis (where you start to refer to principal components as factors) is to rotate the factors as though they were axes on a scatterchart. The original data points remain in place with respect to one another, but the factors are rotated around the point where they intersect.

Because the data points remain in place, the locations where the points project onto the factors change as the factors rotate. The changes due to the rotation often have the effect of clarifying the structure of the factors. Ideally, this clarification approximates something called *simple structure*.

A set of factors that exhibits simple structure has factors whose loadings are either strong (say, 0.80 or greater) or weak (say, 0.30 or smaller). The variables associated with the strong loadings ought to hang together conceptually. So, in a well-known analysis of crime rates in different states, one factor has high loadings on robbery, burglary, larceny, and auto theft, and low loadings with other types of crime. Another factor has high loadings on murder and assault, and low loadings elsewhere. (The sole exception is rape, which displays a moderate loading on both factors.)

The variables that load strongly on each factor are conceptually related: robbery, burglary, larceny, and auto theft are crimes against property, whereas murder and assault are crimes against persons. It's this sort of simple structure that we're looking for when we undertake a PCA in the first place, and subsequently when we extend it to the techniques of factor analysis, such as factor rotation.

I should note that the simple structure in the crime data was achieved only after factor rotation. The initial factor structure after component extraction but before factor rotation yielded one factor on which every crime except murder loaded strongly, and a second factor on which only murder loaded strongly. The principal components analysis achieved one of its purposes, to reduce the seven original variables to a more manageable pair of components. But the variables that define the components were "Not Murder"—that is, all the crimes other than murder—and "Murder." The factor rotation results in an outcome that's conceptually much richer.

> **NOTE** I discuss the crime study in the context of classification in the final section of this chapter.

The Factor.xls workbook that accompanies the downloadable files for this chapter performs a Varimax rotation on the initial principal components. I discuss that later in this chapter. For now, be aware that factor structures of the sort shown in the range B36:D38 of Figure 7.5 often appear uninformative at first, and rotating the factors is necessary before they begin to make sense.

7

Factor Score Coefficients

Factor score coefficients are reported for this example in the range B30:D32 of Figure 7.5. These are the coefficients used to calculate scores on each factor for each original record.

> **NOTE**
> If you provide a correlation matrix rather than raw observations, you still get factor score coefficients for both an unrotated and a Varimax solution. However, you do not get automatically calculated factor scores, rotated or not, because the raw observations can't be derived from the correlation matrix.

You use the coefficients for a given factor by first converting the raw observations to z-scores: Subtract each variable's mean from the actual observation and divide the result by the standard deviation of that variable. (Treat the observations as though they were a population: Use Excel's STDEV.P() function rather than its STDEV.S() function.)

Then, for each record, multiply the z-score on each variable by the corresponding coefficient for the variable on the factor you're calculating. Add the products to get the record's score on that factor.

You don't need to carry out these calculations for records that you supply; the factor scores are calculated and reported automatically. You do need to carry them out for new records that you did not include in the original principal components analysis. Use the means and standard deviations from the original data set. Do not use the new records to recalculate them.

Communalities

A variable's *communality* is the amount of its variance associated with the components that you extract from the correlation matrix. (You sometimes see *communality* symbolized as h^2.) The communalities are the sum of the squared factor loadings from the structure matrix in B36:D38.

The communalities, by the way, are not affected by Varimax rotation. The individual loadings are affected—that's the whole point of rotating the factors. But suppose you call for the analysis to retain two of three factors for the Varimax rotation. The loadings for the first two rotated factors are virtually certain to differ from the loadings for the first two unrotated factors. However, the sum of the squares of the rotated loadings would equal the sum of the squares of the unrotated loadings. The loadings change; the communalities don't.

Bear in mind that loadings are correlations: the correlations between the original variables and the extracted factors. Therefore the squares of the loadings are percents of shared variance, and their sum, a variable's communality, is the amount of variance that a variable contributes to the retained factors. As such, the communality is a measure of the relative importance of a variable to the factors you choose to extract.

Relationships Between the Individual Results

I belabored the issue of the inverse of the R matrix and SMCs in earlier sections for two reasons. One is that there are some differences between PCA and factor analysis that are somewhat difficult to articulate, much less pin down. For example, factor analysis often uses SMCs in the main diagonal of the R matrix (rather than 1.0 values as in PCA). That's one difference between PCA and factor analysis that is both objective and that makes good sense.

The other reason is that relationships exist between the different values calculated by PCA, and an awareness of those relationships is helpful when you're trying to get grounded in what PCA is all about. This phenomenon—that is, the relationships between the calculated results—is similar to the results of LINEST(), which reports (among other results) the values for R^2, the standard error of estimate, the degrees of freedom for the residual, and the sum of squares for the regression and the residual. This is all useful stuff, but when you're considering multiple regression it's even more illuminating to consider relationships such as the following:

- ■ R^2 is the ratio of the sum of squares regression to the total of the sum of squares regression and the sum of squares residual.

- ■ The standard error of estimate is the square root of the result of dividing the sum of squares residual by the degrees of freedom for the residual.

- ■ The F-ratio is the ratio of the sum of squares regression, divided by its degrees of freedom, to the sum of squares residual, divided by its degrees of freedom.

You can find more on these matters in Chapter 3, "Univariate Analysis of Variance (ANOVA)." The point is the results of analyses, taken one by one, are often informative regarding a particular data set, but studying the relationships between those results brings about a greater understanding of the analysis itself.

Using the Eigenvalues and Eigenvectors

Take the eigenvalues once again, reported in the range B20:D20 of Figure 7.5. As I noted earlier, when the R matrix is used as input to PCA (rather than a covariance matrix), the eigenvalues sum to the trace of R, or the number of variables in the R matrix. The effect of the scales of measurement of the variables is removed, and you can assess the importance of each root directly, in terms of the number of variables you have at hand.

Furthermore, the continued product of the eigenvalues equals the determinant of R. Specifically, these two formulas return the same result:

=B20*C20*D20

=MDETERM(B3:D5)

(The range B3:D5 refers to the worksheet shown in Figure 7.3.) The first of the two formulas calculates the continued product of the eigenvalues. The second formula uses Excel's

MDETERM() worksheet function to calculate the determinant of the R matrix in B3:D5. Both formulas return 0.58057, which cell A13 in Figure 7.3 reports is the determinant of the R matrix.

As I point out in Chapter 4, "Multivariate Analysis of Variance (MANOVA)," some matrices are not invertible, a situation that arises when the matrix has a determinant of 0. Because the determinant is the continued product of the eigenvalues, you get a determinant of 0 when one (or more) of the eigenvalues is 0. And that can happen when all the variance available to a root has already been assigned to other roots. There's no available variance because all the variance that could be attributed to the next root has been attributed to roots that have already been removed. Therefore, perfect linear dependence exists somewhere in the original matrix.

As you read in this book and in many other sources, that sort of linear dependence is termed *multicollinearity*, and in the extreme case of complete dependence it results in a matrix that cannot be inverted. The route to understanding that goes through understanding the continued product of the eigenvalues.

Eigenvalues, Eigenvectors, and Loadings

In Chapter 6, "Discriminant Function Analysis: Further Issues," I discuss the use of *structure* coefficients to assess the importance of each predictor variable to each discriminant function.

Both discriminant function analysis and multiple regression analysis term these correlation coefficients *structure coefficients*. In multiple regression analysis, each structure coefficient is the correlation between a predictor variable and the set of predicted values, also termed the best combination of the predictor variables—in Excel, the results of the TREND() function. In discriminant analysis, the structure coefficient is the correlation between a predictor variable and a discriminant function.

In PCA, the structure coefficient is the correlation between any given variable in the R matrix and a component. However, PCA usually refers to that correlation as a *loading*, or a *component loading*. (In factor analysis, the correlation is considered to be between any given variable in the R matrix and a factor. There, it's also termed a *loading* or, occasionally, a *factor loading*.)

In any case, whether it's called a loading or a structure coefficient, whether the context is multiple regression or discriminant analysis or PCA or factor analysis, these coefficients are measures of the importance of a variable to some combination of the available variables: a set of predicted values, or a discriminant function, or a principal component, or a factor.

In PCA, one of the results you generally see is a list of the scores each observation has on each component. The principal components routine, in the workbook named Factor.xls that accompanies this chapter's Excel workbook, puts the component scores on the worksheet named Principal Components. Figure 7.6 shows the component scores along with the original variables.

Figure 7.6
The component loadings in B16:D18 are calculated by correlating the original variable scores with the component scores in E3:G12.

B16 =CORREL(A$3:A$12,E$3:E$12)

	A	B	C	D	E	F	G
1	**Original Scores**			**Factor Scores**			
2	Weight	Age	Height		Factor 1	Factor 2	Factor 3
3	6	32	27		-0.5710	1.0521	0.0871
4	5	25	0		-0.9559	-1.1528	1.6707
5	29	5	21		1.1163	-0.2692	0.9064
6	10	32	26		-0.4580	0.8536	-0.1811
7	1	47	8		-1.7580	-0.2557	-0.2112
8	41	20	22		0.9677	-0.4510	-1.3383
9	42	11	5		0.9583	-1.9142	-0.0637
10	18	45	15		-0.9415	-0.1973	-1.5508
11	11	11	34		0.5716	1.3497	1.3074
12	30	16	36		1.0705	0.9848	-0.6266
13							
14							
15		Factor 1	Factor 2	Factor 3			
16	Weight	0.82893	-0.39653	-0.39452			
17	Age	-0.89740	0.07627	-0.43459			
18	Height	0.45035	0.88184	-0.13981			

Figure 7.6 shows how you can calculate the component loadings by brute force. Most PCA routines, including the one available for this chapter, report component or factor scores: the score calculated for each observation on each derived component or factor. With those scores in hand, you can calculate a simple Pearson correlation coefficient for each original variable with each component. In Figure 7.6, that's done in B16:D18.

Compare the loadings in B16:D18 of Figure 7.6 with the loadings reported in Figure 7.5, in the range B36:D38. The results are identical. But Figure 7.7 shows how the eigenvectors can come into play here.

In Figure 7.7 you can see one way that the eigenvalues interact with their associated eigenvectors. The component loadings shown in the range B14:D16 are identical to those reported in Figures 7.5 and 7.6. But in Figure 7.7, they are calculated by taking the square root of each eigenvalue and multiplying that by each element in the corresponding eigenvector.

For example, the three loadings in the range B14:B16 in Figure 7.7 are calculated as follows:

=SQRT(B$3)*B8

=SQRT(B$3)*B9

=SQRT(B$3)*B10

Recall that the eigenvalue is a measure of the variance in the overall correlation matrix that's attributable to the eigenvalue's component. Multiplying each eigenvector's element by the square root of the corresponding eigenvalue simply scales the eigenvector to that of a continuum of correlation coefficients. So the elements of the eigenvectors actually represent the loadings of each variable on each component.

Figure 7.7
The eigenvalues and eigenvectors combine to show the component loadings.

G19	▾			f_x	{=TRANSPOSE(MMULT(G14:I16,TRANSPOSE(B8:D10)))}				
	A	B	C	D	E	F	G	H	I	J
1	Eigenvalues					Diagonal of Eigenvalues				
2		Factor 1	Factor 2	Factor 3			1.69525	0	0	
3		1.69525	0.94069	0.36406			0	0.94069	0	
4							0	0	0.36406	
5										
6	Eigenvectors					Original R Matrix				
7		Factor 1	Factor 2	Factor 3			Weight	Age	Height	
8	Weight	0.63665	-0.40884	-0.65386		Weight	1	-0.60266	0.07880	
9	Age	-0.68923	0.07864	-0.72026		Age	-0.60266	1	-0.27612	
10	Height	0.34589	0.90921	-0.23172		Height	0.07880	-0.27612	1	
11										
12	Factor Structure									
13		Factor 1	Factor 2	Factor 3		Reciprocals of Square Roots of Eigenvalues				
14	Weight	0.82893	-0.3965	-0.3945			0.768038	0	0	
15	Age	-0.8974	0.07627	-0.4346			0	1.031045	0	
16	Height	0.45035	0.88184	-0.1398			0	0	1.657347	
17										
18						Factor Score Coefficients				
19							0.48897	-0.42153	-1.08367	
20							-0.52936	0.08108	-1.19372	
21							0.26565	0.93744	-0.38404	

Notice also in Figure 7.7 that the original correlation matrix can be recovered from the eigenvalues and eigenvectors. A diagonal matrix, with the eigenvalues in the main diagonal, occupies the range G2:I4. Then this array formula is entered in the range G8:I10:

=MMULT(B8:D10,MMULT(G2:I4,TRANSPOSE(B8:D10)))

In words, postmultiply the diagonal matrix in G2:I4 by the transpose of the eigenvectors in B8:D10. Use the result of that operation to postmultiply the eigenvectors. In the more succinct notation of matrix algebra:

R = VLV'

where:

R is the correlation matrix.

V is the eigenvectors and V' is its transpose.

L is the diagonal matrix with the eigenvalues in the main diagonal.

Eigenvalues, Eigenvectors, and Factor Coefficients

You can get the factor coefficients with a method similar to the one used to reconstruct the R matrix. Instead of using the diagonal matrix with the eigenvalues in the diagonal, use the diagonal matrix with the reciprocals of the square roots of the eigenvalues. I have placed that matrix in the range G14:I16 of Figure 7.7, with these formulas in the diagonal:

Cell G14: =1/SQRT(B3)

Cell H15: =1/SQRT(C3)

Cell I16: =1/SQRT(D3)

Now the factor score coefficients are returned using this array formula in the range G19:I21:

=TRANSPOSE(MMULT(G14:I16,TRANSPOSE(B8:D10)))

Again, using matrix algebra notation, this formula equates to the following:

$$\mathbf{C} = \mathbf{L}^{-1/2}\, \mathbf{V'}$$

where:

$\mathbf{C}$ is the matrix of factor coefficients.

$\mathbf{L}^{-1/2}$ is the diagonal matrix of the reciprocals of the square roots of the eigenvalues.

$\mathbf{V'}$ is the transpose of the eigenvectors.

Compare the values returned in G19:I21 of Figure 7.7 with the factor score coefficients shown in B30:D32 of Figure 7.5. This is yet another example of how the combination of the eigenvalues with the eigenvectors provides a valuable piece of the results of principal components analysis.

Getting the Eigenvalues Directly from the Factor Scores

Figure 7.8 demonstrates another relationship between the eigenvectors and the eigenvalues: in particular, how the eigenvalues express the variance in the data set.

The eigenvalues and eigenvectors appear in Figure 7.8, just as they do in previous figures. The range A12:C21 contains the original data, with each variable standardized to zero mean and unit variance.

The range F3:H12 contains this array formula:

=MMULT($A$12:$C$21,B7:D9)

which scales the standardized values according to the elements in the eigenvector corresponding to each component. If you now calculate the variance of each column in F3:H12, as is done in F15:H15, the result is the eigenvalues. This makes intuitive sense, because the values in A12:C21 have been standardized to zero mean and unit variance. Therefore, multiplying them by the square root of the eigenvalue leaves each variable with a variance that equals the eigenvalue itself.

7

Figure 7.8
The original data values are standardized to z-scores, just as the original variance-covariance matrix is standardized to an R matrix.

	A	B	C	D	E	F	G	H
						F3	▼	f_x {=MMULT($A$12:$C$21,B7:B9)}
1	Eigenvalues					Components		
2		Factor 1	Factor 2	Factor 3		Factor 1	Factor 2	Factor 3
3		1.69525	0.94069	0.36406		-0.74346	1.02037	0.05254
4						-1.24458	-1.11811	1.00808
5	Eigenvectors					1.45349	-0.26111	0.54691
6		Factor 1	Factor 2	Factor 3		-0.59634	0.82789	-0.10926
7	Weight	0.63665	-0.40884	-0.65386		-2.28889	-0.24796	-0.12742
8	Age	-0.68923	0.07864	-0.72026		1.25997	-0.43738	-0.80748
9	Height	0.34589	0.90921	-0.23172		1.24767	-1.85652	-0.03846
10						-1.22590	-0.19136	-0.93573
11	Weight	Age	Height			0.74428	1.30904	0.78887
12	-0.92484	0.55482	0.65841			1.39377	0.95513	-0.37806
13	-0.99438	0.04380	-1.68068					
14	0.67451	-1.41625	0.13861				Variances	
15	-0.64669	0.55482	0.57178			1.69525	0.94069	0.36406
16	-1.27252	1.64985	-0.98761					
17	1.50895	-0.32121	0.22525					
18	1.57848	-0.97823	-1.24751					
19	-0.09040	1.50385	-0.38118					
20	-0.57715	-0.97823	1.26484					
21	0.74404	-0.61322	1.43811					

NOTE You need to use the population version of the variance: For example, the formula in cell F15 is =VAR.P(F3:F12) rather than =VAR.S(F3:F12).

Getting the Eigenvalues and Eigenvectors

By now you've seen that the eigenvalues and eigenvectors of a correlation matrix play a central role in the calculation of principal components: their coefficients, how the original variables load onto the components, how the eigenvalues combine with the eigenvectors, and so on. You might have wondered how the eigenstructure (the full set of eigenvalues and eigenvectors) gets teased out of the correlation matrix.

You can derive the eigenstructure in several different ways. As this book is written in 2013, the method of choice for quite a few years has involved something called *tridiagonalization*, which transforms an input matrix such as a correlation matrix to a tridiagonal matrix. A tridiagonal matrix has zeroes in all its cells with the exception of three diagonals: the main diagonal, the diagonal immediately above the main diagonal, and the one immediately below the main diagonal.

It turns out that the tridiagonal matrix loses none of the information contained in the original input matrix, but it takes many fewer steps to complete the matrix calculations with a tridiagonal matrix. Therefore, the process of determining the eigenstructure is considerably faster. Additional features of modern algorithms for determining eigenstructures include the ability to deal effectively with variables that cause multicollinearity (and therefore matrices that have determinants of zero) via *singular value decomposition*, a process which makes use of QR decomposition, mentioned earlier in this chapter.

But although these approaches are faster and more efficient than older methods, it is difficult to show how they turn out eigenstructures. One of those older and slower methods uses *iteration and exhaustion* to calculate the eigenvalues and the corresponding eigenstructures. I discuss the approach here in general terms because it's conceptually close to the approach as originally conceived by Karl Pearson in the early part of the last century.

Iteration and Exhaustion

The basic idea behind the iteration and exhaustion process isn't at all complex. You start out with an estimate of an eigenvalue based on the sum of the values in the first row of the correlation matrix. Then you combine that eigenvalue with the values in the correlation matrix to make an initial estimate of the corresponding eigenvector.

A series of loops gets you to the point where any improvement from one eigenvalue and eigenvector to the next is extremely small. At that point you decide that you've gotten as close as you can to the structure of the first component—more specifically, the eigenvalue and eigenvector that define it. Now you use the eigenvalue and eigenvector to extract the variance and covariance associated with the component from the correlation matrix. You're left with a *residual matrix*, and you start the process over again, substituting the residual matrix for the original correlation matrix. You calculate a new eigenvalue and eigenvector for a second component, and use them to remove more variance and covariance from the residual matrix. You continue until you have completely exhausted the matrix of variance and covariance and are left with a residual matrix of values that are all either 0 or extremely close to it.

The residual matrices are additive, in the sense that you can take their sum to reconstitute the original correlation matrix. The next few figures show how all this works. Figure 7.9 repeats the correlation matrix for the data set used in this chapter's examples.

Figure 7.9
The initial correlation matrix is in A2:C4.

K2	▼		f_x	{=E2*MMULT(G2:G4,TRANSPOSE(G2:G4))}												
	A	B	C	D	E	F	G	H	I	J	K	L	M	N	O	P	Q
1		R Matrix			Eigenvalues		Eigenvectors				Extraction				Residual		
2	1	-0.603	0.079		1.695		0.637	0	0		0.687	-0.744	0.373		0.313	0.141	-0.295
3	-0.603	1	-0.276				-0.689	0	0		-0.744	0.805	-0.404		0.141	0.195	0.128
4	0.079	-0.276	1				0.346	0	0		0.373	-0.404	0.203		-0.295	0.128	0.797

It's not shown, but here's what happens behind the scenes as the eigenvectors and eigenvalue shown in Figure 7.9 are calculated:

1. The initial values for the initial trial eigenvector are the sums of each row of the correlation matrix.

2. The initial trial eigenvalue is set equal to the first value in the eigenvector.

3. The values in the eigenvector are each divided by the eigenvalue.

4. The values in the eigenvector are multiplied by the sum of the values in the corresponding row of the correlation matrix.

5. If the change in the total of the values of the eigenvector is smaller than a preset criterion supplied by the programmer (for example, 0.00001), the loop terminates and the code moves on to the next principal component. Otherwise, the process continues with Step 2 in this list.

When the loop terminates for the first principal component, the eigenvalue shown in Figure 7.9 in cell E2 is established as the eigenvalue for the first component, and the corresponding eigenvector is as shown in the range G2:G4.

> **NOTE** Notice that the signs of the values in the eigenvector are not the same as those shown for the eigenvector in Figure 7.5. This is due to differences in the algorithms used in the versions of the code that derives the eigenvectors. As I mention in Chapter 6, the signs are arbitrary.

Before moving to the second principal component, though, it's necessary to extract the variance and covariance associated with the first component from the correlation matrix. That variance and covariance—in the standardized scale used by correlations—appears in the range K2:M4 in Figure 7.9. You obtain it by entering this array formula in that range:

=E2*MMULT(G2:G4,TRANSPOSE(G2:G4))

That is, get the result of the postmultiplication of the eigenvector by its transpose and scale the result by the eigenvalue. The resulting matrix in K2:M4 is an expression of the variance and covariance attributable to the eigenvalue and eigenvector in E2 and G2:G4.

To get the residual matrix, just subtract K2:M4 from A2:C4, using this formula in cell O2:

=A2-K2

Copy and paste that formula into P2:Q2, and then into O3:Q4. The result is the residual matrix that's used in place of the original correlation matrix to get the second principal component (see Figure 7.10).

Figure 7.10
The residual correlation matrix is in A6:C8.

K6	▼		*fx*	{=E6*MMULT(H6:H8,TRANSPOSE(H6:H8))}												
	A	B	C	D	E	F	G	H	I	J	K	L	M	N	O	P	Q
1	R Matrix				Eigenvalues		Eigenvectors				Extraction				Residual		
2	1	-0.603	0.079		1.695		0.637	0	0		0.687	-0.744	0.373		0.313	0.141	-0.295
3	-0.603	1	-0.276				-0.689	0	0		-0.744	0.805	-0.404		0.141	0.195	0.128
4	0.079	-0.276	1				0.346	0	0		0.373	-0.404	0.203		-0.295	0.128	0.797
5																	
6	0.313	0.141	-0.295		0.941		0.637	0.409	0		0.157	-0.030	-0.350		0.156	0.171	0.055
7	0.141	0.195	0.128				-0.689	-0.079	0		-0.030	0.006	0.067		0.171	0.189	0.061
8	-0.295	0.128	0.797				0.346	-0.909	0		-0.350	0.067	0.778		0.055	0.061	0.020

Be sure to compare the range O2:Q4 in Figure 7.9 with the range A6:C8 in Figure 7.10. Both contain the residual correlation matrix that remains after accounting for the first principal component. The second principal component is extracted in the same way as the first component, but the work is done using the residual correlation matrix.

In this way, PCA ensures that the principal components are uncorrelated with one another. By the time that the process gets around to extracting the second (and subsequent) components, all the variance and covariance that can be associated with the first principal component has been extracted from the correlation matrix, and there's none attributable to the first component that's left for subsequent components. Therefore, no subsequent component can share variance with the first component, and they must by definition be uncorrelated.

The eigenvalue corresponding to the second principal component appears in cell E6, and the second eigenvector is in the range H6:H8. They are used to derive the matrix of values extracted from the residual correlation matrix in A6:C8, using an array formula analogous to the one used in Figure 7.9. In Figure 7.10, the array formula in K6:M8 is as follows:

=E6*MMULT(H6:H8,TRANSPOSE(H6:H8))

Notice that the first eigenvalue and the first eigenvector play no part in the array formula just given. All the variance and covariance associated with the first component is already gone, and using the first eigenvalue and eigenvector during this step would be both pointless and misleading.

The final component in this example is extracted in the third general step, and the results appear in Figure 7.11.

Figure 7.11
The final residual correlation matrix is in O10:Q12.

	A	B	C	D	E	F	G	H	I	J	K	L	M	N	O	P	Q
	— R Matrix				Eigenvalues		Eigenvectors				Extraction				Residual		
1		R Matrix			Eigenvalues		Eigenvectors				Extraction				Residual		
2	1	-0.603	0.079		1.695		0.637	0	0		0.687	-0.744	0.373		0.313	0.141	-0.295
3	-0.603	1	-0.276				-0.689	0	0		-0.744	0.805	-0.404		0.141	0.195	0.128
4	0.079	-0.276	1				0.346	0	0		0.373	-0.404	0.203		-0.295	0.128	0.797
5																	
6	0.313	0.141	-0.295		0.941		0.637	0.409	0		0.157	-0.030	-0.350		0.156	0.171	0.055
7	0.141	0.195	0.128				-0.689	-0.079	0		-0.030	0.006	0.067		0.171	0.189	0.061
8	-0.295	0.128	0.797				0.346	-0.909	0		-0.350	0.067	0.778		0.055	0.061	0.020
9																	
10	0.156	0.171	0.055		0.364		0.637	0.409	0.654		0.156	0.171	0.055		0.000	0.000	0.000
11	0.171	0.189	0.061				-0.689	-0.079	0.720		0.171	0.189	0.061		0.000	0.000	0.000
12	0.055	0.061	0.020				0.346	-0.909	0.232		0.055	0.061	0.020		0.000	0.000	0.000

K10 f_x {=E10*MMULT(I10:I12,TRANSPOSE(I10:I12))}

The same procedures used in Figures 7.9 and 7.10 are used to extract variance and covariance from what is now the residual matrix in A10:C12. The matrix that results from extracting the third component is in the range O10:Q12. All the variance and covariance has been extracted from the original correlation matrix, and it is now *exhausted*.

In fact, the final residual matrix does contain some vanishingly small values, obscured by the number format that I've applied to the range O10:Q12. For example, the value in cell O10 is actually -0.0000021. The iteration-and-exhaustion code I used to run this analysis is not as accurate as modern methods, but it does have the virtue of coupling the theory of PCA tightly with the code, which makes it much easier to see what goes on during the extraction process.

Figure 7.12 provides one additional view of the results of the extraction process.

Figure 7.12
The extracted matrices in columns K through M are sometimes termed additive slices.

	A	B	C	D	E	F	G	H	I	J	K	L	M	N	O	P	Q
	K15	▾		f_x	=K3+K7+K11												
1		R Matrix			Eigenvalues		Eigenvectors				Extraction				Residual		
2	1	-0.603	0.079		1.695		0.637	0	0		0.687	-0.744	0.373		0.313	0.141	-0.295
3	-0.603	1	-0.276				-0.689	0	0		-0.744	0.805	-0.404		0.141	0.195	0.128
4	0.079	-0.276	1				0.346	0	0		0.373	-0.404	0.203		-0.295	0.128	0.797
5																	
6	0.313	0.141	-0.295		0.941		0.637	0.409	0		0.157	-0.030	-0.350		0.156	0.171	0.055
7	0.141	0.195	0.128				-0.689	-0.079	0		-0.030	0.006	0.067		0.171	0.189	0.061
8	-0.295	0.128	0.797				0.346	-0.909	0		-0.350	0.067	0.778		0.055	0.061	0.020
9																	
10	0.156	0.171	0.055		0.364		0.637	0.409	0.654		0.156	0.171	0.055		0.000	0.000	0.000
11	0.171	0.189	0.061				-0.689	-0.079	0.720		0.171	0.189	0.061		0.000	0.000	0.000
12	0.055	0.061	0.020				0.346	-0.909	0.232		0.055	0.061	0.020		0.000	0.000	0.000
13																	
14	0.000	0.000	0.000								1	-0.603	0.079				
15	0.000	0.000	0.000				Reconstituted R Matrix		-0.603		1	-0.276					
16	0.000	0.000	0.000								0.079	-0.276	1				

You can demonstrate for yourself that the three extracted matrices in columns K through M are in fact additive slices by totaling them. For example, the formula in cell K14 is

=K2+K6+K10

and it is copied and pasted into the remainder of the range K14:M16. Note that the latter range contains values that are identical to those in A2:C4, the original correlation matrix.

Rotating Factors to a Meaningful Solution

I mentioned earlier in this chapter that the Factor.xls workbook that accompanies this chapter also performs Varimax factor rotation.

> **NOTE** Optionally, the Factor.xls workbook performs Quartimax factor rotation instead of Varimax, but it's been decades since Quartimax was used extensively for factor analysis. I included it because it was easy to do so, and it can be enlightening to compare the results of the two approaches.

This section discusses how to use the Factor.xls workbook to obtain a Varimax rotation for a particular number of factors.

Identifying the Factors

The dialog box that appears when you open the Factor.xls workbook and click Principal Components in the Ribbon's Add-Ins tab was shown, in part, in Figure 7.2. The second and final part of the dialog box is shown in Figure 7.13.

Figure 7.13
If you leave the Factors to Retain edit box blank, the value defaults to the number of original variables.

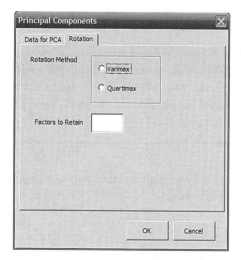

In most situations you want to run the code in Factor.xls at least twice. The first time you want to check diagnostic information such as the sphericity test. You also want to verify that dependency between two or more variables in the original data did not create problems inverting the R matrix. You want to check the eigenvalues, and, if you're using Kaiser's rule about retaining components only if their eigenvalues are greater than 1.0, you want to note the number of those eigenvalues.

For that first run, consider entering the number of variables in your input data set as the number of components to retain in the Factors to Retain edit box shown in Figure 7.13. At this point you don't know how many components to retain.

After you make the checks that I just mentioned, run the code again. Use the Factors to Retain edit box shown in Figure 7.13 to trim down the number of components you decided to retain. Bear in mind that one of the primary purposes for using PCA is to reduce the number of variables without a significant loss of information.

Figure 7.14 shows an R matrix with correlations between seven variables that pertain to wine. The variables are actually the averages of ratings provided by judges who tasted 40 different wines over the course of several weekends.

7

Figure 7.14
If you use a correlation matrix as shown here, it must be square rather than upper- or lower-triangular.

▲	A	B	C	D	E	F	G	H
1		Acidity	Body	Bouquet	Cost	Fruit	Sweetness	Tannin
2	Acidity	1	0.61204	0.11690	0.44069	0.34342	0.69132	0.55443
3	Body	0.61204	1	0.37579	0.54489	0.60985	0.63823	0.41238
4	Bouquet	0.11690	0.37579	1	0.51617	0.81783	0.30035	0.14359
5	Cost	0.44069	0.54489	0.51617	1	0.71977	0.69388	0.55246
6	Fruit	0.34342	0.60985	0.81783	0.71977	1	0.58454	0.37807
7	Sweetness	0.69132	0.63823	0.30035	0.69388	0.58454	1	0.80735
8	Tannin	0.55443	0.41238	0.14359	0.55246	0.37807	0.80735	1

> **NOTE**
>
> Recall that if you base the analysis on a correlation matrix, you get factor coefficients but not factor scores. To get the factor scores, use the coefficients with a raw data set, standardized to zero means and unit variances, to create as many factors as you called for: Multiply the coefficients by the variables and sum the results for each record.

With the worksheet that contains the correlation matrix active, the user clicks Principal Components in the Ribbon's Add-Ins tab and fills out the dialog box shown in Figures 7.2 and 7.13 as follows:

1. Click in the Input Range box and drag through the range B1:H8 to capture both the correlations and the variable names (refer to Figure 7.14).
2. Fill the Variable Labels in First Row check box.
3. Skip the Record IDs edit box.
4. Select the Correlation Matrix option button.
5. Fill in the number of records on which the correlation matrix is based—here, 40 wines were evaluated, so you enter 40 in the Number of Observations edit box.
6. Click the dialog box's Rotation tab and choose the Varimax rotation method.
7. Enter the number of components, also termed *factors*, to retain in the edit box.
8. Click OK.

Figures 7.3 and 7.5 show most of the results of the principal components analysis (although the results are not based on the data used to create the correlation matrix in Figure 7.14). The original loadings appear in the worksheet named Principal Components. The loadings *after* rotation are placed in a different worksheet, named Rotated Loadings. Figure 7.15 shows the eigenvalues for the first three components, plus both the original loadings (termed the *factor structure*) and the loadings after the components have been rotated according to the Varimax method.

Notice that the original factor loadings in the range B7:C13 indicate that the correlation matrix consists of one factor only; you come across this type of result frequently in PCA. Prior to rotation, subsequent components tend to have strong loadings on one variable only.

Figure 7.15
Only two components were retained for the second run per Kaiser's rule for minimum eigenvalues.

	A	B	C	D
1	Eigenvalues			
2		Factor 1	Factor 2	Factor 3
3		4.15820	1.34359	0.63122
4				
5	Factor Structure			
6		Factor 1	Factor 2	
7	Acidity	0.70291	0.47773	
8	Body	0.78476	0.03860	
9	Bouquet	0.58754	-0.74070	
10	Cost	0.83978	-0.14219	
11	Fruit	0.82325	-0.49892	
12	Sweetness	0.89073	0.30630	
13	Tannin	0.72574	0.44976	
14				
15	Rotated Loadings			
16		Factor 1	Factor 2	
17	Acidity	0.84701	-0.06992	
18	Body	0.63480	-0.46299	
19	Bouquet	-0.00823	-0.94539	
20	Cost	0.56403	-0.63822	
21	Fruit	0.32706	-0.90537	
22	Sweetness	0.88543	-0.32129	
23	Tannin	0.84719	-0.10602	

NOTE The loadings that I regard as strong are indicated by shading in their cells. The loadings of around 0.63 are admittedly borderline.

The loadings that are the result of the Varimax rotation of the factors, in B17:C23, are quite different from the unrotated loadings. Combined with the fact that only two eigenvalues exceed 1.0, the rotated loadings suggest that two different factors underlie the observed correlations. What does the Varimax rotation do to bring about this difference in the factor structure?

As the name "Varimax" implies, the purpose of the rotation is to maximize variance—not, as you might initially expect, the variance of the original observations, but the variance of the loadings (actually the variance of the squares of the loadings). The expected result of maximizing that variance is that each factor will have strong loadings on a few variables and weak loadings on the remaining variables.

When you have an outcome such as that, you can often identify what it is that each factor represents. I'm no wine expert. To me, one box of wine is pretty much the same as the next. But someone who knows wine might be able to look at those rotated loadings and conjecture that the first factor represents, say, a wine's age, whereas the second factor represents a wine's commercial value: some combination of the type of grape used and the wine's aroma.

7

The Varimax Rotation

Figure 7.16 shows how a particular variable might load on two factors, after the factors have been extracted (remember that, formally, "factor" is a principal component that has been extracted a little differently, usually with SMCs in the main diagonal instead of 1.0 values).

Figure 7.16
The variable has a moderate loading on both factors.

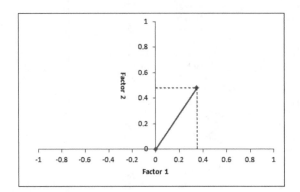

The factors as they are extracted from the correlation matrix are uncorrelated and, therefore, at right angles to one another. They act as the axes of the chart. The variable is represented by the diagonal vector in the plane that's defined by the two factors. The variable has a moderate loading on each factor: roughly 0.35 on Factor 1 and roughly 0.5 on Factor 2. Those loadings don't help us much in determining what it is that each factor represents.

Figure 7.17 shows what might happen to the variable and the factors as the result of a Varimax factor rotation.

Figure 7.17
The rotation causes one loading to increase and the other to decrease.

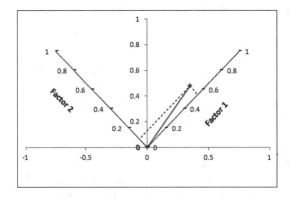

Notice in Figure 7.17 that the factors have rotated approximately 45 degrees from their original positions. They have also remained at right angles to one another. This feature of

Varimax rotation enables the factors to remain uncorrelated with one another. It also clarifies the components' definitions by way of the new loadings.

> **NOTE**
> The fact that the factors are still at right angles is one of the characteristics that define *orthogonal rotations*. Other rotation methods allow the factors to orient themselves at other than 90-degree angles and are termed *oblique* rotations. Many of those who use factor analysis regard oblique rotations as more likely than orthogonal rotations to conform to how factors behave naturally. Others find that factors developed using oblique rotations are substantially more difficult to interpret than are those developed using orthogonal rotations.

The projections (which are the loadings) of the variable onto the rotated factors are different from its projections onto the original factors. The loading on Factor 1 has increased from about 0.35 to about 0.5, and has dropped on Factor 2 from about .5 to just slightly greater than 0.0.

In this particular example, the rotation has not increased an original loading of 0.35 on Factor 1 to a dramatic 0.85. But the new loading of about 0.5 is marginal at worst. Perhaps more important in this case is that the loading on Factor 2 is now essentially 0.0, and that may clarify for you what it is that Factor 2 is actually measuring.

An added point of interest about the Varimax rotation has to do mainly with its derivation. Figure 7.18 has the particulars.

Figure 7.18
The sum of the retained eigenvalues equals the sum of the squares of the loadings.

◢	A	B	C	D
1	Eigenvalues			
2		Factor 1	Factor 2	Factor 3
3		4.15820	1.34359	0.63122
4				
5		=B3+C3	5.50179	
6				
7				
8				
9	Rotated Loadings			
10		Factor 1	Factor 2	
11	Acidity	0.84701	-0.06992	
12	Body	0.63480	-0.46299	
13	Bouquet	-0.00823	-0.94539	
14	Cost	0.56403	-0.63822	
15	Fruit	0.32706	-0.90537	
16	Sweetness	0.88543	-0.32129	
17	Tannin	0.84719	-0.10602	
18				
19		=SUMSQ(B11:C17)	5.50179	

The eigenvalues shown in Figure 7.18, in the range B3:D3, come from the first of two runs of the Factor.xls code against the correlation matrix shown in Figure 7.14. Just two factors were retained in the second run, and the resulting rotated loadings appear in the range B11:C17.

Compare the values that appear in cells C5 and C19. They are identical. Cell C5 contains the sum of the eigenvalues for the two retained factors. Cell C19 contains the sum of the squared, rotated factor loadings. You would get the same result by summing the squares of the factor loadings before rotation. This relationship is used by the code to help derive the Varimax loadings.

Classification Examples

This chapter concludes with a couple of examples, each of which gets a fair amount of play in online discussions of principal components and factor analysis. Both examples highlight the possibilities for classification that PCA brings to the table. Both also demonstrate some of the problems with doing so.

As you examine these two examples, it's a good idea to bear in mind the different purposes of discriminant analysis, cluster analysis and PCA.

- PCA derives variables (variously termed *components* or *factors*) that are uncorrelated with one another. Subsequent rotation of those components may yield loadings that make it clear what each component represents. The main purpose is not classification: To classify cases as a way of making decisions, it is not necessary to work with orthogonal components.

- Discriminant analysis aims to derive a discriminant function, similar in concept to a principal component but which serves a different purpose: The discriminant function is calculated to maximize the separation between groups and to minimize the variability of values within groups. The basic purpose is classification.

- Cluster analysis tries to generate clusters of records purely on the basis of similarity (in some versions, the basis is dissimilarity) on the predictor variables. No prior information about groupings is necessarily assumed. The basic purpose is again classification.

So if a principal components analysis, either before or after rotation, happens to do a creditable job of classifying cases, that may well be due to the idiosyncrasies of the variables that were selected. That doesn't mean that it's necessarily spurious, simply that it might be an unanticipated benefit of putting the data through PCA.

On the other hand, as you'll see, there are good arguments for deriving and rotating principal components from a raw data set, and using those components as inputs to a cluster analysis. I get further into those possibilities in this book's next two chapters.

State Crime Rates

The study of crime rates that I mentioned earlier in this chapter takes its data from the 1972 edition of the *Statistical Abstract of the United States*. The raw information included number of crimes per 100,000 population in each state during 1970 and 1971. These rates are available in a worksheet in the Excel workbook for this chapter. The study has been replicated in various papers and books, using both the original 1970–71 data and data from later years.

If you run a principal components analysis on the state crime rate data, you get two components whose eigenvalues are greater than 1.0 (4.1 and 1.4 with seven original crime rate variables). The loadings for each component appear in Figure 7.19, along with the loadings for the first two components after Varimax rotation.

Figure 7.19
As often happens, the first component has moderate to strong loadings on every variable, and subsequent components are bipolar.

	A	B	C	D
1	**Eigenvalues**			
2		Factor 1	Factor 2	Factor 3
3		4.07678	1.43164	0.63117
4				
5	**Factor Structure**			
6		Factor 1	Factor 2	
7	Murder	0.55748	0.77113	
8	Rape	0.85078	0.13918	
9	Robbery	0.78232	-0.05499	
10	Assault	0.78359	0.54590	
11	Burglary	0.88105	-0.30769	
12	Larceny	0.72760	-0.47966	
13	Auto Theft	0.71447	-0.43801	
14				
15	**Rotated Loadings**			
16		Factor 1	Factor 2	
17	Murder	-0.01467	0.95142	
18	Rape	0.59844	0.62054	
19	Robbery	0.65975	0.42400	
20	Assault	0.30126	0.90624	
21	Burglary	0.89005	0.28059	
22	Larceny	0.86999	0.05098	
23	Auto Theft	0.83455	0.07650	

If you ended your analysis with the unrotated components and their loadings, you would conclude that the first factor consisted of all crimes other than murder, and the second factor consisted of murder. That's how the loadings fall out in Figure 7.19, cells B7:C13.

But if you rotate the factors using Varimax, the rotation cleans up the first two factors. The loadings shown in Figure 7.19, cells B17:C23, indicate that the first factor is defined by robbery, burglary, larceny, auto theft—so-called "property crimes." The second factor is defined by murder, assault, and rape—crimes against persons or "violent crime."

So the first useful outcome from the principal components analysis and the subsequent Varimax rotation is the appearance of two coherent factors. Further, the strong loadings group the variables in ways that make good sense. Notice that there was nothing other than the pattern of the correlations between the original variables to cause those factors to emerge.

The second useful outcome appears when you chart the factor scores against one another. Because we began the analysis using raw data rather than using a correlation matrix, the code in Factor.xls is able to report scores on both factors for each of the 50 records—in this example, each of the 50 states. Figure 7.20 shows a scatterchart of those 50 states, using the *unrotated* factor scores to plot on the chart's two axes.

I divided the 50 states into four regions: North, East, West, and South, and charted each region separately, each region as a different data series, so that it would be possible to distinguish the regions by means of different markers. No pattern is apparent from looking at the chart in Figure 7.20: It's just a random spray of data points, and there's no systemic pattern to how the four regions are located. There is some tendency for the states designated as North and South to cluster toward the bottom of the chart, and for the East and West states to cluster toward its top.

Figure 7.20
The chart of the unrotated factor scores is uninformative.

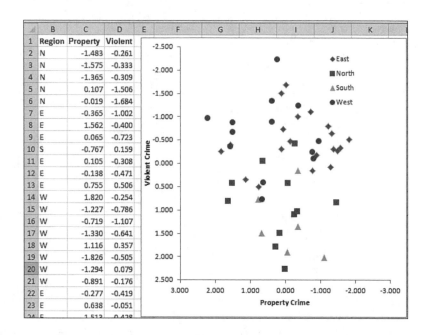

In both Figures 7.20 and 7.21, I reversed the axes so that larger X values are to the left and larger Y values are toward the bottom. I did this so that in Figure 7.21 the Western states would appear on the left of the chart instead of the right, and so that the Northern states would appear toward the top instead of the bottom. In 2007 and subsequent versions of Excel you can reverse the order of the values on the chart axes by right-clicking the axis, choosing Format Axis from the shortcut menu, and filling the Values in Reverse Order check box on the Axis Options page. You can do the same thing in earlier versions but the steps are slightly different.

A chart of the *rotated* factor scores, which shows a different outcome, is in Figure 7.21.

Figure 7.21
I reversed both axes so
that larger X values are
to the left and larger Y
values are toward the
bottom.

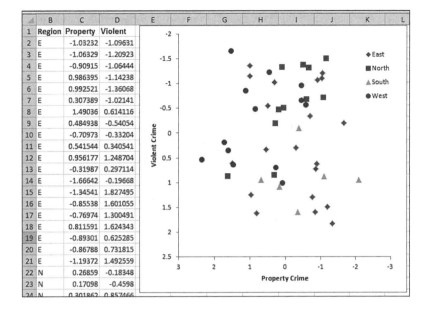

	B	C	D
1	Region	Property	Violent
2	E	-1.03232	-1.09631
3	E	-1.06329	-1.20923
4	E	-0.90915	-1.06444
5	E	0.986395	-1.14238
6	E	0.992521	-1.36068
7	E	0.307389	-1.02141
8	E	1.49036	0.614116
9	E	0.484938	-0.54054
10	E	-0.70973	-0.33204
11	E	0.541544	0.340541
12	E	0.956177	1.248704
13	E	-0.31987	0.297114
14	E	-1.66642	-0.19668
15	E	-1.34541	1.827495
16	E	-0.85538	1.601055
17	E	-0.76974	1.300491
18	E	0.811591	1.624343
19	E	-0.89301	0.625285
20	E	-0.86788	0.731815
21	E	-1.19372	1.492559
22	N	0.26859	-0.18348
23	N	0.17098	-0.4598
24	N	0.301862	0.857466

Although there is no clear, crisp clustering in the chart shown in Figure 7.21, some definite tendencies emerge. The states designated as South mostly remain at the bottom of the chart, but those designated as North generally have been moved by the rotation of the factors to the top of the chart.

Similarly, Western states are now largely on the left half of the chart and the Eastern states mostly on the right half. Again, these are tendencies rather than inarguable classifications; there are plenty of counterexamples, and the classifications would be altered by someone who preferred to categorize, say, Kansas as a Southern rather than a Northern state.

This is the sort of self-classification that cluster analysis is intended to offer. No information about the geographic locations of the 50 states is involved in this principal components analysis. Nevertheless, the following steps led to a chart on which four geographic regions tend to separate themselves from one another:

- The 21 correlations between the seven variables established two principal components.
- The two principal components were rotated to clarify the variables that the components represent: Property Crime and Violent Crime.
- Each of the 50 records was assigned to one of four regions. A score on each of the two components was calculated for each of the 50 records.
- The states were plotted by region on a chart of the Property Crime component by the Violent Crime component.
- States in the North central part of the country are separated from states in the South central region along the Violent Crime axis. States in the West are separated from states in the East along the Property Crime axis.

7

It's intriguing that the principal components analysis resulted in as much separation as it did. Bear in mind the different purposes of different kinds of analysis that I outlined at the start of this section.

Discriminant analysis aims to create a new function—a new combination of the available predictor variables—that maximizes the distance between group centroids and minimizes the variability within groups. Its purpose is classification. *Cluster analysis* aims to find clusters of records by the brute force of trying out new combinations of records until they establish clusters that, it is hoped, stand up with different samples. Again, and although no *a priori* classes are provided to the analysis, the purpose is classification.

The purpose of PCA is *not* to classify records, but to arrange the combination of a larger number of variables into a smaller number of components that explain the variance in the existing data set, such that those components are uncorrelated with one another.

> **NOTE** However, as I point out in this book's final two chapters, recent research has shown that unexpected similarities exist between the math behind principal components analysis and the math behind cluster analysis. These similarities depend largely on the nature of the space occupied by the principal components as compared to the space occupied by the clusters.

In a case such as the state crime rates example, it's an unanticipated (but happy) outcome that not only do the loadings cause the rotated factors to make sense, but that there appear to be regional differences in the principal components. (The analysis has been replicated for years other than 1970 and 1971, with similar results.)

Physical Measurements of Aphids

Jeffers (Jeffers, J.N.R. Two case studies in the application of principal component analysis. *Applied Statistics*, **16**, 225–236) presents a principal components analysis of 19 measures taken on 40 aphids. (You can find the raw data on a worksheet in the Excel workbook for this chapter.) The 19 measures are mainly concerned with the size of the aphid: length, width, length of antenna segments, length of tibia and femur, and so on.

The principal components analysis for this data returns a component that accounts for 72.8% of the variance in the measured variables, and a second component that accounts for an additional 12.5%. The first factor loads heavily on 13 variables that measure size. The second factor loads heavily on 5 of the remaining variables that count structures, such as Number of Hooks and Ovipositor Spines. So it appears that both the first two factors have to do with the size of the aphid, with the first concerned with measured size and the second with counts of body parts.

I'll spare you the grisly details of the analysis, which you can in any case complete yourself using the raw data in the workbook for this chapter in combination with the Factor.xls add-in.

What I want to draw to your attention is the remarkably clear clustering that appears when you chart the first factor against the second (see Figure 7.22).

Figure 7.22
Rotating the factors does not materially improve this clustering.

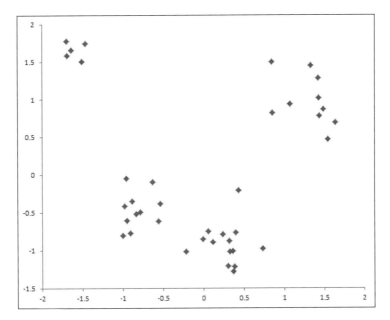

The scatterchart of the two factors displays four beautifully distinct clusters, and analysts who write about this study suggest that the clusters represent different species of aphid. Different sources are coy about the reason that the clusters were not actually mapped to recorded aphid species. Some suggest that the species identity, supplied independently of the principal components analysis, was simply unavailable. Others note that it is difficult to make a sure identification of the species of winged aphids—or was so in 1967.

But several writers point out correctly that although PCA is not designed as a classification procedure, it can simplify a data set. It can, as here, take 19 measured variables (which result in 171 bivariate correlations) and reduce them to just two variables: components that can be easily examined on a two-dimensional scatterchart. In this case, nearly all the analysts who have written about this aphids study speculate that the four clusters that appear on the scatterchart represent four species of aphid.

The charted clusters do present a visually compelling argument that PCA has isolated four clusters that might easily represent four species. Nevertheless, you'd really like to see more data to cross-validate the findings shown in Figure 7.22, or an independent classification of the 40 aphids according to species so that a confusion table of the sort described in Chapter 6 can be constructed. But I can be easily persuaded that people have better uses for their time than counting the number of ovipositor spines found on 40 winged aphids.

7

Cluster Analysis: The Basics

Apart from the brief reviews of logistic regression and univariate ANOVA earlier in this book, all the types of decision analytics discussed so far are characterized by their multivariate nature: the use of several measured variables to derive a new composite such as a discriminant function or a principal component. The classification technique that this chapter and the next discuss is radically different. Instead of rearranging variables into new composites, cluster analysis rearranges records into new clusters.

Cluster Analysis, Discriminant Analysis, and Logistic Regression

As you see in this chapter, cluster analysis is best used as an exploratory technique. You deploy cluster analysis when you have a number of records, possibly ranging from fewer than 100 to tens or even hundreds of thousands, but you don't know how to classify them or even what the classifications might be. You do have access to other variables that describe the records' behavior (number of items purchased and gross margin, for example) and other descriptive measures such as height, weight, cholesterol levels, and so on.

If you know what your categories should be, then you might be able to assign each record to a different category. You could then run a logistic regression analysis or a discriminant analysis as described in earlier chapters of this book. Using logistic regression, your purpose would be to determine how the predictor variables combine to predict a category using maximum likelihood techniques. Or, using discriminant analysis, your purpose might be to discover how your predictor variables work together to bring about the categories that you observe for each record.

In either case you have information about category membership before you undertake the analysis. You might establish your equations using data that includes category information and subsequently apply them using data whose category information is missing. But at some point the analysis takes note of the records' membership and ties the predictor variables to the information about category membership.

Things are different in cluster analysis. You might not have information about membership in different categories, and so cannot deploy either logistic regression or discriminant analysis. Or you might have category information but it's not useful for the purpose you have in mind. It's also possible that you're simply interested in determining whether the predictor variables group the records on their own accord—much as principal components analysis combined with a rotation of some sort can enable underlying factors to emerge from a mass of directly measurable variables.

That's what cluster analysis does, and it's how you can get away without knowing up front what categories might be hidden in an undifferentiated mass of measured variables. The idea is that if you examine how close, or how distant, different records are from one another on the measured variables, clusters will inevitably emerge.

The question that remains is whether the clusters mean anything. Have the measured variables resulted in meaningful groupings of the records? Or are those groupings—or *clusters*—just artifacts of random distances between records that can't be sensibly grouped?

The fact that it's possible to ask those questions is the reason that cluster analysis is usually considered to be an exploratory technique, as distinct from a technique that's used to confirm an existing hypothesis. Certainly, techniques such as logistic regression and discriminant analysis are often used to explore patterns in a data set. But because you have actual grouping data in hand when you undertake a logistic regression or discriminant analysis, the exploring you do is generally limited to learning more about how the predictor variables work to define the groups.

In contrast, cluster analysis is appropriate when you don't know what the categories are, or even if there are any meaningful categories, and therefore it's ideal for exploration. Of course, if you have enough records to arrange for a preliminary analysis and a subsequent cross-validation, it's possible to view cluster analysis as a means of confirming a finding. That's ideal, of course. You're always on much safer ground when you have enough data first to establish a finding, and then to test whether other data supports that finding.

Different methods of cluster analysis exist and find frequent use. One general approach is sometimes termed *agglomerative*, a word that is surely one of the two ugliest found in statistical literature (the other is *homoscedastistic*). Fortunately, it's possible to refer to the methods that follow that general approach as *linkage methods*, although you sometimes see them referred to as *hierarchical*. I discuss two linkage methods, single and complete linkage, in this chapter.

Another general approach, *centroid-based clustering*, is typified by the k-means method. I also discuss k-means in this chapter. Bear in mind that this chapter is intended as an introduction to the basics of cluster analysis. As such, it focuses on the mechanics of how the different methods reach the goal of assigning records to clusters. Chapter 9, "Cluster Analysis: Further Issues," goes into the implications of using the k-means method in greater detail.

Regardless of the method used to establish and populate the clusters, a metric is needed to measure the distance between individual records and the members of existing clusters. Several such metrics exist, and they get fuller treatment in the next chapter, but one of the most frequently used metrics is Euclidean distance, discussed next.

Euclidean Distance

Perhaps the most popular method of measuring distance between objects, or between clusters centroids, is *Euclidean distance*. Euclidean distance is the ordinary distance between two points, typically measured on two or more variables. Figure 8.1 shows the simplest sort of situation.

Figure 8.1
Two objects and two variables provide the smallest possible scope for a distance calculation.

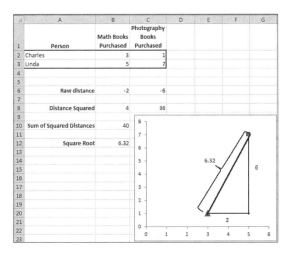

Figure 8.1 displays neither more nor less than the Pythagorean Theorem that you probably recall from Geometry I. You start with two points on the scatterchart: {3,1} corresponding to 3 math books and 1 photography book, and {5,7} corresponding to 5 math and 7 photography. If you drop a line from {5,7} and across from {3,1} you wind up with a right angle at {5,1}. So the vertical line is 6 units high and the horizontal line is 2 units wide. Then the hypotenuse (the diagonal line connecting the two points) is 6.32 units long. Using Excel worksheet syntax, the formula to return the Euclidean distance between Linda and Charles would be

=SQRT((B2-B3)^2+(C2-C3)^2)

Figure 8.2 extends the Euclidean logic to a third variable.

Figure 8.2
Third (and subsequent) variables merely extend the basic Euclidean distance equation.

	A	B	C	D	E
1	Person	Math Books Purchased	Photography Books Purchased	Novels Purchased	
2	Linda	5	7	2	
3	Charles	3	1	4	
4					
5					
6	Raw distance	2	6	-2	
7					
8	Distance Squared	4	36	4	
9					
10	Sum of Squared Distances	44			
11					
12	Square Root of Sum	6.63		6.63	=SQRT((B2-B3)^2+(C2-C3)^2+(D2-D3)^2)

Of course you can carry out the math in just one cell, and that's done in cell D12 of Figure 8.2. The formula is spelled out in cell E12.

The addition of a third variable—here, Novels Purchased—merely adds a term to the equation:

=SQRT((B2-B3)^2+(C2-C3)^2+(D2-D3)^2)

So, if you are concerned with two variables only, Charles is 6.32 units from Linda, but with three variables the distance is 6.63. Bear in mind that adding a variable complicates matters only to the extent of adding another squared distance to the basic equation.

> **NOTE** Squared Euclidean distances are a frequently used variation of the basic Euclidean distance because the squared distance emphasizes outliers more heavily than does the simple Euclidean distance. Obviously, to get the squared Euclidean distance, just remove the SQRT() function from the previous formula.

Adding another person or object is another matter, as Figure 8.3. shows.

In Figure 8.3 a third person, Ellen, has been added. In Figures 8.1 and 8.2 there were just two people to worry about, and therefore only one distance between the two people. But Figure 8.3 has three people and therefore three distances: Linda to Charles, Linda to Ellen and Charles to Ellen.

In general, the number of distances follows an equation that you probably recall from correlation analysis. The number of correlations in an R matrix is returned by

=(X * (X − 1))/2

where X is the number of variables. In situations such as this chapter discusses, the formula is the same, but X represents persons or objects instead of variables. Because the number of distances increases geometrically, it's good that Excel has a feature that saves you a lot of typing. (It's also good that the applications that do cluster analysis calculate the distances on your behalf.)

Figure 8.3
Adding more records increases the number of distances that must be calculated.

	A	B	C	D
1	Person	Math Books Purchased	Photography Books Purchased	Novels Purchased
2	Linda	5	7	2
3	Charles	3	1	4
4	Ellen	6	2	1
5				
6		Linda	Charles	Ellen
7	Linda	0		
8	Charles	6.63	0	
9	Ellen	5.20	4.36	0
10				
11				
12		6.63		
13		5.20	4.36	
14				
15	=SQRT(SUMXMY2(B2:D2,B3:D3))			
16	=SQRT(SUMXMY2(B2:D2,B4:D4))	=SQRT(SUMXMY2(B3:D3,B4:D4))		

In Figure 8.3, the formula in cell B8 is

$$=SQRT((B2-B3)^2+(C2-C3)^2+(D2-D3)^2)$$

It returns the Euclidean distance between Linda on row 2 and Charles on row 3. If you had to replicate this formula nine times, as you would with a total of five people, there would be considerable room for error as well as frustration. Fortunately, Excel offers the SUMXMY2() worksheet function. This function takes an array of values (X), subtracts (M) another array of values (Y), squares the differences (2), and sums the squared differences (SUM).

Still in Figure 8.3, notice that the value in cell B12 is equal to the value in cell B8. But the formula in cell B12 is

$$=SQRT(SUMXMY2(B2:D2,B3:D3))$$

The SUMXMY2() function does the following for you:

- Takes the values in B2:D2 as the X array.
- Takes the values in B3:D3 as the Y array.
- Subtracts the values in B3:D3 from the corresponding values in B2:D2. (The subtraction is abbreviated as M, standing for Minus, in the function name.)
- Squares the results of the subtractions.
- Totals the squared subtractions.

Finally, the SQRT() function is used to get the square root of the result of the SUMXMY2() function.

So you can save a considerable amount of time and grief by using the SUMXMY2() function instead of calling out all the arithmetic operations involved in calculating a Euclidean distance between two people or objects. Furthermore, you can save some additional effort by setting up the first formula to use mixed references, along these lines:

=SQRT(SUMXMY2($B$2:$D$2,$B3:$D3))

The use of the dollar signs makes the B2:D2 reference absolute, but the $B3:$D3 reference is mixed. You can autofill the formula down in its original column to get these results:

=SQRT(SUMXMY2($B$2:$D$2,$B4:$D4))

=SQRT(SUMXMY2($B$2:$D$2,$B5:$D5))

and so on. To get the remaining columns you still need to autofill to the right and make some adjustments to the row numbers, but by anchoring the references to columns B through D you save yourself some editing.

I'm *not* recommending that you undertake cluster analysis routinely using this approach in Excel. I do recommend that you try two or three small analyses with this approach, in order that you develop a better idea of what the applications that do all this on your behalf are up to. There's nothing like doing it by hand, and examining the results, to provide yourself with a hook to hang a concept on.

Mahalanobis' D^2 and Cluster Analysis

The section "Adjusting for the Variance-Covariance Matrix," in Chapter 6 discusses how discriminant function analysis can use an extension of Euclidean distance called Mahalanobis' D^2 to take the covariance between measures into account. The example discussed there is the iris data set, with three known species and four continuous variables (sepal and petal length and width). Recall that for each iris, the Euclidean distances are converted to D^2 by means of this formula:

=MMULT(A3:D3,MMULT($B$3:$E$6,TRANSPOSE(A3:D3)))

where the range A3:D3 (Figure 6.14) contains an iris's deviation from a species centroid on the four continuous measures, and the range B3:E6 (Figure 6.15) contains the inverse of the pooled within-groups variance-covariance matrix.

The use of simple Euclidean distances in discriminant analysis causes problems that also arise in cluster analysis. Suppose you're working with a swarm of data points that configure themselves into a cigar shape—that is, an ellipse with a long axis and, at right angles to it, a short axis.

One of your many data points lies precisely on the long axis, five units from the center of the swarm. Another point lies precisely on the short axis, two units from the center of the swarm. Both points are members of the swarm, but what's the probability of membership of each point?

One point is five units from the center on the long axis, and the other is two units from the center on the short axis. Intuitively, you might conclude that the point that's closer to the center has the higher probability of membership. But that can be misleading. Suppose the standard deviation of the variable on the long axis is 10 units, whereas the standard deviation of the variable on the short axis is 1 unit. Then the first point is 5/10 or half a standard deviation from the center, and the second point is 2/1 or two standard deviations from the center. Now the first point is clearly more likely a member of the swarm than is the second point.

Factoring the within-groups variance-covariance matrix corrects for both the differences in scale discussed in the previous paragraph as well as different covariances between the variables, which alter the angles at which the axes intersect. Those corrections are among the effects of using Mahalanobis' D^2 instead of simple Euclidean distances.

The difficulty involved with trying to use D^2 in cluster analysis is that the groups are not known before the analysis is complete. (In discriminant analysis, of course, the groups and their membership are known at the outset of the analysis.) However, you can't know the deviation of a record's values from a group centroid—such as in A3:D3 in the previous formula—without knowing the group centroid. And that requires knowing the members of the group, which are as yet unknown in cluster analysis.

Similarly, the pooled within groups variance-covariance matrix is also used in the previous formula to get the values in the range B3:E6. Calculating that matrix requires that you pool the variance-covariance matrix for each group. Again, knowledge of group membership is required, and again you don't yet know the composition of the groups.

Different transformations such as the Cholesky transformation are available to attempt to deal with this problem, but none is entirely satisfactory—at least in an exploratory context. In that case, most researchers work with simple Euclidean distance measures until a sensible pattern of clusters is established. At that point it can make good sense to replace the Euclidean distances with D^2 in a confirming sample and run the analysis again.

Finding Clusters: The Single Linkage Method

Cluster analysis has several methods for developing clusters, including single linkage, complete linkage, and average linkage. To give you a sense of how linking takes place, I walk through a single linkage process in this section. Later sections discuss complete linkage and the k-means approach.

Different approaches to linking clusters have different definitions for the term *distance*. These definitions have less to do with the way the distance is measured than with which objects are chosen for assessment. Using single linkage, the distance between two clusters refers to the *minimum* distance between a point in one cluster and a point in the other cluster. After finding that minimum distance, you combine—some say *fuse* or *merge*—the two clusters that exhibit that minimum distance between their points.

Here's an example. Suppose you have a distance matrix of the sort developed in the previous section, and as shown in Figure 8.4.

Figure 8.4
At first, a cluster is a single data point.

⊿	A	B	C	D	E	F
1		Jan	Ken	Lou	Mac	Ned
2 Jan		0				
3 Ken		9	0			
4 Lou		14	6	0		
5 Mac		13	16	5	0	
6 Ned		8	14	12	15	0

It's straightforward to find the smallest distance between points in the distance matrix shown in Figure 8.4. The smallest distance is 5, between Lou and Mac, in cell D5. The next few steps involve these tasks:

1. Find the nearest neighbors to the members, Lou and Mac, of the new cluster.
2. Fuse the Lou point with the Mac point to form a new cluster.
3. Remove Lou and Mac as individual points from the distance matrix.
4. Add a new cluster consisting of Lou and Mac.
5. Rebuild the matrix with the nearest neighbor distances.

First, who are the people with the minimum distances from Lou and Mac? Figure 8.5 repeats the distance matrix from Figure 8.4 and adds an analysis of the distances to Lou and the distances to Mac.

Figure 8.5
Before fusing Lou and Mac into a new cluster, assess the remaining distances.

D9	▾		*f*×	=MIN(B9:C9)		
⊿	A	B	C	D	E	F
1		Jan	Ken	Lou	Mac	Ned
2 Jan		0				
3 Ken		9	0			
4 Lou		14	6	0		
5 Mac		13	16	5	0	
6 Ned		8	14	12	15	0
7						
8		Lou	Mac	Minimum Distance		
9 Jan		14	13	13		
10 Ken		6	16	6		
11 Ned		12	15	12		

Bear in mind that using single linkage, the distance between two clusters is defined as the minimum distance between the points in one cluster and the points in the other cluster. At this point in the example, you have identified Lou and Mac as the members of the first cluster. The remaining three people each still occupy their own cluster. So the task is to find out the smallest distance between Lou and the remaining three, and the smallest distance between Mac and the remaining three.

That's what the matrix in the range B9:D11 of Figure 8.5 does. For example, the distance between Lou and Jan is 14 (cell B9) and between Mac and Jan is 13 (cell C9). Cell D9 gets the minimum of B9 and C9, which of course is the value 13 in C9. So the minimum distance, the single linkage distance, between the Jan "cluster" and either Lou or Mac is 13.

Similarly, the distance between Lou and Ken is 6, and between Mac and Ken it's 16. The single linkage distance between Ken and either Lou or Mac is the smaller of those two distances, 6. And the single linkage distance between Ned and either Lou or Mac is 12.

Be sure you see the reason that Figure 8.5 measures the distances between Lou and Mac, on one hand, and Jan, Ned, and Ken on the other hand. At this point you have identified Lou and Mac as the members of the first cluster to be established. The next task is to find the nearest neighbor from among Jan, Ned, and Ken to the Lou/Mac cluster. But that nearest neighbor could be nearest to Lou or to Mac.

The question of whether to locate the member of an existing cluster that's nearest or most distant distinguishes the single linkage method from the complete linkage method, discussed later in this chapter. In both the single and the complete linkage methods, every step assesses the distances between two records, whether they're already cluster members or not, and whether the nearest or most distant member is sought. That's the reason that Figure 8.5 gets the minimum distances between six different pairings of records. Even though Lou and Mac are now considered to constitute a cluster, it's still necessary to assess their distances as individuals.

With those three single linkage distances (13, 6, and 12) in hand, you can go ahead and fuse Lou and Mac and redraw the distance matrix (see Figure 8.6).

The matrix has lost two rows and two columns to the fusing of Lou and Mac, and has added a row and a column to accommodate their new cluster. The single linkage distances to the new cluster are shown in the range B15:B17 of Figure 8.6, and are obtained from the range D9:D11 (already derived in Figure 8.5, D9:D11).

The remaining values in the distance matrix in B14:E17 of Figure 8.6 are carried forward from the matrix in B2:F6—that is, 9 for Jan to Ken, 8 for Jan to Ned, and 14 for Ken to Ned.

Figure 8.6 completes the first stage in this single linkage process. At this point we have four clusters instead of the five we started with: Rather than five clusters with one person each we have one cluster that contains two people and three that contain one person each.

Figure 8.6

The matrix has one fewer row and column after fusing Lou and Mac.

	A	B	C	D	E	F
1		Jan	Ken	Lou	Mac	Ned
2	Jan	0				
3	Ken	9	0			
4	Lou	14	6	0		
5	Mac	13	16	5	0	
6	Ned	8	14	12	15	0
7						
8		Lou	Mac	Minimum Distance		
9	Jan	14	13	13		
10	Ken	6	16	6		
11	Ned	12	15	12		
12						
13		Lou/Mac	Jan	Ken	Ned	
14	Lou/Mac	0				
15	Jan	13	0			
16	Ken	6	9	0		
17	Ned	12	8	14	0	

We continue as we did in Figure 8.4, looking for the smallest existing distance. That value is in cell B16 of Figure 8.6, between the Ken "cluster" and the Lou/Mac cluster. Ken is to be assigned to the Lou/Mac cluster, and in preparation for that we obtain the smallest single linkages between the members of Lou/Mac/Ken, and the remaining single members, Jan and Ned (see Figure 8.7).

Figure 8.7

Bear in mind that the single linkages depend on the smallest distances between the members of existing clusters.

	A	B	C	D	E
1		Lou/Mac	Jan	Ken	Ned
2	Lou/Mac	0			
3	Jan	13	0		
4	Ken	6	9	0	
5	Ned	12	8	14	0
6					
7		Lou/Mac	Ken	Minimum Distance	
8	Jan	13	9	9	
9	Ned	12	14	12	
10					
11					
12		Lou/Mac/Ken	Jan	Ned	
13	Lou/Mac/Ken	0			
14	Jan	9	0		
15	Ned	12	8	0	

We've already established the single linkage distances between Lou/Mac and Jan, and between Lou/Mac and Ned, in Figure 8.6; in Figure 8.7 they are repeated in cells B3 and B5, and again in cells B8 and B9. The distances from Jan to Ken and from Ned to Ken are taken from the distance matrix in B2:E5 of Figure 8.7. The idea here is to determine whether moving Ken into the Lou/Mac cluster alters the single linkage distance between the Lou/Mac cluster and either Jan or Ned.

As it happens, adding Ken to the Lou/Mac cluster does alter the distance between Lou/Mac/Ken and Jan. It was 13, as shown in cell B3. But adding Ken to Lou/Mac changes the minimum distance between the cluster and Jan from 13 to 9. This is because Jan is closer to Ken (their distance is 9) than to either Lou or Mac (the distances are 14 and 13, respectively).

The single linkage distance from Lou/Mac/Ken to Ned remains at 12; adding Ken to the Lou/Mac cluster does not alter that single linkage distance.

So you can remove Ken's row and column from the distance matrix, moving him into the Lou/Mac cluster. The minimum distances established in the range D8 to D9 are used for the linkages between Lou/Mac/Ken and Jan, and Lou/Mac/Ken and Ned, in cells B14 and B15.

There's just one person-to-person distance left in the matrix, 8 between Jan and Ned in cell C15. But that value, 8, is the smallest single linkage distance left, smaller than the 9 for Lou/Mac/Ken and Jan, or the 12 for Lou/Mac/Ken and Ned. So you have a new two-person cluster consisting of Jan and Ned.

But you're not quite finished, even though you have now assigned every single person in the original distance matrix to a cluster: Lou/Mac/Ken and Jan/Ned. You still need to determine the distance between those two clusters (see Figure 8.8).

Figure 8.8
The final step is to determine the minimum distance between Lou/Mac/Ken and the members of Jan/Ned.

	A	B	C	D	E	F
1		Jan	Ken	Lou	Mac	Ned
2	Jan	0				
3	Ken	9	0			
4	Lou	14	6	0		
5	Mac	13	16	5	0	
6	Ned	8	14	12	15	0
7						
8		Lou/Mac	Jan	Ken	Ned	
9	Lou/Mac	0				
10	Jan	13	0			
11	Ken	6	9	0		
12	Ned	12	8	14	0	
13						
14		Lou/Mac/Ken	Jan	Ned		
15	Lou/Mac/Ken	0				
16	Jan	9	0			
17	Ned	12	8	0		
18						
19		Lou/Mac/Ken	Jan/Ned			
20	Lou/Mac/Ken	0				
21	Jan/Ned	9	0			

In Figure 8.8, the range B16:B17 assesses the distance from Lou/Mac/Ken to Jan (9) and to Ned (12). The smaller of these is 9, so the single linkage distance between Lou/Mac/Ken and Jan/Ned is 9. If you look back to Figure 8.4, you see that this distance is due to the distance between Ken and Jan (Figure 8.4, cell B3). Once again, recall that the definition of the single linkage distance is the minimum distance between a point in one cluster and a point in the other cluster. In this case, those two points are Ken in Lou/Mac/Ken and Jan in Jan/Ned.

The results of these steps are conventionally represented in a special type of chart called a *dendogram* (see Figure 8.9).

Figure 8.9
The dendogram can tell you the sequence in which individual observations were assigned to clusters.

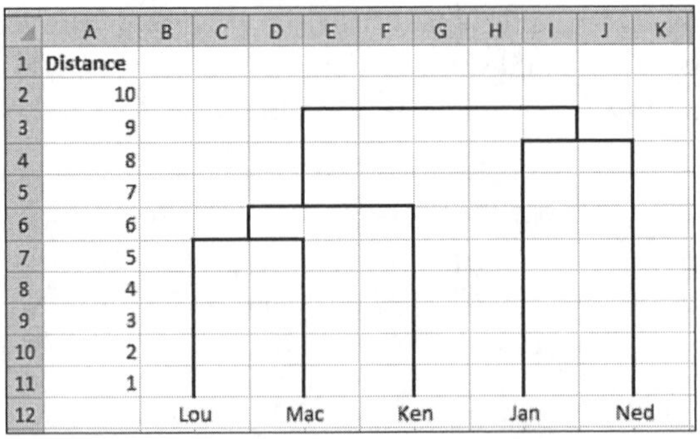

Because single linkage starts with the shortest available distance in the matrix, it's easy to tell from the dendogram which individual observations fused earlier and which ones later, and of course which observations fused with which others.

It might also be enlightening to note the distances at which the clusters acquired new members. For example, the dendogram makes it clear that Lou and Mac fused at a distance of 5, but Jan and Ned fused at a distance of 8. The difference between those distances might illuminate your theory, depending on what it is that the distances measure. It might also shed light on how Lou and Mac resemble one another, and how that differs from the ways that Jan and Ned resemble one another.

The Self-Selecting Nature of Cluster Analysis

These matters—distances at which clusters are established and the nature of the similarities between members of the same cluster—highlight one of the aspects of cluster analysis, which, depending on the use you make of it, can be either illuminating or misleading. Lou and Mac were fused into one cluster early in the process. Does that fact fit in with what else you know about Lou and Mac?

Suppose that Lou and Jan, who did not share a cluster until the final step that merged everyone, both belong to an interest group pertaining to the use of digital cameras. Suppose further that Ned and Mac, who also shared no cluster until the final step, both belong to an interest group that focuses on the programming language C#. If the distance measures are based on each person's height in inches, it would not be at all surprising to find that people who share a particular interest wind up in different clusters.

But if the distance measures are based on number of cameras owned, you might be surprised to find that Ned and Mac do not share a cluster until the final step. You might not even be able to explain that outcome in the context of the theory you're working with.

This sort of problem is hardly specific to cluster analysis. If you have two sets of numeric values you can run a t-test to assess the reliability of the difference between the means of the two sets. If you have three sets of values you can run an ANOVA instead of a t-test, with the same end in mind. If you have sets of binary outcomes you can run a chi-square test to decide whether classifications in a contingency table are independent of one another.

And it's all a waste of time, energy, and microprocessor cycles if you don't have a handle on how the data was gathered. You can always run the numbers if you have the numbers to run. Excel, Minitab, SAS, R, and similar applications will always churn out the sums of squares and the probabilities. But the inferences that you might make about populations on the basis of how the samples behave are *meaningless* without a sound experimental design to back them up, to give the numbers a context. Cluster analysis is worse than other types of classification analysis (such as logistic regression and discriminant analysis) in this regard, because you're letting the numbers form groupings instead of the other way around. This is the sort of thing that we scorn as "capitalizing on chance" in such approaches as multiple regression analysis.

But at the same time cluster analysis is not as misleading as other approaches, because it's never far from your mind that you're working without a net—that you don't have the structure of experimental design to keep the inferences grounded in reality. If that doesn't worry you, perhaps it should.

The arguments I've just advanced don't mean that cluster analysis is pointless. It's not. Used properly it's a wonderful *exploratory* technique, one that can draw your attention to hypotheses that you can subsequently test in more formal ways. And there's always the possibility of cross-validation if you have access to sufficient numbers of observations. As an exploratory technique cluster analysis can be a valuable tool, so long as you don't ask more of it than it can provide. But you're usually better off using more formal design and analysis techniques if your purpose is to explain results instead of devising hypotheses.

I've written about this before, but it's such a great example of what can go wrong that it deserves more exposure, particularly in a book about decision analytics. In the early 1970s, the University of California at Berkeley encountered considerable bad press concerning the relative admissions rates of men and women into different graduate programs. Lawsuits alleging sex discrimination were brought against the university, with the evidence that appears in Figure 8.10 as the basis for the actions.

The data in Figure 8.10 comes from Bickel, Hammel, and O'Connell, "Sex Bias in Graduate Admissions: Data From Berkeley" (*Science* 187, 1975, pps. 398–404). In Figure 8.10, the range B3:C4 shows the actual numbers of men and women who were admitted or denied admission to graduate programs at Berkeley for the fall quarter of 1973.

Figure 8.10

Men were accepted to graduate programs at rates clearly higher than were women.

| C8 | ▾ | f_x {=SUM((B3:C4-H3:I4)^2/H3:I4)} |

◢	A	B	C	D	E	F	G	H	I	J
1			Observed						Expected	
2			Admitted	Denied	Total	Percent admitted			Admitted	Denied	Total
3	Men	3738	4704	8442	44%		Men	3461	4981	8442
4	Women	1494	2827	4321	35%		Women	1771	2550	4321
5	Total	5232	7531	12763	41%		Total	5232	7531	12763
6										
7										
8		Chi-square	111.25							
9		Probability	<.001							

The marginal totals for admission status and sex are used to create the expected frequencies shown in the range H3:I4. The chi-square statistic is obtained by combining the observed with the expected frequencies, as shown in cell C8. The probability of obtaining a chi-square value as large as 111.25, with 1 degree of freedom, is less than .001.

The conclusion is that it's very unlikely to be due to chance that 44% of the male applicants were admitted when only 35% of the female applicants were admitted, when in some population representing different years and different applicants the admission rates would be much closer to one another.

And so it is, other things being equal. But Bickel, Hammel, and O'Connell analyzed the department-by-department data behind the summary findings you see in Figure 8.10 and found that other things weren't equal at all. Departments varied in the competitiveness of the admissions process. Some departments admitted nearly two-thirds of their applicants, and some admitted only one-third or one-fourth. One department admitted only one in sixteen.

The authors of the paper also found that women were disproportionately more likely to apply to the more competitive departments. Ten times more men than women applied to the noncompetitive departments. In one instance, twice as many women as men applied to a department that accepted only one-fourth of its applicants.

In general, it turned out that when the department-by-department data was considered rather than the summary graduate school data, women were being admitted to graduate programs in numbers that reflected their frequency in the population of applicants.

This phenomenon, where unequal cell frequencies are masked or even reversed when the cells are combined into larger collections, is sometimes termed the *Yule-Simpson effect*, after statisticians who had taken note of it earlier in the twentieth century. It appears not only in educational administration but in politics, bioinformatics, and many other substantive areas.

The danger is clear: It's unwise to apply inferential statistical methods, even ones as simple as a chi-square test for independence of classifications in a contingency table, without a basic understanding of how the numbers got there. It's all too easy to assume that causality is operating when category frequencies contradict our expectations.

My point is not that there was no sex bias in how admissions to the Berkeley graduate school were conducted in the 1970s. Even given the contradictory evidence unearthed by the researchers and statisticians who examined the department-level data, it's possible that sex bias was at work. It's also entirely possible that it wasn't.

My point is that because a sturdy experimental design was not employed to obtain the data, it's impossible to tell what happened. In that case, when you can't attribute an outcome to an identifiable cause that you can manipulate, probability statements are pointless. The outcome shown in Figure 8.10 might indeed be 1000-to-1 against, but you still don't know why.

It's true that designing and carrying out a convincing experiment would not be feasible. Random selection and assignment are simply not possible when the treatment groups consist of applications for admission to different departments in a prestigious graduate school. The experimenter can't just draw names from a hat and direct Ellen to apply to the PhD program in biochemistry and John to apply for a Master's degree in Russian.

Still, just because a true experiment with random selection and random assignment to groups is impossible or unethical does not mean that a convenience sample is a credible source of information for a test of statistical inference. And that's exactly what the data source in the Berkeley study consisted of: a conveniently available count of the number of men and women who applied to, and were either admitted or denied admission to, graduate study at Berkeley. As such the students were self-selected.

That's precisely what goes on with cluster analysis. The linking approaches use distance measures to assign individual records to clusters. The experimenter is out of the picture, and in an exploratory context that's the whole point. You don't know what clusters the records might already belong to—if you did, you might well apply logistic regression or discriminant function analysis. You're hoping that the data you do have, your distance measures, will help you determine the data you don't have, the cluster membership. You're not exerting assignment to groups as you would do with a truly independent variable in a classic randomized experiment. You're allowing the records to classify themselves. And in that case you have no basis for inferring that an experimental treatment was responsible for the outcome you observe—no matter how unlikely the outcome is in the context of a null hypothesis.

Finding Clusters: The Complete Linkage Method

Another hierarchical method of cluster analysis is a close cousin of the single linkage method called *complete linkage*. The complete linkage approach avoids a problem in single linkage sometimes referred to as the *chaining phenomenon*.

Recall that in the single linkage approach, you define the distance between two clusters as the smallest distance between two members of the different clusters. So, if Cluster A consists of Utah and Colorado and Cluster B consists of Kansas and Missouri, the distance between the two clusters would be the distance from Colorado to Kansas. Geographically, those two states are closer together than are any other two states such that one state is in Cluster A and the other is in Cluster B.

But complete linkage defines the distance between two clusters as the *largest* distance between two members of the different clusters. With complete linkage, the distance between Cluster A and Cluster B would be the distance from Utah to Missouri, not Colorado to Kansas. You can't get two states, one from each of those two clusters, farther apart than Utah and Missouri.

With single linkage, it's entirely possible to wind up with clusters that are a small single linkage distance apart, but that are otherwise dissimilar. The distances of the other members of Cluster A from Cluster B are not taken into account: just the two closest members factor into the distance calculation.

With complete linkage, you're not finding the minimum of the smallest distances between cluster members, as you are with single linkage. Instead, you find the minimum of the *largest* distances between cluster members. The result is that you arrange clusters so that their most dissimilar members are as close as the arrangement can make them. Complete linkage seeks to minimize the distances between clusters by arranging for the distances between the most dissimilar members to be as small as possible.

Complete Linkage: An Example

Let's take a look at how complete linkage works out in practice, using the same data set that was used earlier to illustrate single linkage. Figure 8.11 shows the complete linkage process at its outset.

Figure 8.11
The main difference between single and complete linkage is that the maximum instead of minimum values are found in the range D9:D11.

	A	B	C	D	E	F
		Jan	Ken	Lou	Mac	Ned
1						
2	Jan	0				
3	Ken	9	0			
4	Lou	14	6	0		
5	Mac	13	16	5	0	
6	Ned	8	14	12	15	0
7						
8		Lou	Mac	Maximum Distance		
9	Jan	14	13	14		
10	Ken	6	16	16		
11	Ned	12	15	15		

D9 — f_x =MAX(B9:C9)

Compare Figure 8.11 with Figure 8.5. In both cases you see that Lou and Mac comprise the first cluster, with a distance of 5 (cell D5), just as with single linkage. The range B9:C11 pulls together the distances between the other three members and the two that will merge as the first cluster. In Figure 8.5, the *minimum* distances between the observations are picked up in the range D9:D11, whereas the complete linkage approach in Figure 8.11 picks up the *maximum* distances between the observations.

The effect of this distinction isn't immediately apparent, but it soon will be. First, though, Figure 8.12 shows how the maximum distances from D9:D11 are moved into the new distance matrix in B14:E17, which loses two individual rows and columns and gains a new cluster row and column.

Figure 8.12

The maximum values from D9:D11 are placed in the new column for the Lou/Mac cluster.

	D9	▾	*fx*	=MAX(B9:C9)		
◢	A	B	C	D	E	F
1		Jan	Ken	Lou	Mac	Ned
2	Jan	0				
3	Ken	9	0			
4	Lou	14	6	0		
5	Mac	13	16	5	0	
6	Ned	8	14	12	15	0
7						
8		Lou	Mac	Maximum Distance		
9	Jan	14	13	14		
10	Ken	6	16	16		
11	Ned	12	15	15		
12						
13		Lou/Mac	Jan	Ken	Ned	
14	Lou/Mac	0				
15	Jan	14	0			
16	Ken	16	9	0		
17	Ned	15	8	14	0	

In Figure 8.6, which illustrates single linkage, the minimum distances between members are moved into the first column of the distance matrix; in Figure 8.12, which illustrates complete linkage, the maximum distances between members are used.

The first phase is complete, and it's time to find the next candidate for cluster placement (see Figure 8.13).

In Figure 8.7, the next candidate for a cluster is Ken: His distance of 6 from the Lou/Mac cluster is the smallest remaining in the distance matrix. The single distance algorithm proceeds to add Ken to the Lou/Mac cluster.

But in Figure 8.13, the smallest remaining distance is 8, between Jan and Ned in cell C5. That distance is the same as it is in Figure 8.7. But because maximum distances rather than minimum distances were used to fill out the range B3:B5 in Figure 8.13, Ken's distance from the Lou/Mac cluster is no longer 6 but 16. That distance of 16, cell B4 in Figure 8.13, is no longer the smallest distance available, and the next step does not merge Ken into the Lou/Mac cluster. Instead, a new cluster that consists of Jan and Ned is created, because their distance of 8 is the smallest remaining in the distance matrix.

Figure 8.13
The complete linkage maximum distances link Jan and Ned earlier than single linkage.

	A	B	C	D	E
1		Lou/Mac	Jan	Ken	Ned
2	Lou/Mac	0			
3	Jan	14	0		
4	Ken	16	9	0	
5	Ned	15	8	14	0
6					
7		Jan	Ned	Maximum Distance	
8	Lou/Mac	14	15	15	
9	Ken	9	14	14	
10					
11					
12		Jan/Ned	Lou/Mac	Ken	
13	Jan/Ned	0			
14	Lou/Mac	15	0		
15	Ken	14	16	0	

As a result, you need to assess the distances between Jan and Ned on one hand, and Lou/Mac and Ken on the other. That's done in the range B8:C9 in Figure 8.13, and once again the maximum distances are reported in the range D8:D9.

The new Jan/Ned cluster is formed, Jan and Ned are dropped as individuals from the distance matrix, and the new Jan/Ned cluster is added, with the maximum distances in the Jan/Ned column (see Figure 8.14).

Figure 8.14
Complete linkage puts Ken in a different cluster than does single linkage.

	A	B	C	D
1		Jan/Ned	Lou/Mac	Ken
2	Jan/Ned	0		
3	Lou/Mac	15	0	
4	Ken	14	16	0
5				
6		Jan/Ned	Ken	Maximum Distance
7	Lou/Mac	15	16	16
8				
9		Jan/Ned/Ken	Lou/Mac	
10	Jan/Ned/Ken	0		
11	Lou/Mac	16	0	

Figure 8.14 shows the conclusion of the process. The smallest distance in the matrix in the range B2:D4 is 14, between Ken and Jan/Ned. Ken is added to the Jan/Ned cluster, but first the remaining distances are assessed in B7:C7. The maximum remaining distance, 16 between Ken and Lou/Mac, is assigned as the distance between the Lou/Mac cluster and the Jan/Ned/Ken cluster. The resulting dendogram appears in Figure 8.15, along with the dendogram built from single linkage and originally shown in Figure 8.9.

Figure 8.15
It's typical for the dendogram for complete linkage to be taller than the dendogram for single linkage.

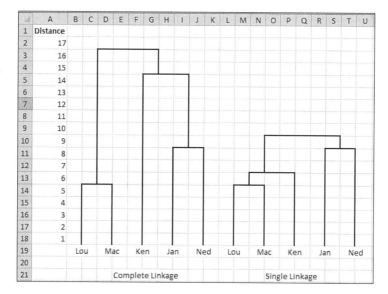

If you compare the two dendograms in Figure 8.15 you first note that the dendogram from complete linkage is taller than the dendogram from single linkage. The reason, of course, is that the distances between clusters are defined differently: minimum distances for single linkage and maximum distances for complete linkage. This means that the individual records and the clusters are fused at greater distances with complete linkage.

It's also clear that the cluster membership is different in the two dendograms, with Ken joining Lou and Mac in the single linkage approach but joining Jan and Ned in the complete linkage approach. As I emphasized in the previous section's rant about statistical analysis in the absence of experimental design and cross-validation, cluster analysis in and of itself does not enable you to make inferences about the causes of the linkages—and certainly not without information about what it is that the distances are measuring.

Other Linkage Methods

The examples presented in this chapter's section on single linkage and complete linkage are terribly sparse. I haven't provided any information about what the distances measure, or any pertinent characteristics of the individuals (Jan, Ken, and so on) themselves. The sole purpose has been to illustrate the mechanics of identifying the next linkage and recalculating the distances after another record has been added to a cluster.

With that information in hand, you can easily generalize the single linkage and the complete linkage approaches to the average linkage approach. Instead of using the minimum distance between the members of a cluster and remaining unassigned individuals (single linkage) to measure distance, or the maximum distance (complete linkage), the average linkage method uses the average distance.

But bear in mind that the average distance is defined as the average of the distances of *all* the members of a cluster and an as-yet-unassigned individual, or between all the members of one cluster and all the members of another cluster. As such the computational burden can become much greater than with single or complete linkage, and it becomes counterproductive to work out by hand an example of average linkage with even as few as five original records.

Finding Clusters: The K-means Method

The k-means method of cluster analysis is a popular approach to the problem of classifying people or objects when you don't have existing information on class membership (or when you withhold that information to test the procedure's accuracy). The k-means method is similar in some ways to the linkage methods that this chapter has looked at—for example, it depends on measures of proximity such as the Euclidean distances that this chapter also discussed. But k-means also differs from the linkage methods in some major respects, such as the use of a cluster's centroid rather than its individual records as the criterion.

> **NOTE**   The term *k-means* comes from early writings on the topic in the 1960s, in which the letter "k" simply refers to the number of clusters or their mean values.

Characteristics of K-means Analysis

The k-means method requires that you specify at the outset the number of clusters that you want formed. Some regard this requirement as a drawback because the underlying point of cluster analysis is to allow the data to dictate the structure of the clusters, and that structure ought to include the number of clusters.

On the other hand, you often have some notion as to the number of clusters you expect to emerge from the analysis. That notion might come from the theory of the situation you're examining, or from your informal observations, or from the stark reality of binary outcomes (such as likely or unlikely to survive 12 months). In such cases it matters less whether k-means analysis can determine the optimal number of clusters, and more whether k-means can accurately assign cases to those clusters.

Another feature of k-means analysis is that the initial composition of the clusters is random. The analysis proceeds by calculating the Euclidean distances between unassigned records and the means or centroids of the existing clusters. Therefore the clusters must be initialized with means or centroids at the outset so that the distances can be calculated. There are a couple of ways to accomplish the initialization, and both involve random assignment.

As a result, it's entirely possible to run a k-means analysis more than once on precisely the same set of data and obtain different results. The outcomes are due to differences in how the randomization takes place at the outset. It's not unusual to run the analysis several times in an effort to reach consensus on the composition of the clusters. (But it also happens that the same end solution is reached even when the clusters are initialized randomly.)

A K-means Example

The next few figures give you a sense of how the k-means method takes place. The actual calculations and comparisons used in applications that automate the analysis are somewhat different from those shown here, but the basics appear in this example. Chapter 9 discusses the procedures used in the applications in somewhat more detail. (That chapter also includes in its downloads from the publisher's website an Excel workbook that carries out k-means analysis.)

Suppose that you have seven records with two measures on each record, as shown in Figure 8.16.

Figure 8.16
At the outset you have seven unclassified records with two test scores each.

	A	B	C	D	E
1			Person	Test 1	Test 2
2			1	0.2	1.8
3			2	7.9	4.4
4			3	6.5	9
5			4	8.6	7.5
6			5	9.3	4.2
7			6	2.8	2.5
8			7	6.6	5.6

Because each record has two measures, k-means compares each unassigned record to the clusters' centroids.

> **NOTE** Recall from Chapter 4, "Multivariate Analysis of Variance (MANOVA)," that a centroid is simply a vector of means, such as {2,4} where 2 and 4 are both means.

To keep things straightforward, assign each of the seven records to one of two clusters. If you choose two records at random you can use them to initialize those two clusters. There are procedures in k-means analysis that enable the reassignment of records to different clusters if things change. Therefore, even if the random selection of two records for initialization purposes causes them to occupy different clusters when they should share a cluster, the opportunity exists to reassign them later on.

So, Step 1 assigns a randomly selected Person 1 to Cluster 1 and Person 4 to Cluster 2. Because they are the only records in each cluster, their values on Test 1 and Test 2 establish the two cluster centroids (see Figure 8.17).

Figure 8.17
The clusters are initialized with two randomly selected records.

	H13	▾		f_x	=D5				

	A	B	C	D	E	F	G	H	I
10				Cluster 1				Cluster 2	
11				Centroid				Centroid	
12			Person	Test 1	Test 2		Person	Test 1	Test 2
13 Step 1			1	0.2	1.8		4	8.60	7.50
14									
15			Person	Test 1	Test 2	d(Cluster 1)	d(Cluster 2)		
16			2	7.9	4.4	8.127	3.178		
17			3	6.5	9	9.567	2.581		
18			5	9.3	4.2	9.411	3.373		
19			6	2.8	2.5	2.693	7.658		
20			7	6.6	5.6	7.443	2.759		

Because Person 1 and Person 4 have been assigned to clusters they are removed from the available records that appear in the range C16:E20 in Figure 8.17. Use the distance matrix in the range F16:G20 to find the next record to assign to a cluster, as well as which cluster to use.

The entries in the distance matrix are calculated using the Euclidean distance formula discussed in earlier sections of this chapter. For example, the formula in cell F16 is

=SQRT((D16-$D$13)^2+(E16-$E$13)^2)

The formula finds the difference between Person 2's score on Test 1 and the current mean of Test 1 in Cluster 1 (D16 - $D$13), and squares that difference. To that value it adds the squared difference (E16 - $E$13) between Person 2's score on Test 2 and the current mean of Test 2 in Cluster 1. The formula then returns the square root of that sum, which is 8.127 in cell F16. The Euclidean distance between Person 2 and the current centroid for Cluster 1 is 8.127.

By making the references to D13 and E13 absolute, you can copy it down through F17:F20.

Similarly, you calculate the Euclidean distance between Person 2 and the current centroid for Cluster 2 with this formula, in cell G16:

=SQRT((D16-$H$13)^2+(E16-$I$13)^2)

And again, it can be copied and pasted through G17:G20. The distance matrix after initializing the clusters with randomly selected records is now complete, and you can choose the next record to assign to a cluster, as well as the cluster to use.

Simply select the smallest value in the distance matrix. That value's place in the matrix identifies the next person to assign and the cluster to assign him to. In this case, as shown in Figure 8.17, the smallest remaining value is 2.581 in cell G17. That cell represents the intersection of Person 3 and Cluster 2, so the next step is to assign that person to that cluster (see Figure 8.18).

Figure 8.18
By Step 2 there are only
four persons left to
assign.

	H25			f_x	=AVERAGE(D4,D5)				
	A	B	C	D	E	F	G	H	I
22				Cluster 1				Cluster 2	
23				Centroid				Centroid	
24			Person	Test 1	Test 2		Person	Test 1	Test 2
25 Step 2			1	0.20	1.80		3, 4	7.55	8.25
26									
27			Person	Test 1	Test 2	d(Cluster 1)	d(Cluster 2)		
28			2	7.9	4.4	8.127	3.866		
29			5	9.3	4.2	9.411	4.412		
30			6	2.8	2.5	2.693	7.458		
31			7	6.6	5.6	7.443	2.815		

At Step 2, the composition of Cluster 1 has not changed. It still consists only of Person 1 and so its centroid in the range D25:E25 in Figure 8.18 remains the same as in D13:E13 in Figure 8.17.

In Figure 8.18, however, Person 3 has been added to Cluster 2. Notice that cell G25 shows that the current membership of Cluster 2 is Person 3 and Person 4. The Cluster 2 centroid is now updated to take account of the membership's scores on the two tests. The value in cell H25 is

=AVERAGE(D4,D5)

and the formula in I25 is

=AVERAGE(E4,E5)

The cell references in the latter two formulas are to the original seven records shown in Figure 8.16. And the Cluster 2 centroid, which started out as {8.60, 7.50}, is now {7.55, 8.25}.

The distance matrix is also updated, to take account of the fact that the Cluster 2 centroid has changed since step 2. (Because the Cluster 1 centroid did not change in step 2, its centroid can simply be carried forward. Compare the range D25:E25 in Figure 8.18 with D13:E13 in Figure 8.17.)

The update of the distance matrix is fully analogous to the update that takes place in Figure 8.17. For example, in Figure 8.18, the formula in cell F28 is

=SQRT((D28-$D$25)^2+(E28-$E$25)^2)

This formula returns the Euclidean distance for Person 2 from the Cluster 1 centroid. After the update of all four persons in the distance matrix, the smallest value is in cell F30. The next person to enter a cluster is Person 6, into Cluster 1 (see Figure 8.19).

Figure 8.19

Cluster 1 gets its second member.

	D36	▼		*fx*	=AVERAGE(D2,D7)				
	A	B	C	D	E	F	G	H	I
33				Cluster 1				Cluster 2	
34				Centroid				Centroid	
35			Person	Test 1	Test 2		Person	Test 1	Test 2
36	Step 3		1, 6	1.50	2.15		3, 4	7.55	8.25
37									
38			Person	Test 1	Test 2	d(Cluster 1)	d(Cluster 2)		
39			2	7.9	4.4	6.784	3.866		
40			5	9.3	4.2	8.065	4.412		
41			7	6.6	5.6	6.157	2.815		

Figure 8.19, cell C36, shows that Person 6 has entered Cluster 1. As shown in Figure 8.19, the centroid for Cluster 1 is updated using these formulas in cell D36:

   =AVERAGE(D2,D7)

and in cell E36:

   =AVERAGE(E2,E7)

Again, you can find the original values in rows 2 and 7 in Figure 8.16. With the centroids updated, the distance matrix is recalculated as in Figure 8.19, and the smallest value in the matrix, 2.815, is in cell G41.

By this point you see the pattern:

1. Find the smallest value in the distance matrix, which tells you the next record to be added to a cluster and which cluster to add it to.
2. Recalculate the cluster centroids. (In fact, you need to recalculate only the centroid of the cluster that just got a new member.)
3. Drop the record that has just been added to a cluster from the distance matrix.
4. Recalculate the distance matrix according to the current values of the cluster centroids.

Let's skip to the conclusion of Step 6 in Figure 8.20.

Figure 8.20 shows that all seven records have now been assigned to the two clusters, two records to Cluster 1 and five records to Cluster 2. It's handy at this point to be able to confirm that the cluster memberships are as they should be, so the distance matrix is updated once more, this time with all seven records in it as shown in F68:G74 of Figure 8.20.

You can tell from the distance matrix that Persons 1 and 6, who were assigned to Cluster 1, have lower values in the distance matrix for Cluster 1 than they do for Cluster 2; therefore, they remain correctly assigned. Similarly, Persons 2, 3, 4, 5 and 7 have lower values in the distance matrix for Cluster 2 than they do for Cluster 1; therefore, they also remain correctly assigned.

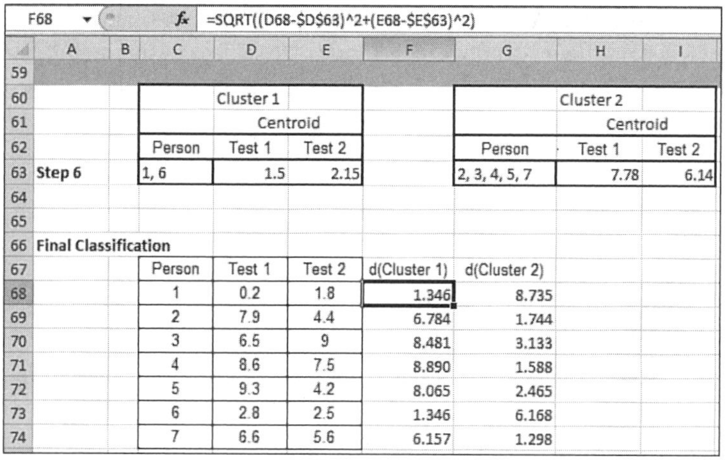

Figure 8.20
You can find Steps 4 and
5 in the downloaded
workbook for Chapter 8.

It can happen, during the looping that assigns members to clusters and that updates the distance matrix, that a record that earlier belonged to, say, Cluster 1 would now be assigned to Cluster 2, because the values of the clusters' centroids have changed in the interim. The algorithms followed by the code that automates k-means cluster analysis typically perform checks for that sort of reassignment.

Benchmarking K-means with R

Chapter 6, "Discriminant Function Analysis: Further Issues," describes how to obtain and install the R freeware statistical application on your computer. R has a k-means function that I occasionally find useful for the purpose of benchmarking results I get in Excel. It's a good idea to familiarize yourself with R's offering regardless of the software you use to actually carry out k-means cluster analysis. When it's possible to get different results for a cluster analysis despite using the same inputs time after time—because of the random ways that the cluster centroids are initialized—it's wise to check your results against a different application.

Here's how to obtain a k-means cluster analysis using R. I use the same data set, seven records and two variables, that is used in the previous section.

I assume that you have already obtained and installed R. As I did in Chapter 6, I show what you are expected to type in **boldface** and R's responses in `this typeface`.

Begin by saving a .csv file with the data as shown in the range C1:E8 of Figure 8.16. You can move the data into A1:C8 if you want. I'll assume that you save the .csv file to your C:\ root, and that the data file is named kmeans.csv. Start R and enter these commands:

```
> indata <- read.csv("C:/kmeans.csv", header=TRUE, row.names=1)
> km <- kmeans(indata,2,20)
> print(km)
```

The *kmeans* arguments specify the data frame (*indata*), the number of clusters to establish (*2*), and the maximum number of iterations (*20*). The maximum number of iterations is set so as to avoid a situation in which the code enters an assignment-and-allocation loop that it can't otherwise terminate.

R responds with the following results:

```
K-means clustering with 2 clusters of sizes 5, 2

Cluster means:
  Test.1 Test.2
1   7.78   6.14
2   1.50   2.15
```

Compare the preceding cluster means with the cluster centroids shown in Figure 8.20, D63:E63 and H63:I63. The cluster numbers are reversed, probably because of how R initialized the clusters with random selections. However, the ending centroids are identical.

```
Clustering vector:
1 2 3 4 5 6 7
2 1 1 1 1 2 1
```

Records 1 and 6 are assigned to Cluster 2, and the remaining five records are assigned to Cluster 1. Again, the cluster identifiers are the reverse of those established in Figures 8.16 through 8.20.

Chapter 9 goes into the meanings of the remaining components of the k-means results, including the within, between, and total sums of squares called out next in the R results.

```
Within cluster sum of squares by cluster:
[1] 23.140  3.625
 (between_SS / total_SS =  74.7 %)

Available components:

[1] "cluster"      "centers"      "totss"       "withinss"
"tot.withinss"
[6] "betweenss"    "size"
```

You can access these components using the following syntax:

```
> kmeans(indata,2)$totss
[1] 105.8486
> kmeans(indata,2)$betweenss
[1] 79.08357
> kmeans(indata,2)$withinss
[1] 23.140  3.625
```

Let's move on now beyond the pure mechanics of the k-means method. Chapter 9 looks at some of the finer points of this type of cluster analysis, as well as its relationships to other methods that I haven't covered here.

Cluster Analysis: Further Issues

Chapter 8, "Cluster Analysis: The Basics," covers some introductory aspects of cluster analysis and discusses two fundamentally different approaches: linkage or hierarchical methods, and centroid distances methods, particularly the popular k-means procedures. The focus in Chapter 8 is on the mechanics of each approach.

This chapter focuses exclusively on the k-means approach. An Excel workbook named Kmeans Cluster Analysis.xls accompanies this chapter, and it contains code that performs a k-means analysis on data that you supply. The first portion of this chapter walks you through the steps involved in using the workbook and the information that it returns.

The second half of the chapter explores two examples of using cluster analysis in conjunction with principal components analysis. It points out some of the traps that can mislead you if you don't keep in mind what it is that you're up to. It also shows how it's possible to obtain much more powerful results from cluster analysis if you precede it with a principal components analysis that returns useful data reductions.

Using the K-means Workbook

The Kmeans Cluster Analysis.xls workbook, which can be downloaded with this chapter, contains code that carries out a k-means analysis on data that you supply. Let's walk through how to use it, with the state crime data as an example. Figure 9.1 shows a portion of that data set (which is included in the Excel workbook that you can download from the publisher's website for this book).

Figure 9.1
Including meaningful
record identifiers can help
in a variety of ways.

	A	B	C	D	E	F	G	H
1	Murder	Rape	Robbery	Assault	Burglary	Larceny	Auto Theft	State
2	12.2	26.1	71.8	168	790	2183	551	AK
3	11.7	18.5	50.3	215	763	1125	223	AL
4	10.1	17.1	45.6	150	885	1211	109	AR
5	9.5	27	120.2	214	1493	3550	501	AZ
6	6.9	35.1	206.9	226	1753	3422	689	CA
7	6.2	36	129.1	185	1381	2992	588	CO
8	3.5	9.1	70.4	87	1084	1751	484	CT
9	7.7	18.6	105.5	196	1056	2320	559	DE
10	12.7	22.2	186.1	277	1562	2861	397	FL
11	15.3	10.1	95.8	177	900	1869	309	GA
12	3.6	11.8	63.3	43	1456	3106	581	HI
13	1.9	6.2	28.6	48	507	1743	175	IA
14	4.6	12.3	20.5	86	674	2214	144	ID
15	9.6	20.4	251.1	187	765	2028	518	IL

There's just one rigid requirement for your input data. It should be laid out like an Excel list or table, with each row representing a different record and each column representing a different variable.

If you want to include variable names in the first row, by all means do so. The Kmeans Cluster Analysis.xls code makes provision for them, but if you don't supply variable names, then the output uses default values such as Variable 1, Variable 2, and so on.

It's also helpful to supply record IDs, such as the state abbreviations shown in Figure 9.1. They can be placed to the right or to the left of the main data set, but not within it. For example, also in Figure 9.1, the state names could be in column A instead of column H, with the main data set moved from columns A through G into columns B through H.

Begin by opening the Kmeans Cluster Analysis.xls workbook, and then open or switch to the worksheet that contains the data you want to cluster. If the Add-Ins tab was not already visible on the Ribbon, you should see it there after opening the Kmeans workbook.

Click the Add-Ins tab and then click the Kmeans item. (If you're using a version of Excel prior to Excel 2007, look instead in Excel's Data menu.) You see the dialog box shown in Figure 9.2.

I recommend that you use record identifiers, such as state abbreviations used here, with your own data sets. If you run a cluster analysis using two or more different applications (such as R or SPSS), it's much easier to track down the reasons for discrepancies in the results if record IDs are available to compare the outcomes. The record identifiers also turn out to be helpful if you first extract principal components from the original data set, as I illustrate later in this chapter. In that case, you might need a way to link the records in the principal components analysis to the original records. Unique record identifiers are necessary for that.

Most important, using record identifiers can help you determine what the clusters represent if you know which specific records were placed in each cluster. That process, which is usually a subjective rather than objective or empirical one, is always easier when the records have meaningful identifiers instead of numeric or text codes.

Figure 9.2
Leave the Record IDs box blank if you aren't using them.

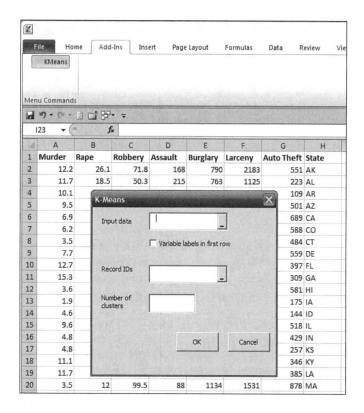

With the data as laid out in Figure 9.1, you would complete the dialog box in Figure 9.2 as follows:

- Input Data box: The address should be A1:G51. Include the first row of variable names, but omit the record IDs in column H.
- Select the Variable Labels in First Row check box.
- Record IDs box: The range address should be H2:H51. Leave the box blank if you have not supplied record identifiers.
- Number of Clusters box: Enter the number of clusters you want the code to establish.

Deciding on the Number of Clusters

The fact that you must supply the number of clusters, a largely subjective and sometimes ambiguous choice, is generally regarded as a genuine drawback in the theory of k-means cluster analysis. Hierarchical linkage methods do not impose this requirement on you. Instead, as Chapter 8 demonstrates, both the clusters themselves and the number of clusters emerge from the nature of the linkages that are found, as well as the location on the dendogram where you focus your attention.

It's true that picking a number of clusters for k-means to deal with can be a problem. Some who have written on the theory of cluster analysis recommend a two-stage process: a first stage that deploys one of the linkage methods discussed in Chapter 8, and a second stage that consists of a k-means analysis. The idea is that the linkage analysis (which does not require that you specify the number of clusters to return) informs you how many clusters to specify for the second, k-means stage.

There are a couple of good reasons that this two-stage approach makes little sense. One is that the linkage methods start with as many clusters as they have records, and end up with just one cluster. (See, for example, Figure 8.15.) Writers who espouse this approach recommend specifying as many clusters for the second stage as there are "major" clusters identified in the first stage. Left unstated is the criterion to apply for the identification of a major cluster.

The second reason to avoid this approach is that nothing more than simple arithmetic is involved in the identification of clusters using the linkage methods. It's always up to the researcher—as it should be—to decide if the composition of the clusters makes sense and, if so, which clusters are sensible. But if exploratory work via a linkage method suggests a meaningful cluster structure, there must be enough meat on the bones of the underlying theory to suggest, at least roughly, how many clusters make sense. Else it wouldn't be possible even to decide whether a cluster was meaningful.

Some have recommended, and have implemented in R scripts, an approach to k-means analysis that calculates the sum of squared errors, or SSE, for different numbers of clusters of the same set of data. In other words, the script repeats the cluster analysis for two clusters, then three clusters, then four and so on, recording the SSE for each analysis.

This procedure expects that as the number of clusters increases, the SSE decreases. The reason is that when there are more clusters, the distances of each point to its cluster's centroid decrease. In the extreme, when there are as many clusters as there are records, each record constitutes its own cluster and each record's Euclidean distance to its own centroid is zero.

Using a line chart, the SSE figures are then plotted against number of clusters to form a graph that looks much like a scree chart in principal components analysis. Sometimes an elbow appears in the chart, where the rate of decrease in the SSE abruptly slows, indicating that the returns from larger numbers of clusters have begun to diminish. The theory suggests that the number of clusters in use where the elbow appears is the number of clusters to specify.

Strictly as a matter of personal preference, I'm not a fan of this approach. I suppose that it's better than a blind guess, because it at least has some empirical rationale behind it. And it's similar to an approach, one that I use, to determine the constant to employ in exponential smoothing. (See *Predictive Analytics: Microsoft Excel*, Que, 2012, Chapter 4.)

But I'm much more comfortable choosing a number of clusters that is suggested by the theory of the situation. Obviously I would call for three clusters, for example, if I were using cluster analysis with the Iris data set discussed in Chapter 6 on discriminant function analysis—three species of irises, so look for three clusters.

Sometimes, though, you don't have such a clear criterion to guide you. In those cases I think that you need to face the fact that you're in a highly exploratory situation that requires you to bring more thought and less automation to the results. Look at the composition of your clusters—which records each cluster includes—and decide whether they make sense in terms of the nature of your data and your understanding of the relationships involved. If not, try again with a different number of clusters. Unfortunately there's no automatic scree chart that plots meaningfulness against number of clusters.

For the purpose of this example, I called for three clusters in the dialog box shown in Figure 9.2. When you have finished with the dialog box, click OK. After the code completes, you will find new worksheets in your workbook. They are discussed in the next several sections.

The Cluster Members Worksheet

The Cluster Members worksheet consists of three columns, as shown in Figure 9.3.

Figure 9.3
The records are sorted by
Record ID within cluster.

	A	B	C	D	E	F
1	Record IDs	Clusters	Distances			
2	AL	1	74.523			Records in Clusters
3	AR	1	118.469		1	14
4	KY	1	83.102		2	10
5	ME	1	37.535		3	26
6	MS	1	188.935		Grand Total	50
7	NC	1	125.473			
8	ND	1	145.928			
9	NE	1	181.519			
10	NH	1	77.962			
11	PA	1	77.716			
12	SD	1	123.848			

The column contents are as follows:

- Column A contains the record identifiers. These are either the identifiers you have supplied (Column H in Figure 9.2) or the default identifiers supplied by the k-means code.

- Column B contains the cluster numbers. These numbers are arbitrary and are assigned by the code. If you benchmark the results from the Kmeans Cluster Analysis.xls workbook against the results from another application, the cluster identifiers will likely be

different. This is why it's a good idea to supply your own meaningful record identifiers: else, you might have difficulty matching up the records returned by two different
analyses.

■ Column C contains the Euclidean distance of each record from the centroid of the
cluster it's assigned to.

The data is automatically sorted, first by cluster number and then by record identifier
within cluster number.

Note also that a pivot table is supplied, showing the number of records assigned to each
cluster.

The distances in Column C are the Euclidean distances discussed in Chapter 8. The *basis*
of each state's distance is the difference between its values from the means of the associated variables for the record's cluster: for example, the state's murder rate less the average
murder rate for the state's cluster. But the *distances reported* in Figure 9.3 are an expression
of each variable's distance, appropriately squared and then added to the other variables'
squared distances. The sum is divided by the number of variables and the square root is
taken. (These steps are called out in detail in Chapter 8.)

The process of computing the distances is awkward to express in words but straightforward to express in figures. Figure 9.4 has an example of how the distances in Figure 9.3 are
calculated.

Figure 9.4
The distance reported in
Figure 9.3 for Alabama.

				E13	▼	f_x	=AVERAGE(A11:G11)	
	A	B	C	D	E	F	G	H
1	Murder	Rape	Robbery	Assault		I rceny	Auto Theft	State
2	11.70	18.50	50.30	215.00	763.00	1125.00	223.00	AL
3								
4	Murder	Rape	Robbery	Assault	Burglary	Larceny	Auto Theft	Cluster
5	6.33	11.04	40.66	115.21	598.57	1114.00	183.21	1
6								
7	Differences							
8	5.37	7.46	9.64	99.79	164.43	11.00	39.79	
9								
10	Squared Differences							
11	28.85	55.72	92.98	9957.19	27036.76	121.00	1582.90	
12								
13	Average of squared differences:				5553.63			
14								
15			Square root of average:		74.523			

The process as shown in Figure 9.4 is just an extension to seven variables of the steps discussed in Chapter 8 for one- and two-variable situations. The elements are illustrated in
Figure 9.4:

■ The data in row 2 consists of the crime rates in the state of Alabama in the early 1970s.

■ The data in row 5 consists of the mean crime rates for the states in cluster 1.

■ Row 8 contains the differences—the univariate distances—between Alabama's crime rates and cluster 1's crime rates.

■ Row 11 contains the squared differences.

■ Cell E13 takes the average of the squared differences, and cell E15 takes the square root of that average.

Compare the value in cell E15 of Figure 9.4, which is 74.523, with the value in cell C2 of Figure 9.3, the distance for Alabama as calculated by the Kmeans Cluster Analysis.xls code. They are identical.

> **NOTE**   In the context of worksheet formulas, it's worth noting that you could use Excel's SUMXMY2() function instead of taking the individual steps shown in Figure 9.4. For example, this formula:
>
> =SQRT(SUMXMY2(A2:G2,A5:G5)/7)
>
> entered on the worksheet shown in Figure 9.4 would return the same value, 74.523, as shown in cell E15. The SUMXMY2() function would find the differences between the values in A2:G2 and those in A5:G5, square the differences, and return the sum of the squared differences. It remains only to divide by the number of variables, 7, and take the square root.

The Cluster Centroids Worksheet

The centroids for each cluster are shown in the Cluster Centroids worksheet (see Figure 9.5).

Figure 9.5
Each numeric entry is the mean value for a given cluster.

	A	B	C	D
1		Cluster 1	Cluster 2	Cluster 3
2	Murder	6.329	6.860	7.142
3	Rape	11.036	22.570	15.408
4	Robbery	40.657	148.970	116.023
5	Assault	115.214	162.800	135.769
6	Burglary	598.571	1450.600	909.769
7	Larceny	1114.000	3038.300	1969.346
8	Auto Theft	183.214	489.200	420.615
9				

Taken together, the mean values in the range B2:B8 in Figure 9.5 constitute the centroid for cluster 1. The centroid for cluster 2 is in C2:C8 and for cluster 3 in D2:D8.

Each mean value, such as the mean of 6.329 for Murder in cluster 1 (cell B2), is the actual mean on a given variable for the records assigned to that cluster as of the final iteration of the Kmeans Cluster Analysis.xls code. As I mention in Chapter 8, the k-means procedure begins by establishing random cluster membership. The procedure iterates through steps that reassign records to different clusters with the goal of reducing the distances, reported in Figure 9.3, within each cluster. Each time a cluster's membership changes, through gaining or losing a record, the centroids are recalculated to accurately reflect the current membership.

The iterations stop when the reassignment procedure completes without having reassigned any records. It's at this point that the model is frozen, centroids are finalized, and ending distances calculated.

It's easy enough to verify these centroids (and therefore the distances in Figure 9.3, which are based on the centroids). Figure 9.6 calculates the centroids outside the context of the cluster analysis.

Figure 9.6
The pivot table entries are identical to the values in Figure 9.5.

	A	B	C	D	E	F	G	H	I
1		Clusters ▼							
2	Values	1	2	3					
3	Murder	6.329	6.860	7.142					
4	Rape	11.036	22.570	15.408					
5	Robbery	40.657	148.970	116.023					
6	Assault	115.214	162.800	135.769					
7	Burglary	598.571	1450.600	909.769					
8	Larceny	1114.000	3038.300	1969.346					
9	Auto Theft	183.214	489.200	420.615					
10									
11									
12	Cluster	Murder	Rape	Robbery	Assault	Burglary	Larceny	Auto Theft	State
13	3	12.2	26.1	71.8	168	790	2183	551	AK
14	1	11.7	18.5	50.3	215	763	1125	223	AL
15	1	10.1	17.1	45.6	150	885	1211	109	AR
16	2	9.5	27	120.2	214	1493	3550	501	AZ

In Figure 9.6 I attached the cluster assignments to the original data set shown in Figure 9.1. Then I built the pivot table report shown in the range A1:D9, putting Cluster in the pivot table's Column area and each of the crime rate variables in the Σ Values area. Of course, you need to choose to show each crime rate variable as an Average rather than the default Sum.

TIP

By default Excel lays out a pivot table with multiple Σ Values fields strung out side by side, left to right. You can override this default and lay out the table with the Σ Values fields arranged vertically, as shown in Figure 9.6. To do so, right-click any cell in the pivot table and choose Show Field List from the shortcut menu. Click any field's name in the Σ Values area of the Pivot Table Field List dialog box (or click the drop-down arrow to the right of the field's name). You get another shortcut menu. One of its items is Move to Row Labels. Click that item to move the Σ Values field to the Row Labels area.

The Cluster Variances Worksheet

One way to view how tightly the individual records in a cluster surround the cluster's centroid is by way of the cluster variances. These are shown for the state crime rate analysis in Figure 9.7.

Figure 9.7
The variances are based on the sum of the variables' Euclidean distances.

	A	B	C
1	Cluster	Variance	
2	1	100736.6	
3	2	136214.9	
4	3	161897.0	
5			

The smaller the variance, of course, the more tightly the records swarm around the cluster's centroid. The variance for cluster 1 is considerably smaller than for cluster 2 or cluster 3. An imaginary scatterchart with seven axes would show the 14 records in cluster 1 surrounding the centroid much more closely than the remaining records surround their own centroids. If we were working with two variables instead of seven, a standard scatterchart might show the states in cluster 1 form a cigar shape around the trendline. Other scattercharts might show the states in clusters 2 and 3 forming shapes closer to a circle around their trendlines.

The cluster variances are closely related to the individual states' distances given in Figure 9.3. Figure 9.8 shows how to get from one to the other.

Figure 9.8
Calculating the variance for cluster 1 from its individual states' distances.

	A	B	C	D	E	F
1	Record ID	Clusters	Distances			
2	AL	1	74.523		=C2^2*7	38875.4
3	AR	1	118.469		=C3^2*7	98243.6
4	KY	1	83.102		=C4^2*7	48342.0
5	ME	1	37.535		=C5^2*7	9861.9
6	MS	1	188.935		=C6^2*7	249876.3
7	NC	1	125.473		=C7^2*7	110203.9
8	ND	1	145.928		=C8^2*7	149065.8
9	NE	1	181.519		=C9^2*7	230645.1
10	NH	1	77.962		=C10^2*7	42546.2
11	PA	1	77.716		=C11^2*7	42278.2
12	SD	1	123.848		=C12^2*7	107367.6
13	TN	1	97.967		=C13^2*7	67182.3
14	VT	1	81.778		=C14^2*7	46813.0
15	WV	1	155.385		=C15^2*7	169011.8
16						
17					=AVERAGE(F2:F15)	100736.6

The states assigned by the cluster analysis to cluster 1 are shown in Figure 9.8. The process I describe here to calculate the individual states' distances from the cluster centroid is not used by the Kmeans Cluster Analysis.xls code, but it serves to show the relationship between the distances and the variances.

The first step is to undo some of the work done in constructing the distances. The distances are squared and multiplied by the number of variables in the centroid. Recall from the discussion of the process that is carried out in Figure 9.4 that the final step is to take the square root of the average squared distance. We reverse part of that by squaring the distance. And we convert the result, the average squared distance, to the total squared distance by multiplying by the number of squared distances—in this case, 7, one for each crime rate variable.

Those two calculations, squaring the distance and multiplying by 7, are carried out in Figure 9.8 in the range F2:F15. (The formulas are spelled out in the range E2:E15.)

We now have in F2:F15 the squared distance of each state in cluster 1 from the centroid of cluster 1. There's a useful analogy here: When you calculate the variance of a single variable, you find the deviation of each case's value from the mean of the variable, and you square each of the deviations. In a multivariate context that's what's happening in F2:F15. Each of those values is the squared Euclidean distance between a state's values on the seven crime rate variables and the cluster's centroid, summed over the seven variables.

We then find the average of the squared Euclidean distances in cell F17. Again the relationship to the calculation of a univariate variance is clear: The univariate variance is the average squared deviation of individual values from their mean. The variance of a cluster is the average squared Euclidean distance of the record's values (here, crime rates) from the cluster's centroid.

TIP Again, a more concise way of calculating the centroid's variance from the states' distances is by way of this array formula (entered using Ctrl+Shift+Enter instead of simply using Enter):

=AVERAGE(C2:C15^2*7)

But breaking it out into its constituent steps makes the relationship between the multivariate and the univariate variance much more crisp.

The F-Ratios Worksheet

The code in the Kmeans Cluster Analysis.xls workbook also produces a worksheet named *F-Ratios*. The worksheet contains the building blocks for F-ratios, as well as the F-ratios themselves, for each variable used in carrying out the cluster analysis.

You might be accustomed to seeing F-ratios used in the context of inferential statistics. In an ANOVA, for example, a calculated F-ratio is compared to a distribution of F-ratios that could come about under the null hypothesis of no differences in the means of different groups.

You might then get an F-ratio that's so large, given its degrees of freedom, that it's irrational to conclude that there are no differences between the group means in the population. Or you might get an F-ratio that's so small that it provides no rationale for concluding that the group means in the population are anything but identical.

But that sort of use of the F-ratio, to make inferences about population means from sample means, is just one rationale. As a ratio of variances—and that's what an F-ratio is—it is perfectly useful as a descriptive statistic, like a mean or a standard deviation. And the F-ratio is particularly useful in the evaluation of the results of a cluster analysis.

Take a step back from the minutiae of the worksheet contents discussed in the last few sections of this chapter and refocus on the purpose of cluster analysis, whether that's performed using a linkage method or a centroid-based approach such as k-means. The idea is to find clusters of records with the characteristics that members of the same cluster are relatively close to one another, and that different clusters are relatively distant from one another.

Given that perspective, an F-ratio is a handy way of looking at the differences between clusters *on a univariate basis*. An example using the crime rate data appears in Figure 9.9.

Figure 9.9
The F-ratios are used as descriptive rather than as inferential statistics.

	A	B	C	D	E	F
1	Variable	SSB	DFB	SSW	DFW	F-Ratio
2						
3	Murder	6.025767	2	719.516	47	0.196807
4	Rape	778.4156	2	1867.392	47	9.795892
5	Robbery	79843.86	2	327651.5	47	5.726605
6	Assault	13215.61	2	214492.6	47	1.447914
7	Burglary	4258682	2	2128808	47	47.01175
8	Larceny	21636222	2	3052802	47	166.5523
9	Auto Theft	696911.9	2	1255442	47	13.04515

Recall that to calculate an F-ratio in the context of ANOVA, you divide the mean square between by the mean square within. The term *mean square* is just a traditional way of referring to a variance. As I discuss in Chapter 3, "Univariate Analysis of Variance (ANOVA)," the *mean square between* is an estimate of the variance in a data set that is based on the differences between group means—in the context of cluster analysis, that's the distance between clusters.

The *mean square within* is another way of estimating the variance in the data set, but it is independent of differences between group means. It is the average of the variance within each group—and in the context of cluster analysis, that's the variability between the records in a cluster.

So an F-ratio, the result of dividing the variance between clusters by the variance within clusters, is an excellent way to assess the results of a cluster analysis. It tells you, in one number, whether the clusters are far apart from one another relative to the variability within the clusters.

The F-ratios reported in Figure 9.9 are obviously univariate F-ratios. They are not the sort of multivariate F-ratios that are related to Wilks' lambda and discussed in Chapter 4, "Multivariate Analysis of Variance (MANOVA)." The F-ratios in Figure 9.9 tell you whether clusters are close or are far apart on the basis of Murder rates, Burglary rates, Larceny rates, and so on. As such, they can help you decide whether to retain a given variable in a subsequent and similar cluster analysis.

For example, the F-ratios for Murder (cell F3) and for Assault (cell F6) suggest that those two variables are not of much help in distinguishing the clusters that the analysis has established. If you were considering replicating the analysis using data from a different year, you might consider first dropping Murder and Assault from the data set and rerunning the analysis with the data that is otherwise the same. It is possible that the presence of Murder and Assault is doing nothing but making the clusters more difficult to distinguish.

Apart from the absence of p-values (because the F-ratios are being treated as descriptive rather than inferential statistics), the analyses shown in Figure 9.9 are nothing more than stripped-down, univariate ANOVAs. For example, Figure 9.10 shows a standard univariate ANOVA in which the three identified clusters are the independent variable, and Auto Theft is the dependent variable.

Figure 9.10
Compare this analysis with that for Auto Theft in Figure 9.9.

	A	B	C	D	E	F	G	H	I
1	Cluster				Anova: Single Factor				
2	1	2	3						
3	223	501	551		SUMMARY				
4	109	689	484		*Groups*	*Count*	*Sum*	*Average*	*Variance*
5	346	588	559		Cluster 1	14	2565	183.214	9405.258
6	146	397	309		Cluster 2	10	4892	489.200	18608.400
7	78	581	175		Cluster 3	26	10936	420.615	38627.926
8	169	464	144						
9	91	661	518						
10	292	333	429		ANOVA				
11	172	316	257		*SV*	*SS*	*df*	*MS*	*F*
12	340	362	385		Between Groups	696911.9	2	348455.955	13.04515
13	94		878		Within Groups	1255442	47	26711.534	
14	289		548						
15	124		346		Total	1952354	49		

Figure 9.10 arranges the Auto Theft rates by cluster in columns A through C. The range E1:I15 contains the results of the Data Analysis add-in's ANOVA: Single Factor tool, run using the data in columns A through C.

Notice that the F-ratio in cell I12 of Figure 9.10 is identical to the F-ratio in cell F9 of Figure 9.9. The same is true of the sum of squares between and within, and the degrees of freedom between and within. Therefore, if you were to calculate the mean squares between and within for Figure 9.9 you would find that they were equal to the mean squares reported in Figure 9.10.

Why have I omitted the p-values that you would normally see in a univariate ANOVA? For one of the same reasons that you might prefer to precede several univariate ANOVAS by a MANOVA. When you have more than one dependent variable measured on the same beings or objects, it's normal for the dependent variables to be correlated, and the correlations have effects—effects that can't be quantified—on the probabilities of obtaining the observed F-ratios. P-values associated with multiple, univariate F-ratios based on the same subjects have no meaning, and it's pointless to include them.

Nevertheless, the F-ratios can be useful in a cluster analysis when, as here, you regard them as descriptive rather than inferential statistics.

Reporting Process Statistics

The final worksheet produced by the Kmeans Cluster Analysis.xls workbook is named Process Summary. It recaps the information already shown in the other four worksheets and adds a bit of data regarding the process of establishing the clusters. I don't find the information useful all the time by any means, but it saves me some grief every so often.

Figure 9.11 shows the Process Summary worksheet for the state crime rate cluster analysis.

Figure 9.11
This sheet helps jog my memory as to the number of records and variables I used.

	A	B	C	D
1	Summary statistics:			
2				
3	3 iterations were required			
4	3 clusters were requested			
5	50 records were clustered			
6	7 variables were analyzed			
7				
8	Cluster	Records in cluster	Percent records in cluster	Variance
9	1	10	20.0%	136214.9
10	2	26	52.0%	161897.0
11	3	14	28.0%	100736.6
12				
13	Total	50	100.0%	139635.7

The first piece of new information is the number of iterations required, shown in cell A3. As I mentioned in Chapter 8, as records are moved into and out of clusters, the cluster centroids change. When the centroids change, it often happens that a record that belonged to a cluster with an earlier centroid no longer should belong to that cluster; a different cluster's centroid is now closer to the record.

Therefore the code enters a loop after the initial assignment of records to clusters. Every pass through the loop recalculates the cluster centroids and reassigns records accordingly. After a pass through the loop during which no records change clusters, the clusters are regarded as stable, the loop terminates, and the reports are written to the worksheets.

On rare occasions it can happen that the reassignment loop would not terminate because a record changes clusters in such a way that when the centroids are recalculated, that record or another is moved back to the cluster it occupied during an earlier iteration. Therefore, to keep the loop from executing interminably I have established a maximum number of iterations: 50. Very rarely will you encounter a situation in which you need more than 50 iterations. (I have never encountered one, but the need to cover something requires me to use the phrase "very rarely.")

The Process Summary worksheet gives you the actual count of the number of iterations that were needed to reach a stable set of clusters.

You're also given the number of clusters you requested, and the number of records and the number of variables in your input data. Certainly you could get this information by summarizing the data in the Cluster Members worksheet and in the Cluster Centroids worksheet. But it's a lot quicker to find it in the Process Summary worksheet.

Why would you want easy access to this information? Cluster analysis is usually exploratory, and you wind up running it multiple times, looking for the outcome that makes the most sense (if in fact there is one). You often change the number of input variables when you do so—for example, if you try the analysis both with raw data and with derived principal components; see the next section for more on that. You also change the number of clusters you ask for, in an attempt to find the optimal number. There are also occasions when the number of records changes, particularly when you're in a position to cross-validate an outcome.

Excel worksheets and workbooks lend themselves well to documenting such issues. But documentation is often the last thing on your mind when you're looking for a compelling finding. Having access to statistics such as these, automatically provided, can help you backtrack to the data set that was behind a particular result.

Cluster Analysis Using Principal Components

Chapter 7, "Principal Components Analysis," discusses the notion of principal components and how principal components analysis can reduce a large, perhaps unmanageable number of measured variables to a smaller and workable number of components. Factor rotation can further enable you to make better sense of what the components are measuring. Chapter 7 also discusses how principal component analysis can sometimes result in dimensions that enable you to classify records without prior knowledge of the categories.

If that sounds anything like cluster analysis, it should. In fact, in recent years (say, 2004 and later) theorists have explored the relationship between k-means cluster analysis and principal components analysis. It's well beyond the scope of this book to dive into the mathematical underpinnings of that relationship, but if you're interested and have the necessary background you might find Ding and He's "K-means Clustering via Principal Component Analysis," *Proceedings of the International Conference on Machine Learning*, pages 225–232, a good place to start learning about how principal components and k-means cluster analysis are equivalent in several ways.

The basic notion is that both principal components analysis and k-means cluster analysis are data-reduction techniques. Principal components analysis performs the data reduction by deriving relatively few components from relatively many measured variables, based on how the measured variables load on the components. Then the locations of individual records can be examined, on the basis of each record's score on the components that are retained. If n components are retained, they define an n-dimensional space in which each record can be located.

K-means cluster analysis goes at the problem of data reduction from the other end, creating a space that's defined by the distances of individual records from the centroids of clusters.

(In fact, Ding and He refer to that space as *classification space*.) You don't get the same results using the two approaches on the same data set, for a variety of reasons; not the least of the reasons is the set of decisions made by the analyst regarding such issues as the number of clusters to establish. Nevertheless, the approaches are in many ways equivalent.

Furthermore, it's definitely possible and often profitable to combine the two approaches. One such combination has been used for decades, and it involves the extraction of principal components as a first step and the establishment of clusters, based on component scores, as a second step. I explore that approach—both its advantages and its drawbacks—in the remainder of this section.

Principal Components Revisited

Chapter 7 takes a look at the states' crime rate data from the point of view of principal components analysis. Among other results, the states' scores on two principal components are presented and charted: Two components are chosen because only the first two eigenvalues have values of 1.0 or greater. (Other criteria are available for choosing components, of course, but the 1.0 criterion is so popular that many applications use it as the default option. And it makes good sense, both empirically and in theory.)

Before rotation using the Varimax method, the two principal components are pretty clearly All Crimes Except Murder (the first component) and Murder (the second component). That's not at all an unusual outcome in principal components analysis. You wind up with a first component that carries high loadings on most of the measured variables, and subsequent components that each have only one, or possibly two, moderately high loadings.

So it's normal to rotate the components—that is, the axes—and that's also done in Chapter 7. Doing so tends to clarify what the components represent by redistributing the loadings across them, often in a way that makes the meaning of the components more interpretable. In the case of the state crime rates, the result of the rotation is an adjustment of the loadings so that the first component represents property crimes (burglary, larceny, auto theft, and so on) and the second component represents the violent crimes of murder and assault.

Each state's scores on the two principal components are shown in scattercharts in Chapter 7. The purpose there is to determine whether principal components tend to classify the states into identifiable regions of the country. The component scores prior to rotation do not classify anything. After rotation, the scatterchart hints that the component scores might classify states by region, but things remain somewhat messy, as they often do.

One of the purposes of principal components analysis is to set irrelevant variation to one side. That's the point of working only with components whose eigenvalues are at least 1.0. At some point in the extraction process you extract the final component that has an eigenvalue greater than or equal to 1.0. Components that are extracted subsequently, with eigenvalues smaller than 1.0, often represent a mix of measurement error and sampling error. They can also represent variability that's particular to a specific variable, a situation contrary to the whole idea of principal components and factor analysis.

But principal components analysis is in the business of reducing the number of variables to a manageable number, without significant loss of information, by finding components that are combinations of the measured variables. From that point of view, a component that represents one measured variable only is suspect.

So the notion of using the selected principal components, those with eigenvalues of 1.0 or greater, as the basis for a k-means cluster analysis is an attractive one. The components are uncorrelated (refer to Chapter 7 for a discussion of this aspect of principal components analysis), and that characteristic might help make the resulting clusters more interpretable. The cluster analysis will not be dealing with irrelevant variation in its derivation of the clusters because, as just noted, unshared error variance and variance attributable to one variable only have been set aside along with components that have low eigenvalues.

With all those arguments going for it, the use of retained components to derive clusters ought to work beautifully. To look further into the state crime rate data, I took the unrotated component scores from Chapter 7 and ran them though a k-means cluster analysis. I specified four clusters, and the results are shown in Figure 9.12.

Figure 9.12
Each cluster is represented by a different marker shape in the chart.

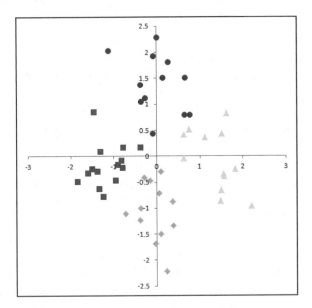

The members of the four clusters are shown with different markers, and it's clear that the cluster analysis has separated the 50 states into four distinct clusters. However, if you project the points in any one cluster onto either the vertical or the horizontal axis (which are the components property crime and violent crime), it's also clear that neither by itself successfully distinguishes the clusters.

Well, that's what rotation is for. Figure 9.13 shows the same data after Varimax rotation. The k-means cluster analysis was repeated using the rotated component scores and the results charted with the same markers to represent the four clusters.

Figure 9.13
The rotation clarifies where the clusters locate on the principal components.

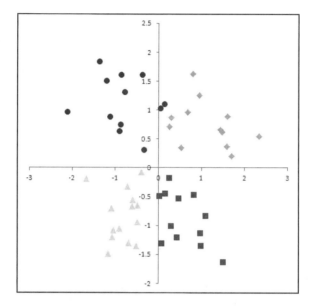

Notice first in Figure 9.13 that there is no longer any significant overlap in the projections of the cluster members onto the axes. Two states represented by circles sneak (barely) into the upper-right quadrant of the chart, while the remainder of that cluster is in the upper-left quadrant.

Furthermore, the clusters are identical in Figure 9.12 and Figure 9.13; the same states are assigned to each cluster whether the data are unrotated or rotated. That's as you'd expect, because the data points' positions with respect to one another don't change—only the positions of the axes shift in response to the Varimax rotation. It follows that the distances from each record in a cluster and the cluster's centroid are the same for both the rotated and the unrotated scores. (That's easy to check if you want, because the Factor.xls workbook that accompanies Chapter 7 provides both the unrotated and the rotated versions.)

Figure 9.13 is a beautiful representation of the sort of thing you hope for in cluster analysis. The clusters are mutually distinct, and they're arranged so as to make good sense; each cluster is on one side of the vertical axis and also on one side of the horizontal axis. Just what I hoped for: The states sort themselves out into four clusters, based on their rates of property and violent crime.

What substantive meaning can we extract from this analysis? The first task is to check the cluster membership. Here are the states that belong to the first cluster: Arizona, California, Colorado, Delaware, Florida, Illinois, Maryland, Michigan, Missouri, New Mexico, Nevada, and New York. Does anything strike you as common to those 12 states? The western part of the country is well represented, with five in the Pacific and Mountain time zones. But the mid-Atlantic is there too, with Delaware, Maryland and New York. So is the central part of the country with Illinois, Michigan, and Missouri.

I'm afraid that no regional influences are apparent in the first cluster, and the same is true of the other three. In fact, the only common thread among the 12 states in the first cluster is that they're all above average in violent crime and property crime rates. Figure 9.14 shows the confusion table for the derived clusters and the preassigned regions.

Figure 9.14
The relationship between Region and Cluster is a random one.

	A	B	C	D	E	F
1	Region	Cluster ▼				
2		▼	1	2	3	4 Grand Total
3	E		4	4	5	7 20
4	N		2	4	5	11
5	S		1		1	4 6
6	W		5	4	3	1 13
7	Grand Total		12	12	14	12 50

And if you consider the steps taken to get to the chart in Figure 9.13, the results you see in Figure 9.14 are just about what you should expect, even in the absence of any meaningful clustering. The principal components analysis and subsequent rotation left us with two retained components, and the loadings after rotation made the nature of each component clear. The two components were uncorrelated, as they must be when they are extracted. Because the rotation method was Varimax, an orthogonal rotation in which the angles between the axes are left alone, the components remain uncorrelated after the rotation.

Because the basis for the principal components analysis was a correlation matrix derived from the raw data (rather than a covariance matrix), the component scores are standardized to zero mean and unit variance, and furthermore they're symmetric. Half the states are above a value of zero on one of the two components. Another quarter of the states are above a value of zero on both components, and another quarter below zero on both.

> **NOTE**
> The outcome described in the previous paragraph is a consequence of the way that I wrote the code that extracts the principal components. The Principal Components add-in that accompanies Chapter 7 always passes a correlation matrix to the extraction routine. Unlike its alternative, the variance-covariance matrix, the correlation matrix has had the effects of different scales of measurement removed from its elements. The result is that the component scores have a mean of zero and both a standard deviation and a variance of 1.0.

Therefore the cluster analysis gives us exactly what we see in Figure 9.13. When you request four clusters, and the two variables are standardized and uncorrelated, you're likely to get clusters above and below, to the left and to the right of each axis.

This outcome underscores the importance of supplying information about the identity of your records to the cluster analysis. At the very least you need to be able to identify each record in each cluster when the analysis has finished. Otherwise, you won't be able to decide whether the membership in each cluster tells you anything about what the cluster represents.

You can easily get the beautiful separation and classification that appears in Figure 9.13. But suppose you didn't have at hand the information that enables you to link each observation to an entity whose characteristics are known, such as a geographic, economic or political region. Then you might think that the clusters represent something meaningful in theory rather than a simple artifact of how the data got derived.

But don't let the outcome described in this section discourage you. It's entirely possible that a slightly different outcome could have been more suggestive. For example, suppose that each cluster had comprised states that, although they were from different regions, disproportionately represented one region. You might have, say, 75% Western states in Cluster 1, 70% Eastern states in Cluster 2, and so on. Or, shifting from regional to economic influences, you might find that Cluster 1 consists of states whose average unemployment rate is 6%, Cluster 2 has states that average 8% unemployment, and so on. Or you might notice that political party affiliation follows, even if only roughly, the assignment of states to clusters.

That's precisely the sort of outcome that makes cluster analysis so valuable as an exploratory tool. You often find that clusters describe dimensions that had not necessarily occurred to you when you were compiling your list of variables for the principal components analysis.

This has been a lengthy and somewhat winding discussion. The two points that I hope you take from it are

- Don't let graphic evidence that clusters exist in your data convince you all by itself that the clusters have any inherent meaning.
- Use unique record identifiers that enable you to link records in each cluster to people or objects whose characteristics are known.

Let's revisit the topic of wine. It will provide a somewhat brighter outcome than we get from studying murder and assault rates.

Clustering Wines

Chapter 8 uses a simplistic data set regarding wine to introduce some concepts and procedures in cluster analysis. A much more sophisticated database containing information about wine is kept by the University of California at Irvine, and I have adapted it from its text format and included it in the Excel workbook that accompanies this chapter (see the worksheet named Wine Data).

The data set consists of 178 records, each record representing a different wine. It also contains 13 variables descriptive of those 178 wines, ranging from Alcohol content to something called Proanthocyanins to Color Intensity. The wines are all made from one of three different cultivars (*cultivar* is how the database represents the concept of *grape variety*), and the idea here is to see whether the 13 descriptive variables can successfully cluster the wines into groups that accurately represent the three cultivars.

For comparative purposes I ran a k-means cluster analysis on the raw data before repeating it on principal components. I called for three clusters and got the results shown in Figure 9.15.

Figure 9.15
These results, based on the raw measured data, are unimpressive.

▲	E	F	G	H	I	J
1						
2		Count of Clusters	Column Labels ▼			
3		Row Labels ▼	Cultivar 1	Cultivar 2	Cultivar 3	Grand Total
4		Cluster 1	46	1		47
5		Cluster 2		50	19	69
6		Cluster 3	13	20	29	62
7		**Grand Total**	59	71	48	178
8						
9		Count of Clusters	Column Labels ▼			
10		Row Labels ▼	Cultivar 1	Cultivar 2	Cultivar 3	Grand Total
11		Cluster 1	78.0%	1.4%	0.0%	26.4%
12		Cluster 2	0.0%	70.4%	39.6%	38.8%
13		Cluster 3	22.0%	28.2%	60.4%	34.8%
14		**Grand Total**	100.0%	100.0%	100.0%	100.0%

Figure 9.15 shows two pivot tables that compare the agreement of the clusters I obtained from a k-means analysis with the actual cultivar values. The first pivot table, in the range F2:J7, shows the actual counts. The second pivot table, in the range F9:J14, shows the same data but as a percent of the column total. Thus, k-means assigned 78.0% of the wines identified as Cultivar 1 to Cluster 1 (see cell G11).

A hit rate of 78% isn't bad at all. It's more than twice what you'd expect if wines were assigned to three clusters on a purely random basis. But the results for Cultivars 2 and 3 are much less promising.

The cluster designations are arbitrary; there is no reason to expect that the cluster designated as Cluster 1 should represent the same records identified as Cultivar 1. It's necessary to examine the agreement between the two classifications, and find the cell (within a particular cultivar, for example) with the highest percentage of the known classification. In Figure 9.15, for Cultivar 1, that cell is G11, so you might tentatively conclude that Cluster 1 represents Cultivar 1. To verify that conclusion, it would be necessary to refer to the individual record IDs and to check their actual cultivar membership. That step of course presupposes that you are using a training sample and therefore know which wine belongs to which cultivar. Otherwise you have no criterion to verify your results. This uncertainty is typical of the use of cluster analysis in purely exploratory situations, where it can be useful as a means of developing hypotheses. But at some point, to confirm those hypotheses you'll need classifications, obtained independently, to test against the derived clusters.

You also need to make sure that you don't assign a cluster to more than one actual classification. For example, in Figure 9.15, cells H12:I12 show that 70.4% and 39.6% of the records in Cultivars 2 and 3 belong to Cluster 2. If those percentage values were much closer to one another—say, 60% and 65%—sheer carelessness might cause you to assign Cluster 2 to both Cultivar 2 and Cultivar 3. Or it might be that either you, *or the k-means analysis itself*, are simply unsure which cultivar it is that Cluster 2 actually represents. In that and similar cases, you need some basis to decide which cultivar is represented by Cluster 2. The basis is normally specific record IDs in combination with independently obtained record classifications.

Figure 9.16 shows what happens when you run the cluster analysis on principal components instead of the raw data used in Figure 9.15.

Figure 9.16

The principal components provide a surprisingly accurate classification.

Count of Cultivar	Column Labels			
Row Labels	Cultivar 1	Cultivar 2	Cultivar 3	Grand Total
Cluster 1		4	48	52
Cluster 2	58	4		62
Cluster 3	1	63		64
Grand Total	59	71	48	178

Count of Cultivar	Column Labels			
Row Labels	Cultivar 1	Cultivar 2	Cultivar 3	Grand Total
Cluster 1	0.0%	5.6%	100.0%	29.2%
Cluster 2	98.3%	5.6%	0.0%	34.8%
Cluster 3	1.7%	88.7%	0.0%	36.0%
Grand Total	100.0%	100.0%	100.0%	100.0%

Begin by running the code in Factor.xls on the same wine data used for Figure 9.15. The Factor.xls code returns the wines' scores on the first three components, on the worksheet named Principal Components.

> **NOTE**
> As noted earlier, it makes no difference to cluster analysis whether you use rotated or unrotated scores. The number of components you use, however, does make a difference, as it normally does whether you're using directly measured variables or derived components.

The example in Figure 9.16 uses three principal components, in part because they each have an eigenvalue greater than 1.0, but primarily because there are three cultivars to identify.

Then, running the Kmeans Cluster Analysis.xls code on the components results in three (requested) clusters that each match the independently recorded cultivars almost perfectly. Hit rates in the 95% range are remarkable, and it's hard not to chalk up the results to a cleaner data set due to basing the analysis on principal components. The data set, as discussed earlier, contains less interference from the various sources of error and idiosyncratic, single-source variation than is the case with the full 13-variable data set.

Further, you have independent confirmation of the composition of the clusters in the form of the cultivar classification. That information is not used in the cluster analysis and yet the agreement is very high. This outcome is in sharp contrast to the results of the previous example of state crime rates, converted to principal components. In that case, the separation of the clusters is even more crisp than with the analysis of the wine data—but the state clusters have no intrinsic meaning.

If you trust the source of the data, it's difficult to avoid the conclusion that the raw variables, trimmed down to a few underlying principal components—or, if you prefer, factors—can accurately classify the wines by cultivar when you run them through a k-means cluster analysis.

Cross-Validating the Results

The previous section shows how the assignment to clusters, based on the principal components derived from Alcohol Content to Proline (an amino acid), agrees strongly with the assignment to cultivars, presumably based purely on knowledge of the plant the grapes, and therefore the wines, came from. With such a powerful outcome it might seem pointless to cross-validate the finding, and perhaps it is. But if you have access to another data set, gathered and recorded similarly, it often costs relatively little to replicate the analysis on the second data set and determine whether the results are similar.

One way to go about a cross-validation is to split your data into two randomly selected halves, and run a separate cluster analysis on each half. If you're using principal components rather than measured variables, you might as well derive the principal component scores before splitting the data set in half.

The approach I've always found best for randomly splitting the data set is illustrated in Figure 9.17.

Figure 9.17
Use the RAND() function to assign records to cross-validation groups.

	E2 ▾	f_x =IF(RAND()<0.5,0,1)					
◢	A	B	C	D	E	F	G
1	Record	Factor 1	Factor 2	Factor 3	Random assignment		
2	1	1.528952051	0.913478143	0.137830036	1		
3	2	1.018516595	-0.210986623	1.68516416	0		89
4	3	1.160164034	0.652553188	-0.817291633	1		
5	4	1.731927916	1.744337597	0.146525376	1		
6	5	0.465085518	0.550464853	-1.685354226	1		
7	6	1.406102647	1.343135986	0.523400194	1		
8	7	1.1289786	0.743488888	0.812537336	1		
9	8	0.949356917	1.01821371	-0.121640131	1		
10	9	1.157459997	0.580988143	1.472707866	1		
11	10	1.269364402	0.499585013	0.818484194	0		
12	11	1.604085085	0.824165691	0.351542484	1		
13	12	0.808904009	0.387281061	0.990314664	0		

Note the contents of the Formula Box in Figure 9.17, where the formula for cell E2 is

=IF(RAND()<0.5,0,1)

The RAND() function returns random numbers in the range 0.0 through 1.0. If the RAND() function returns a value less than .5, the IF() function causes the cell to store a value of 0, and a value of 1 otherwise. Copy and paste the formula down the worksheet so that all records are accounted for.

With an appreciable number of records—say, 100 or more—close to half of them will have values of 0, and the others will of course have values of 1. You'd like to get exactly half if you have an even number of records, plus or minus one with an odd number of records. So, simply total the results in Column E as shown in cell G3 of Figure 9.17, using this formula:

=SUM(E2:E179)

The wine data contains 178 records, so if half of them have a randomly assigned 1, then the total of E2:E179 will be 89.

Simply enter the nested IF(RAND()) formulas on the worksheet as shown, get their sum as in cell G3, and press the F9 key to force the recalculation of the formulas (and therefore the recalculation of the RAND() functions) until the sum of the results is half of your record count.

Then select the range of cells that contain the IF(RAND()) formulas, click the Copy button on the Ribbon, and then press the Alt+E+S+V combination (or choose to Paste Special Values from the Ribbon's Paste drop-down) to paste the formulas into the selected range as values.

You can then sort the data set on the randomly assigned 1s and 0s (again, Column E in Figure 9.17). Split the results into two separate ranges and run the Kmeans Cluster Analysis.xls code once on each range. I have done so with the wine data and obtained the results shown in Figure 9.18.

Figure 9.18
The two tables return similar results.

Count of Clusters	Column Labels			
Row Labels	1	2	3	Grand Total
Cluster 1		2	24	26
Cluster 2	33			33
Cluster 3		30		30
Grand Total	33	32	24	89

Count of Clusters	Column Labels			
Row Labels	1	2	3	Grand Total
Cluster 1	2	4	24	30
Cluster 2	24	9		33
Cluster 3		26		26
Grand Total	26	39	24	89

The results are similar, but that's nearly certain to occur when the analysis of the combined records returns such high hit rates, as in Figure 9.16.

> **NOTE** Of course, you could instead use the RAND() function by itself and dispense with the IF(), the 1s and the 0s. Copy the RAND() formulas, paste them as values, and then sort on the results. Select the first half of the records and treat them as one of your samples. I recommend the IF(RAND()) approach because it's more convenient when you want to create three or more groups of randomly selected records. For example:
>
> =IF(RAND()<.33,1,IF(RAND()<.66,2,3))

Bear in mind that the cluster *designations* are arbitrary: A cluster that one analysis might designate as Cluster 1 might be designated as Cluster 2 in a different analysis of similar records. Therefore you might need to redesignate a cluster identifier before you can compare the two pivot tables directly.

The title of this section, "Cross-Validating the Results," is an apt way to summarize a topic that I've tried to make thematic throughout this book. We often want to develop decision rules by figuring out how classifications work with a given set of subjects or variables. These decisions have to do with the likelihood that a loan will be repaid, that a product will be purchased, that a medical treatment will be successful, that a manufactured product is made with plant or animal material from a particular species...the list of possibilities is endless.

If we're going to make empirically based decisions about people, business strategies, and products, we need to have confidence in our classifications. One approach, a useful one, employs inferential statistics as a guide for our decisions. We investigate the probability that we would once again get an outcome we observe if we were to repeat an experiment— but we don't expect to repeat it. We're working instead with a hypothetical population of repeated experiments.

Nevertheless, for a variety of reasons, we sometimes can't resort to statistical inference. Or even if we can, it's reasonable to go beyond the initial inferential statistics. (An example discussed in this book is the use of discriminant function analysis to follow up a MANOVA.)

One powerful way to build on statistical inference is cross-validation, which is just another term for replication. If we observe a given outcome with one set of data, we'd like to validate that finding with a different, but similarly obtained, set of data. We'd like to confirm our observation.

One of the true giants of statistical theory in the twentieth century was John Tukey. I'll finish this book in a sort of homage to Tukey, and to William Cooley and Paul Lohnes, who finished one of their books (*Multivariate Data Analysis*, John Wiley & Sons, 1971) with a quote from Tukey: "Confirmation comes from repetition."

Index

M

T

U

DECISION ANALYTICS:

Microsoft® Excel®

que·

Conrad Carlberg

Safari
Books Online

FREE
Online Edition

Your purchase of *Decision Analytics: Microsoft® Excel®* includes access to a free online edition for 45 days through the **Safari Books Online** subscription service. Nearly every Que book is available online through **Safari Books Online**, along with thousands of books and videos from publishers such as Addison-Wesley Professional, Cisco Press, Exam Cram, IBM Press, O'Reilly Media, Prentice Hall, Sams, and VMware Press.

Safari Books Online is a digital library providing searchable, on-demand access to thousands of technology, digital media, and professional development books and videos from leading publishers. With one monthly or yearly subscription price, you get unlimited access to learning tools and information on topics including mobile app and software development, tips and tricks on using your favorite gadgets, networking, project management, graphic design, and much more.

Activate your FREE Online Edition at
informit.com/safarifree

STEP 1: Enter the coupon code: YPMBXAA.

STEP 2: New Safari users, complete the brief registration form.
Safari subscribers, just log in.

If you have difficulty registering on Safari or accessing the online edition,
please e-mail customer-service@safaribooksonline.com